Compassion and Empathy in Educational Contexts

This book is dedicated to Emilie.

Acknowledgements

The editors would like to acknowledge all of the contributors to this book. They also thank all of the reviewers involved throughout the journey of this book, without whom the book would not be possible.

About the Book

Compassion and empathy are key attributes to living a healthy and happy life. Surprisingly, there is little written about how these qualities can be taught to children and young people, as well as how teachers can model these traits in their teaching practice. This book fills this void by exploring compassion and empathy in educational contexts. The book shares a number of models of compassion and empathy that can be implemented in schooling contexts. Some chapters also examine how compassion and empathy are presented in texts such as children's picture books, films and games. Personal insights are also shared about successful practices that are necessary in today's world due to bullying and individualism. Finally, some authors also present practical approaches to improve people's awareness and use of compassionate and empathetic approaches to others. Overall, the book supports the work of all educators in early childhood settings, schools, universities and communities.

Contents

Notes on Contributors

Richard G. Bagnall is a Professor Emeritus at Griffith University, Australia. His scholarly work is in the social philosophy of adult and lifelong education, with particular emphasis on the ethics and epistemology of educational theory, advocacy and policy. He has published extensively in these areas, major works including *Cautionary Tales in the Ethics of Lifelong Learning Policy and Management: A Book of Fables* (2004) and *Discovering Radical Contingency: Building a Postmodern Agenda in Adult Education* (1999).

Margaret Baguley is Associate Professor of Arts Education at the University of Southern Queensland. Her contribution to quality learning, teaching and research has been recognised through a series of awards including a national citation for her outstanding contribution to student learning. Baguley is also a practicing artist who has received a number of significant awards throughout her career including the Australia Council's New Media Residency to Banff, Canada. Her work is part of an international touring exhibition funded by the Australia Council for the Arts and is being shown as part of the *Ten Days on the Island* statewide arts festival in Tasmania. Baguley is President of Art Education Australia (AEA), the peak body for visual art education in Australia. She has published extensively and recently co-edited *The Palgrave Handbook of Artistic* *and Cultural Responses to War Since 1914* (Kerby, Baguley, & McDonald, 2019).

Georgina Barton is Associate Professor of Literacies and Pedagogy in the School of Education at the University of Southern Queensland, Brisbane, Australia. She has experience as a programme director for preservice teachers and teaches English and literacy education in higher education. Before being an academic, Barton taught in schools for over 20 years including teaching English in South India with Australian Volunteers International. She has been an acting principal, coordinator of international students, and a lead teacher in the areas of literacy and numeracy. Barton also has extensive experience in teaching the arts in schools and universities and often utilises the arts to support students' literacy learning outcomes. She has over 90 publications in the areas of the arts and literacy and her most recent book is titled *Developing Literacy and the Arts in Schools.*

Casey Burkholder is an assistant professor at the University of New Brunswick, interested in critical teacher education and participatory visual research. In choosing a research path at the intersection of youth resistance and activism, gender, inclusion, DIY media-making and social studies education, Burkholder believes her work may contribute to 'research as intervention' (Mitchell, 2011) through participatory approaches to equity and social change.

Melissa Cain is a lecturer in the School of Education at the Australian Catholic University, Brisbane. She teaches in inclusive education and arts education. She has experience as a school teacher and head of department for 22 years in Australia and in Asia through the international school system. Cain's PhD centred on the challenges teachers face when implementing culturally diverse arts education examining a range of case studies in Australia and Singapore. Her research covers initial teacher education, inclusive education and creative pedagogies with a current focus on hearing the voices of students with vision impairment in mainstream schools. She has managed three large-scale national learning and teaching projects and has produced an international MOOC—'Deep

Learning through Transformative Pedagogies' through EdX and Microsoft. Cain has received several higher education teaching awards and is the recipient of the Callaway Doctoral Award.

Susan N. Chapman has worked professionally as an actor and musician. She has recently completed her PhD dissertation through Griffith University and has experience in teaching the arts in primary, secondary and tertiary sectors. In her capacity as a practicing registered teacher and sessional lecturer, she continues to use integrated learning in the classroom and to deliver professional learning to other educators. Her published work focuses on integrated interdisciplinary learning, specifically with and through the arts. After beginning her undergraduate study at the Queensland Conservatorium of Music, she has broadened her research to include other arts disciplines (dance, drama, media arts and visual art). She is undertaking a Research Fellowship in STEAM (science, technology, engineering, arts, mathematics) at Griffith University, where she works with a team of researchers who represent these various disciplines.

Paul Darvasi is an educator, game designer, speaker and writer whose work looks at the intersection of games, culture and learning. He teaches English and media studies in Toronto, Canada, and is a doctoral candidate at York University. His research explores how commercial video games can be used as texts for critical analysis by adolescents. He has designed pervasive games that include *The Ward Game*, based on Ken Kesey's *One Flew Over the Cuckoo's Nest*, and *Blind Protocol*, a cyberwarfare simulation that instructs on online security, privacy and surveillance. Darvasi has worked with the US Department of Education, UNESCO, foundry10, Consumers International, iThrive and Connected Camps and has participated in several international research projects. He recently wrote a working paper for UNESCO on how commercial video games can be used for peace education and conflict resolution. Darvasi's work has been featured on PBS, NPR, CBC, the *Huffington Post*, Polygon, Killscreen, Gamasutra, Sterne, Engadget, EdSurge, Edutopia and MindShift.

Josélia Mafalda Ribeiro Fonseca is an assistant professor in the Department of Education, Faculty of Social Sciences and Humanities, University of the Azores. She has a degree in history and philosophy from the University of the Azores, as well as a Masters in Child Studies from the University of Minho, specialising in personal and social development. In the scope of the Master's degree, she carried out a study entitled *Education for Values: Conceptions and Practices of Educators*. She holds a PhD in Philosophy of Education from the University of the Azores. Her doctoral thesis is titled *Citizenship as an Educational Project: A Reflexive and Reconstructive Approach*. Fonseca has developed research in the area of education for citizenship, responsibility ethics and action research. She supervised several teacher-educator internships, in the field of education for citizenship and education of values. She collaborates with the School of Health of Angra do Heroísmo in Ethics and Health.

Susanne Garvis is a professor at Gothenburg University and a guest professor at Stockholm University, Sweden. She works within the field of quality and policy development within early childhood education. Garvis has been involved in international and national research projects, worked with private organisations, governments and NGOs around access, quality and inequality in early childhood education. She has worked with teachers, children, families and policy makers.

Heidi Harju-Luukkainen holds a PhD in education, special education, a teacher qualification and a qualification in leadership and management from Finland. She has published more than 100 international books, journal articles and reports as well as worked in more than 25 projects globally. Harju-Luukkainen has worked at top ranked universities in the USA like UCLA, USC as well as in many Nordic research universities. She has developed education programmes for universities, been a PI of PISA sub-assessments in Finland and functioned as board professional. Her research areas are early childhood education, justice in education and international student assessment.

Jaakko Antero Hilppö is a postdoctoral researcher at the Faculty of Educational Sciences, University of Helsinki. His research has focused on children's sense of agency in educational institutions and everyday life and co-participatory research methods with children. More recently, Hilppö's attention has focused on children's projects as manifestations of their agency in and across different settings and especially on compassionate projects and the learning taking place within them. Hilppö is a high baritone and a beltalowda.

Martin Kerby is Senior Lecturer in Education at the University of Southern Queensland. His research focuses on historical and educational areas. His interest is in understanding the effect of educational and sociopolitical changes on people and institutions. He has an extensive publication history with his most recent publication being *The Palgrave Handbook of Artistic and Cultural Responses to War Since 1914* (Kerby, Baguley, & McDonald, 2019). Kerby has received numerous awards and grants including a 2017 Queensland Government Anzac Centenary Spirit of Service grant, which encompassed a regional music tour and accompanying children's picture book with a culminating performance at the State Library of Queensland. In July 2018 Kerby was awarded a 12-month Q ANZAC 100 Fellowship at the State Library of Queensland for his project 'A War Imagined: Queenslanders and the Great War'.

Neha Kulkarni completed her Masters in Clinical Psychology from the Savitribai Phule Pune University, Pune, in 2015 and then joined Leeds University Business School in 2017 for pursuing an MSc in Organisational Psychology. She is working as a research assistant at the Centre for Mental Health Law and Policy at Indian Law Society, Pune. She is working on a peer counselling project which, based on research, will identify, train, mentor and support youth volunteers in the age group of 12–16 years, to provide support to their peers facing mental health distress in their schools. It will enable the youth volunteers to identify their peers in distress, learn ways to reach out to them to provide support. This initiative will build a network among the peers for them to articulate their distress in a safe environment, thus enabling them to develop positive coping mechanism that will have an impact on their personal space.

Amélie Lemieux is Assistant Professor of Literacy and Technology Education at Mount Saint Vincent University. Her research interests include digital literacy practices and maker education informed by phenomenological and post-humanist perspectives. A Lieutenant-Governor's Medal Recipient (Quebec) for academic excellence and community engagement, she received SSHRC and FRQSC funding to investigate digital literacy practices and meaning-making processes. Her combined work in multimodality and literacy has allowed her to raise federal funding, a Quebec Lieutenant-Governor Medal for academic excellence and community engagement, the 2017 McGill award for community engagement, as well as the Tim Casgrain Award for excellence and innovation in literacy research.

Lasse Lipponen is Professor of Education, with special reference to early childhood education, at the Faculty of Educational Sciences, University of Helsinki. His research work is directed to cultures of compassion, children's agency and play.

Lai Kuen Brenda Lo has formally retired after working as a senior secondary school principal in Hong Kong, migrating back to Australia to complete her PhD studies. As a lifelong learner, she earned her Bachelor of Counselling and an MEd from the University of New England, Australia; Master of Arts (Special Educational Needs) from University of Newcastle Upon Tyne, England; and a PhD (Education) from Griffith University, Australia. Besides being an educational administrator, she is an experienced teacher in youth education, vocational education, special education and teacher training. She has participated in various research projects over the past ten years, including projects on education for non-engaged youth, curriculum development for non-Chinese-speaking students in Hong Kong and the present study of teacher stress, burnout and resilience. Recently she has been a student of ageing support at Victoria University, to enrich her knowledge of the third-age learning. She continues working as a casual education advisor and a nanny of her three grandsons settled in Melbourne.

Abbey MacDonald is Senior Lecturer in Arts Education at the University of Tasmania, where she specialises in visual art curriculum, pedagogy and practice. MacDonald is a qualitative researcher with an interest in the applications of storying and arts-based methodologies to support participant, researcher and teacher engagement in and with relational art inquiry. Her research contexts include professional learning collaboration, teacher embodiment and enactment of curriculum, interdisciplinarity and exploration of the intersections and spaces between practice, pedagogy and methodology. Her classroom teaching experience includes secondary visual arts, media arts and English, as well as residential education leadership. MacDonald is a curator and visual artist, working in oils and cross media. She is Vice President of Art Education Australia (AEA) and Councillor of the Tasmanian Art Teachers Association (TATA).

Sairaj M. Patki is Assistant Professor of Psychology at the Department of Social Sciences, School of Liberal Education, FLAME University, Pune (India), and teaches courses including biological bases of behaviour, experimental psychology, abnormal psychology and cognitive psychology. He has over seven years of teaching experience including undergraduate and post-graduate departments at prominent educational institutes in Pune. He strongly emphasises the use of innovative teaching-learning-evaluation practices that are designed with a student-centric approach aimed at making students an integral part of the process and aimed at holistic development. His research interests lie in diverse areas, including adolescent well-being, emotional intelligence and organisational behaviours. He has also guided several post-graduate students for their research projects. Besides being an active researcher, Patki conducts workshops on emotional intelligence and attempts linking his hobby of photography and cinematography with psychology in his free time.

Antti Rajala is a postdoctoral researcher at the Faculty of Educational Sciences, University of Helsinki. His research has addressed dialogic pedagogy, educational change and agency in education. He is working in the project Constituting Cultures of Compassion in Early Childhood Education (funded by Academy of Finland, 2016–2020).

Geoff Taggart has a background in primary and early year education. He is interested in the affective aspect of ethical practice and the way in which universities may be able to cultivate this aspect in students as part of preparation for leadership in 'caring professions'. As an ordained interfaith minister, Taggart has a particular interest in the way in which contemplative pedagogies may contribute to this process and, in his own teaching, focus a lot upon the use of imagery, story and metaphor as tools of transformative learning. Most of Taggart's publications are on the theme of care, compassion and professionalism in early childhood education.

Liisa Uusimaki joined Göteborgs Universitet, Sweden, in January 2013. Her areas of teaching include both International and Swedish postgraduate and undergraduate courses (e.g. pedagogical/educational leadership, mentoring/supervision, globalisation and comparative education). She is a sought-out speaker both locally and internationally pertaining to internationalisation and inclusive education. Based on her interest and expertise in teaching and learning in higher education, she received in 2018 an Excellent Teacher award (equivalent to Associate Professor of Teaching and Learning) from the Faculty of Education at the University of Gothenburg, Sweden. Uusimaki has also extensive teaching and research experience in Teacher Education from several Australian universities, including Charles Sturt University, Albury, Queensland University of Technology (QUT) and the University of the Sunshine Coast (USC). Her research areas are internationalisation, inclusion, cross-cultural studies, international student and staff mobility, mentoring, educational/pedagogical leadership and educational psychology.

Justin H. G. Williams After graduating from Newcastle upon Tyne in Medicine in 1988, I worked in the UK and Australia, before taking some time out to study behavioural ecology. I have always been interested in the evolutionary processes that shaped the human mind, and my research career commenced collaborating with Andrew Whiten in St Andrews, who pioneered the study of social learning in non-human primates. Our first joint publication was a paper (now widely cited) linking imitation and 'theory of mind' problems in autism to impaired 'mirror neuron' functioning. In 2000, I was appointed to my current post as a child and adolescent psychiatrist as both clinician and academic. In my research, I seek better routes to implement our rapidly expanding knowledge of neuroscience to improve children's mental health and well-being. In recent years I have become especially interested in the assessment and promotion of neurodevelopmental health within broader public health contexts.

Tina Yngvesson holds an MSc in International Business, a BSc (Hons) in Social Sciences and is undertaking a BSc in Education as well as an MSc in International Educational Research at the University of Gothenburg, where she is writing her thesis on parental engagement in the Swedish preschool. Alongside her studies and various research projects in child and youth sciences, she also works as a recreational teacher in a Swedish primary school.

List of Figures

List of Tables

Part I

Compassion and Empathy Can Be Learnt

1

Theorizing Compassion and Empathy in Educational Contexts: What Are Compassion and Empathy and Why Are They Important?

Georgina Barton and Susanne Garvis

Introduction

The world is in constant change with growing inequality and access. When you watch the news, you are confronted with national disasters, wars/conflicts, waves of refugees and other crimes against humanity. At a national level, many countries have a changing political landscape that has seen a rise in fundamentalist nationalist parties leading to a discourse of "problematic immigrants". We also witness the decline of democratic ideals and the ethos of supporting people in society as politicians are influenced by capitalist ideals and individual gain. In essence, the world appears to be becoming meaner, with little understanding shown to others. When did values change?

G. Barton (✉)
School of Education, University of Southern Queensland, Brisbane, QLD, Australia
e-mail: georgina.barton@usq.edu.au

S. Garvis
Department of Education, University of Gothenburg and Stockholm University, Göteborg and Stockholm, Sweden
e-mail: susanne.garvis@gu.se

© The Author(s) 2019
G. Barton, S. Garvis (eds.), *Compassion and Empathy in Educational Contexts*,
https://doi.org/10.1007/978-3-030-18925-9_1

3

Changes can also be observed at a personal level for many people in their daily encounters with each other and social media. The rise in bullying and negative statements appears the norm in workplaces and social media. For example, there are some apps that allow anonymous feedback on people that is emailed to them. Likewise, children can access apps that send hurtful messages to each other without adult detection. We do not know the long-term consequences of such apps, but there have been news stories related to suicide and self-harm of the recipients of hurtful posts as well as other consequences. What we can learn from this example is that the old saying "treat others how you would like to be treated" is not enacted by all. A question we must ask ourselves is how would we like to be treated or how would we like our children to be treated? If the answer is "respectfully," we must model appropriate behaviour to others.

One could argue that the lack of role models in society also causes the decline in compassion. The behaviour of politicians, celebrities, sports stars and other high-profile people suggests a decline in moral and ethical standards. This is worrying considering young children learn from role models. We know from research that when children are exposed to positive role models, they learn prosocial behaviour described as "voluntary behaviour intended to benefit another" (Eisenberg, Fabes, & Spinrad, 2006, p. 646). The need for children to learn prosocial behaviour is perhaps greater than ever before.

At the heart of these changes in society lies the importance of compassion to bring about change, to create a better world for all. As Armstrong suggested in her creation of the Charter for Compassion (2008):

> The principle of compassion lies at the heart of all religious, ethical and spiritual traditions, calling us always to treat all others as we wish to be treated ourselves. Compassion impels us to work tirelessly to alleviate the suffering of our fellow creatures, to dethrone ourselves from the centre of our world and put another there, and to honour the inviolable sanctity of every single human being, treating everybody, without exception, with absolute justice, equity and respect.

It calls upon:

> all men and women to restore compassion to the centre of morality and religion, to return to the ancient principle that any interpretation of scripture that breeds violence, hatred or disdain is illegitimate, to ensure that youth are given accurate and respectful information about other traditions, religions and cultures, to encourage a positive appreciation of cultural and religious diversity, to cultivate an informed empathy with the suffering of all human beings—even those regarded as enemies.

The Charter for Compassion is based on the central tenet that compassion is essential for a just and peaceful world. The Charter presents compassion as practical-acquired knowledge that can be taught and developed through reflection and practice. This suggests that compassion is learnt and can be continually developed within educational contexts. As editors, we follow this tenet and argue that compassion and empathy should be embedded within all educational practices and curriculum.

Compassion and empathy are key attributes to living a healthy and happy life (Hubbert, 2017) yet surprisingly there is little written about how we can teach these qualities and how teachers can best display these traits in and through their teaching practice. In a similar way, not much is known about how teachers can be supported in their everyday professional lives through compassionate and empathetic understanding. Much research that exists is from a psychological perspective—investigating the personal attributes of compassion and empathy—rather than on the social and cultural influence these dispositions can potentially have on society (Raab, 2014).

This book therefore aims to provide some robust studies and cases in analysing and understanding how compassion and empathy work in educational contexts from across the globe. Education is often seen as an important tool for teaching the future generation skills that are necessary for survival and societal advancement, based within compassionate and empathetic understanding.

It may be argued that schools already engage many children in compassionate understanding in a variety of ways—such as, the school ethos and values, relationships shown in school (teacher-student relationships, student-student relationships and parent-teacher relationships), extra-curricular activities as well as actual curriculum content that focuses on compassion. However, we argue that a specific focus on embedding compassion across the curriculum is needed with examples of reflection and practice. Teachers need to be aware of how they can create activities with young people to support the development of compassion and empathy. Through such a focus, schools can support the development of moral, ethical, political and social capabilities of students.

Defining Compassion and Empathy

Compassion and empathy are linked; however, they refer to slightly different attributes within the human condition. According to Jiménez (2017) there is a distinct difference between compassion and empathy even though they stem from the same desires—what Jiménez refers to as "to better relate and understand others' experiences" (p. 1). Compassion has been defined as "the emotion one experiences when feeling concern for another's suffering and desiring to enhance that person's welfare" (Halifax, 2012, p. 1751). Compassion usually creates some distance between people and focuses on how we can help others but also step back from situations and assess how best to deal with challenges (MacBeth & Gumley, 2012). Empathy on the other hand allows us to feel what others are feeling and be sympathetic towards them or "the ability to walk in another's shoes" (Wiggins & McTighe, 2005, p. 98).

Compassion is in many ways better for our own wellbeing and resilience (Jiménez, 2017), whereas empathy has the potential to burn us out if we do not have the skills to recognize when to distance ourselves from emotions such as hurt and pain. It is, therefore, important that skills such as compassion and empathy are taught in schools but also that teachers and preservice teachers have these attributes in order to teach students more effectively in our complex world (Aronson, 2002; Aronson, Sikes, Blaney, & Snapp, 1978).

Other concepts related to compassion and empathy are morals and ethics. According to Cam (2012), moral experiences grow out of children's own explorations and, therefore, begin at home. Once in care prior to school, children have direct interaction with an extended peer group and other adults. Cam (2012) suggests that:

Mixing with other children throughout the day, in both structured activities and free play, provides constant opportunities for moral development in an environment that is likely to have a greater focus on social learning than will be the case at school. (p. 17)

The development of compassion and empathy, however, lasts throughout one's lifetime (Wei, Yu-Hsin Liao, Ku, & Shaffer, 2011). Much research has explored these attributes from a psychological perspective whereby "distinct appraisal processes attuned to undeserved suffering, distinct signaling behavior related to caregiving patterns of touch, posture, and vocalization, and a phenomenological experience and physiological response that orients the individual to social approach" (Goetz, Keltner, & Simon-Thomas, 2010, p. 351) can be carried out. Goetz et al. (2010) share a comprehensive review of literature that analyses compassion as an affective experience and oriented state. This perspective relates to a number of theorized models offered in the literature.

Models of Compassion and Empathy

Not surprisingly, a number of scholarly researchers have explored the notions of compassion and/or empathy in different environments. Halifax's (2012) model of enactive compassion, for example, acknowledges that "compassion is an enactive, emergent process of factors in the attentional and affective domains, the intentional and insight domains, and the embodied and engaged domains of subjective experience" (p. 2). These are known as A, I and E axis. According to Halifax (2012), this psychological model involves the notion of people's attention or mental processing resources to everyday objects. Attention, for example, can be focused or dispersed, and Halifax (2012) notes that this idea determines people's ability to acknowledge and respond to others suffering. For Halifax (2012), attention should be "nonjudgmental, nonreactive, not contracting in relation to adversity, and nongrasping in terms of the desire for a particular outcome" (p. 2). In this sense, people are capable of listening attentively to others' concerns without having to always offer solutions to problems.

The other element to an enactive model of compassion is affect. Halifax (2012) explains that the affective domain involves two emotional states: kindness and equanimity. These are defined as:

> Kindness and equanimity are essential affective processes associated with compassion. Kindness is characterized by a dispositional tenderness toward others as well as genuine concern. Equanimity is a process of stability or mental balance that is characterized by mental composure and an acceptance of the present moment. (p. 3)

Halifax (2012) believes that in order to cultivate the affective process, including balance, both kindness and equanimity are required. Another feature of this model is the I axis which involves intention and insight. This involves the ability to intentionally guide the mind and have insight about people's suffering. Intention and insights operate in alignment with affect and attention. They assist with compassionate balance when interacting with others. Halifax believes that "the intention to transform suffering is one of the features that distinguish compassion from empathy" (p. 5). The insight domain involves the capacity to develop metacognitive perspectives. This includes self-awareness and access to memory.

The final axis to this model includes embodiment and engagement. Halifax states that the E axis is based on an enactive process. This is when the mind, body and the environment come together to enhance compassion. Embodiment is the felt sense of someone else's suffering. Engagement is when the embodied mind is in a state of readiness to support this suffering. Halifax's enactive model of compassion provides an excellent resource for those working with others, particularly those who need support. In educational contexts, it is important for educators to consider ways in which to work with others by being mindful of each of the elements outlined here: attention, affect, intention, insight, embodiment and engagement.

Another model offered in the literature is that of Gerdes and Segal (2009). They presented a social work model of empathy that reflected a sense of social justice. They explained that the model involved three components: (1) the affective response to another's emotions and actions; (2) the cognitive processing of one's affective response and the other person's perspective; and (3) the conscious decision-making to take empathic action. They argued that the affective component of empathy required healthy neural pathways and that the cognitive processing includes perspective-taking, self-awareness and emotion regulation. Without an effective understanding of these processes—both affective and cognitive—as well as action that moves beyond them, then empathetic responses are possibly limited.

Kristeller and Johnson's (2005) study explored how mediation can support compassionate and empathetic thinking and doing. They proposed a two-staged model that explains the effect of mediation practice on developing these skills. The model highlights how meditative practice supports not only individual's self-awareness but also their wellbeing and self-regulation. This includes a decrease in self-attachment which leads to more empathy for others. Kristeller and Johnson's (2005) model has significance for educational contexts where the focus on learning and teaching is on thinking about others before oneself (ACARA, n.d.). Indeed, a number of studies have explored how mindfulness and meditation can enhance these practices in the classroom (Fuertes & Wayland, 2015; Hartel, Nguyen, & Guzik, 2017).

Similarly, Singer and Klimecki (2014) note that we use a range of communication modes to express emotion and social abilities such as empathy. They argue that compassion and empathic distress stem from empathy itself and present a schematic model that differentiates between two empathic reactions to the suffering of others (see Table 1.1).

They argue that "an empathic response to suffering can result in two kinds of reactions: empathic distress, which is also referred to as personal distress; and compassion, which is also referred to as empathic concern or sympathy" (p. 875). This means that empathy relates to human capacity to resonate with others' emotions and distress means we can or do not.

Table 1.1 Compassion and empathic distress (Singer & Klimecki, 2014)

Compassion	Empathic distress
Other-related emotion	Self-related emotion
Positive feelings: e.g. love	Negative feelings: e.g. stress
Good health	Poor health, burnout
Approach and prosocial motivation	Withdrawal and non-social behaviour

Compassion, they state, on the other hand is a feeling of concern for others. It is important to consider the difference between compassion and empathy from a cognitive perspective but also in relation to people's dispositions and whether or not they can be learnt and developed skills (Windham, 2016). The next section therefore outlines a number of studies exploring compassion and empathy in context.

Studies About Compassion and Empathy

Compassion and empathy, as both philosophical and theoretical notions, have infiltrated the literature. Unsurprisingly, these concepts have featured in discourse related to different disciplines including business, education, law, medicine and other health areas such as nursing and psychiatry. Birnie, Speca and Carlson's (2010) study, for example, explored how a mindfulness-based stress reduction programme impacted on people's self-compassion and empathy. Their study involved participants who suffered from chronic medical conditions. They found that both self-compassion and empathy increased after participation in the programme and that "self-compassion and aspects of empathy revealed strong associations with psychological functioning" (p. 1). This finding has implications for those working in educational contexts as increasingly students and/or adult learners attend to education with a range of personal or physical concerns. Mindfulness has proliferated the research literature in the past decade and many studies are developing strong evidence-bases related to its significance in building compassion and empathy (O'Brien et al., 2016).

Another study by Stojiljković, Djigić and Zlatković (2012) asked whether empathy is connected with teachers' self-assessment of success in and through their work. Their work explored personality traits and dispositions of successful teachers. This included effective pedagogical leadership and management in the classroom. Stojiljković et al. (2012) argued that teachers' work is very complex and involves a number of roles. One of these roles is supporting the personal growth of students. For Stojiljković et al. (2012) this included the development of compassion and empathy as personal attributes. Another role mentioned was connected with the acquisition of knowledge. They argued that "contemporary school is treated as the institution that should support the overall cognitive and personal development of each student and society contribute to social development of the society in whole" (p. 961). This means that skills such as compassion are critical in contributing to cultural and social growth.

Stojiljković et al. (2012) continued to explain that empathy is an important feature of successful teachers. As such, empathy enables effective communication between teachers and students. Empathy is a skill that helps teachers deal with the multiple roles that they face including interacting with parents in the community. Their study argued that a clear definition of empathy is lacking. Some information provided defined empathy as ranging from caring for other people and having a desire to help them, as well as experiencing the same emotions that others do. Findings from this study (Stojiljković et al., 2012) showed that empathy is an important personal capacity for an effective teacher. In order to carry out their roles successfully, they had to understand the way that students thought as well as how they interacted with others. This included students' learning styles and strategies. Their study highlighted that a "teachers' life and professional experience, as well as appropriate professional education, contribute to the intention and competences for performing different professional roles, primarily those related to social relationships and affective communication in the classroom" (p. 965).

In the field of service-learning, Everhart (2016) shows how students can build their skills through experiences in diverse workplaces. Twelve higher education students completed self-assessments and reflective entries related to critical incidents. Environments that students completed their work experience included schools, medical clinics and service agencies such as for domestic and substance abuse. Themes related to empathy development such as change and student metacognition were explored through the data. The author showed that observation of emotional experiences of others and increased responsibility in communities have the potential of changing empathy levels for service-learning students.

A further two-phase study carried out with adults who worked in a range of contexts and recruited through Amazon.com's Mechanical Turk (Study 1, $n = 124$ and Study 2, $n = 121$) found that respondents who reported higher levels of self-compassion showed a greater willingness to help hypothetical people but with reduced empathy. In addition, self-compassion related only to "feeling less personal distress in response to someone else's emergency" (p. 54). Overall, both studies found that both self-compassion and empathy were distinctly aligned with the participants' willingness to help people in need.

Another interesting exploration of compassion and empathy in the literature is how they relate to mindfulness and wellbeing. Raab (2014), for example, investigates the literature in relation to perceived connections between mindfulness and self-compassion in the health sector. Raab (2014) highlights how such ideals have the potential to reduce stress for health workers as well as enhance compassion in regard to the care of patients. The review reveals how health care professionals are particularly prone to stress overload, impacting on compassionate thinking and behaviour. The examination shows that both mindfulness and self-compassion can promote improved "curiosity and nonjudgment towards one's experiences" (p. 95). Further, it was found that mindfulness learning has the potential to increase self-compassion, decrease stress levels of health care workers and hence care of clients.

References

ACARA. (n.d.). *Australian curriculum: General capabilities—Personal and social capabilities*. Australia: Australian Government.

Armstrong, K. (2008). *Charter for compassion*. Retrieved September 10, 2018, from   http://www.charterforcompassion.org/index.php/charter/charter-overvew

Aronson, E. (2002). Building empathy, compassion, and achievement in the jigsaw classroom. In J. M. Aronson (Ed.), *Improving academic achievement: Impact of psychological factors on education* (pp. 209–225). San Diego, CA: Academic Press.

Aronson, E., Sikes, J., Blaney, N., & Snapp, M. (1978). *The jigsaw classroom*. Beverly Hills, CA: Sage.

Birnie, K., Speca, M., & Carlson, L. (2010). Exploring self-compassion and empathy in the context of mindfulness-based stress reduction (MBSR). *Stress and Health, 26*(5), 359–371.

Cam, P. (2012). *Teaching ethics in schools: A new approach to moral education.* Camberwell, VIC: ACER Press.

Eisenberg, N., Fabes, R. A., & Spinrad, T. L. (2006). Prosocial development. In W. Damon & R. Lerner (Eds.), *Handbook of child psychology. Vol. 3: Social, emotional, and personality development* (6th ed., pp. 647–702). Hoboken, NJ: Wiley.

Everhart, R. S. (2016). Teaching tools to improve the development of empathy in service-learning students. *Journal of Higher Education Outreach and Engagement, 20*(2), 129–154.

Fuertes, A., & Wayland, M. (2015). Cultivating mindfulness through meditation in a classroom setting from students' perspective. *Innovations in Teaching and Learning Conference Proceedings, 7.* https://doi.org/10.13021/G8WK5F

Gerdes, K. E., & Segal, E. A. (2009). A social work model of empathy. *Advances in Social Work, 10*(2), 114–127.

Goetz, J. L., Keltner, D., & Simon-Thomas, E. (2010). Compassion: An evolutionary analysis and empirical review. *Psychology Bulletin, 136*(3), 351–374. https://doi.org/10.1037/a0018807

Halifax, J. (2012). A heuristic model of enactive compassion. *Current Opinion in Supportive and Palliative Care, 6*(2), 228–235.

Hartel, J., Nguyen, A.-T., & Guzik, E. (2017). Mindfulness meditation in the classroom. *Journal of Education for Library and Information Science, 58*(2), 112–115. https://doi.org/10.3138/jelis.58.2.112

Hubbert, C. (2017). *Compassion stories.* Retrieved from www.compassion.com.au

Jiménez, J. M. (2017). *Compassion vs. empathy: Emotional leadership can be exhausting, but compassionate leadership doesn't have to be.* Retrieved from https://www.thriveglobal.com/stories/9842-compassion-vs-empathy

Kristeller, J. L., & Johnson, T. (2005). Cultivating loving kindness: A two-stage model of the effects of meditation on empathy, compassion, and altruism. *Zygon, 40*(2), 391–407.

MacBeth, A., & Gumley, A. (2012). Exploring compassion: A meta-analysis of the association between self-compassion and psychopathology. *Clinical Psychology Review, 32*(6), 545–552.

O'Brien, M., Wade Leeuwen, B., Hadley, F., Kelly, N., Kickbusch, S., Talbot, D., & Andrews, R. (2016). *Professional experience, mentoring and transformative spaces in initial teacher education: A praxis perspective.* In AARE 2016, Melbourne, VIC.

Raab, K. (2014). Mindfulness, self-compassion, and empathy among health care professionals: A review of the literature. *Journal of Health Care Chaplaincy, 20*(3), 95–108.

Singer, T., & Klimecki, O. M. (2014). Empathy and compassion. *Current Biology, 24*(18), R875–R878.

Stojiljković, S., Djigić, G., & Zlatković, B. (2012). Empathy and teachers' roles. International conference on education and educational psychology. *Procedia—Social and Behavioral Sciences, 69*, 960–966.

Wei, M., Yu-Hsin Liao, K., Ku, T.-W., & Shaffer, P. A. (2011). Attachment, self-compassion, empathy, and subjective well-being among college students and community adults. *Journal of Personality, 79*(1), 191–221. https://doi.org/10.1111/j.1467-6494.2010.00677.x

Wiggins, G., & McTighe, J. (2005). *Understanding by design* (2nd ed.). Alexandria, VA: Association for Supervision and Curriculum Development ASCD.

Windham, E. (2016). Compassion, empathy, education, and uniqueness. *Home Healthcare Now, 34*(8), 467. https://doi.org/10.1097/NHH.0000000000000423

2

Empathy as Special Form of Motor Skill That Can Be Trained

Justin H. G. Williams

Introduction

If I was to ask you if you are an empathic sort of person, how would you consider that question? When you walk past a homeless person begging in the street, do you give them money? When you read a detective novel, are you quick to figure out the plot? Are you always ready to talk through a friend's problems? Do you get moved by emotional scenes when you watch movies? These are the sorts of questions that we tend to ask in when considering whether a person is empathic, and which constitute the many self-report empathy questionnaires that are available (e.g. Baron-Cohen & Wheelwright, 2004; Davis, 1980). In these questionnaires, empathy is defined as the ability to vicariously experience and understand the emotions of others. It is concerned with the ability to appreciate the emotions and feelings of others, both in terms of the ability to share the emotional experience of another person, and also the cognitive capacity

J. H. G. Williams (✉)
University of Aberdeen, Aberdeen, Scotland, UK
e-mail: justin.williams@abdn.ac.uk

© The Author(s) 2019
G. Barton, S. Garvis (eds.), *Compassion and Empathy in Educational Contexts*,
https://doi.org/10.1007/978-3-030-18925-9_2

to infer thoughts and beliefs (but see below). However, this might not be the most helpful way to think about empathy.

In this chapter, I will take an 'embodied cognition' perspective and propose that we shift the emphasis, and consider how empathy may be better considered as a quality of emotional communication. Rather than some higher level of cognitive functioning, or a cognitive/emotional state hidden in the mind, I will argue that empathy is something that you experience in the room as you interact with another person. It is a sensorimotor skill which you can develop and demonstrate in your expression through gesture and tone of voice. It is also founded upon non-verbal patterns of interaction and the linguistic modality is secondary to action in its functioning. This is not to dispute the more cognitively oriented perspective, but to suggest that if we consider empathy in terms of affective response and patterns of affective behaviour, we can get a better grasp on how we might be able train or improve it.

Traditional Empathic Concepts

Debate is ongoing about how we define empathy. Cuff, Brown, Taylor and Howat (2014) identified 43 discrete definitions. Undoubtedly, it is a multi-faceted concept and most would agree that it is a constellation of abilities (Decety, 2011). Some claim that one can separate 'cognitive' empathy and 'emotional' empathy (Cuff et al., 2014; Reniers, Corcoran, Drake, Shryane, & Vollm, 2011), whilst others emphasise the importance of distinguishing between emotion identification and emotion sharing (Coll et al., 2017). This is not the place to go into this literature in depth, but we can be clear that there are several components which may be more or less present, depending upon the situation. Firstly, there is the aspect of emotional contagion, which means that the expression of an emotion by one person, is sensed by another, and so engenders a similar feeling in the other person (Hatfield, Cacioppo, & Rapson, 1993). A second element would be a conscious awareness of such an experience (de Vignemont & Singer, 2006). Thirdly, there is the 'meta-representation' of the experience, by which the individual can attribute some meaning to it. Whilst a conscious experience of contagion may simply mean that a person can feel the other's emotion and be aware of it, this does not mean that he or she has any control over it or has any understanding of it. This is required for one to understand *why* someone might be feeling and behaving the way they are. Finally, there is the question of whether the perceiver is motivated sufficiently, and is equipped with appropriate judgement and skills in expression to respond accordingly and appropriately. Whilst definitions and concepts of empathy may vary, nearly all conceptualise it as an invisible cognitive function. Coll et al. (2017) refer to an 'information processing' model of empathy. Secondly, whilst definitions may concern themselves with whether empathy occurs in a particular social interaction, empathy is also thought to be a 'fairly stable personality trait' (Reniers et al., 2011) by which it is meant that the likelihood of an individual acting empathically in any particular situation is predictable, because it is a stable feature of their behaviour.

An Alternative Perspective

In this chapter, I am going to argue that viewing empathy as a relatively fixed and impervious cognitive function is problematic and that we can perceive it differently. Psychology has seen a big shift in recent years and wide acceptance of so-called embodied cognition theory (Niedenthal, 2007) which argues against a psychology characterised by distinct 'cognitive' and 'sensorimotor' functions but instead recognises the sensorimotor mechanisms as integral to function as a whole. Rather than try and explain the theory in detail, this chapter will seek to illustrate how it is applied in the case of empathy.

Although I won't question the idea that empathy is multi-layered, by which I mean there are mechanisms which control it that are not directly observable, I will argue that these 'higher' cognitive mechanisms are part of a sensorimotor hierarchy that develops so much in tandem with the sensorimotor and therefore behavioural aspects of empathy, that they are not usually separable. Empathy is therefore something in the here and now, which you can assess directly when you meet someone. Second, rather than viewing it is a fixed trait, I will argue that we can consider empathy like motor skills. We are better off thinking of empathy, just as we think about the ability to play a sport like football. Yes, there are some inherent motor skills required, but the ability is honed over many years of training, and the training you receive is highly dependent upon your place in society and your culture. Thirdly, whilst most sensorimotor control is about 'goal-directed action', that is, performing actions with a hierarchy of tangible goals in mind, the object of empathic action is much less tangible but relates to value placed on relationships.

Evolutionary Aspects

A useful perspective is to consider how the architecture of the brain has evolved to serve empathy. Some years ago, it was suggested that empathy was served by very specific module of the brain called the 'theory of mind module' (Baron-Cohen, 1997). This notion, which was prevalent shortly before the advent of brain imaging, gave rise to many scientific experiments showing that there could be a 'theory of mind' functions in the medial frontal cortex and the temporoparietal lobe (Saxe, 2006). However, another perspective, the Machiavellian intelligence hypothesis (Byrne & Whiten, 1988), predicted that social cognition is an adaptive property of the whole brain. This is based on research into populations of non-human primates in wild or semi-wild situations and sought to ask what evolutionary pressures drove the rapid expansion of cerebral cortex that occurred over 200,000 years. Given that the brain has such a high metabolism, and is so expensive to maintain in terms of the amount of extra energy required, cortical expansion must have conferred major selective advantages. Byrne and Whiten (1988) suggested that these pressures were driven by social interactions. In primates, reproductive success depends upon dominance within a group. The authors found that dominance within primate groups required behaviour comparable to that seen in human politics; whereby social success was dependent upon behaviours requiring both cooperation and deception. Becoming dominant requires an individual to be socially smarter than other members of the group. Then, being dominant would result in distribution of those genes predisposing towards successful social behaviours throughout the group, resulting in an overall increase in the social intelligence of the whole group. Consequently, an evolutionary arms race is thought to have occurred as each generation would select the socially most able members of the group to spread his and her genes. This led to the massive and rapid expansion of cerebral cortex to serve socially advantageous behaviours. Evidence in support of the hypothesis came from work showing that among different primate species, group size showed a linear relationship to brain size (Dunbar, 2003), and furthermore, the large size of human groups corresponded to much larger cortex size following the same linear equation. Later, as thinking developed and primate research continued, the importance of imitation and culture for transmitting behaviour patterns came to be recognised (Whiten & Byrne, 1997). This is further discussed below.

If the Machiavellian intelligence hypothesis is correct, the unique nature of human intelligence is an adaptation for successful social interaction. One capacity that differentiates us especially from other animals, which is arguably most underrated, and which depends on many parts of our cortex working together, is our sensorimotor coordination. As agile as most other animals are, having far superior motor skills for specific abilities such as climbing or jumping, no other species has the motoric versatility that comes close to that of a human. Consider that dogs and horses even struggle to walk backwards. Non-human primates are undoubtedly highly agile. They can sometimes appear quite human-like in their actions, and can be taught to perform crude sign language, but none could come close to being elegant in a Tango or able to use a needle and thread! A limited number of species have a capacity for flexible vocal expression—in particular, some of the songbirds. But none have the power of speech and language anywhere close to that of a human. Similarly, whilst we are seeing massive and impressive advances in artificial intelligence in recent years, as computers become increasingly able to 'think' like a human, the ability to make robots behave like humans remains very poor. The versatility and complexity of human motor skill is without parallel in the rest of the animal or mechanical world.

Motoric Aspects of Empathy

So why should motor skills be important for empathy? Firstly, feelings and emotion are communicated in actions, whether these are facial expression, hand gestures or bodily postures. If ever you read about the communication of emotion in successful novels, you will see the principle of 'show, don't tell' taught to writers. The communication of emotion in a novel is best achieved by a description of the action which conveys it. This is because the versatility of action allows an emotion to be conveyed in a highly variable and nuanced fashion, and as discussed further below, because our brains are wired to view action as the primary means of perceiving the meaning of others. If you ask someone how they are feeling, and they say they are 'fine', you are likely to rely on the body posture, hand gesture, facial expression and tone of voice to judge their actual feeling state than what they actually say. In any emotional communication situation, the number of types of action that can be used to communicate emotion is considerable. Combinations of facial expression, posture and gesture will tend to occur together and can all serve to increase the effectiveness of expression. Similarly subtle shifts in gaze may be used to control subtle differences in emotion communication. For example, whilst direct and averted gaze will affect perception of a fearful expression (Adams et al., 2012), subtle shifts in head position and directness will affect the meaning attributed to a smile (Lobmaier & Perrett, 2011).

The Hierarchical and Sensorimotor Nature of Intentional Action

The development of sensorimotor behaviour was first described by the great developmental psychologist Piaget. At first, the infant has a reflex action, as you place your finger in her palm, so she closes around it with an instinctive grasp. The next stage is for the infant to see the object and to anticipate that this will result in a grasp. This leads to the first reaching action and the earliest intentional behaviour. The reach-to-goal is the earliest behaviour that has its origins in intention. Nearly everything you do stems from this. When you perform any conscious action, you start with a goal and you plan the actions you must do in order to achieve it. Most actions exist within hierarchies. In other words, you have an overall plan that covers a series of actions that you must do in order to achieve it, so that the plan can then be broken down into further sub-goals, which may then be broken down into further sub-goals until we come to the constituent actions. At the moment I am sitting on a train, typing into a computer. I am addressing two goals—one to write this book chapter and the second to reach my destination. Of course, the meeting that I am due to attend has its own series of goals associated with it. Each typing action I perform consists of its own individual reach and press goal-directed action, so that they build up in hierarchies of words, sentences and then paragraphs. The train journey has required a whole hierarchy of intentional actions that started with me getting up and getting dressed, walking to the railway station (following a planned route), purchasing tickets, grasping them between my thumb and forefinger and feeding them through the ticket barrier.

So development of motor skills develops in hierarchies with multiple levels of intention, merging into levels that are eventually distal from actual bodily actions, but which are nonetheless connected to them. Because of the way that sensorimotor coordination develops, the perception and enactment of actions also develops in tandem. We recognise patterns of behaviour in others that we enact ourselves, and then we rehearse and refine them, making them more sophisticated, effective and culturally tuned as we develop within a culture. A critical aspect of development is this mapping of perceived actions onto our own coding for action-planning.

However, a topic that seems to receive relatively little attention is whether there can be more than one overarching, ultimate motivation. Action hierarchies are considered in terms of physical goals and it is assumed that social actions will follow corresponding hierarchies. Therefore, if we go back to the infant between one and three months, we also see an intentional smile appearing at the same time as the intentional hand action. The intentional smile is clearly different from a sort of reactive smile that may be seen at birth. Parents often report that this captivating smile appears just as they are being driven to exhaustion by their new baby, and it transforms their relationship. One could argue that the intentional smile is still a goal-directed action, planned purely in self-interest, because it will elicit a favourable behaviour by the adult. However, it seems unlikely to me that such Machiavellian planning could be occurring in a six-week old, given that such planning is not evident in other actions. Rather, I would suggest there is a second overarching system governing the organisation of goal-directed action, in which the ultimate goal is no more than to please others rather than the self. There is an innate mechanism in humans that fosters the development of actions and behaviours that simply have the goal of being valued by others and this will be further discussed below.

Social Learning

Culture for many people is a word used to describe the things that sophisticated people do, or alternatively for practices that are specific to certain societies. Animal behaviourists on the other hand use it to describe those behaviours that animals learn from one another (Whiten, Hinde, Laland, & Stringer, 2011). At one time, it was considered that the only species capable of learning by imitation was *Homo sapiens*. It was argued that a number of species could mimic and in this respect the ability of birds (and especially parrots) to mimic quite complex sounds was acknowledged. However, in the last 20 years, a profusion of research has documented an extensive range of behaviours that are transmitted between animals. Even fruit flies have been shown to be capable of social learning (Danchin et al., 2018).

As with empathy, there has been much debate about what constitutes social learning, and differences between imitation, mimicry and emulation. A 'taxonomy' of different social learning mechanisms has been documented (Whiten, 2006) and imitation is considered the most cognitively advanced form of cultural transmission. This involves copying the form of an action by relating its underlying motivation and goal through some sort of cognitive representation of the causal relationship. For example, many of the studies that have investigated imitation in primates (humans and non-humans) have involved 'puzzle' boxes in which an observer learns to copy those actions that are pertinent to open the boxes to obtain rewards (e.g. Flynn & Whiten, 2008). Among non-humans, most imitation concerns practical tasks such as tool use, such as learning to use a probe to remove termites from a tree trunk for food. Gestural communication is relatively sparse. Among humans, however, there is an extensive role of imitation for the purposes of social communication. Language is the obvious example but consider also gesture and facial expression. We use a broad repertoire of actions for social communication that include posture, facial expression and manual gestures. These might be thought instinctive and, for many years, at least since the time of Darwin, it was argued that facial expressions were universal among man and animals (Darwin, 1872, 2009). Whilst it is probably true that the there is a universality to a degree, in so far as you are unlikely to mistake happiness and anger whatever culture you are in, there is also a large and varied dictionary of variants (Jack, Garrod, Yu, Caldara, & Schyns, 2012). When we try to use emoji's in our messages, we would be very impoverished if we were only able to access the six basic expressions. And for me personally, most of the time I can't find one that quite captures the facial expression I want to convey. Not only are our facial expressions locally modified to local culture, but they are also subtly modulated. Actors are paid large sums of money because they can get the expression just right for the situation. Furthermore, social communication by gesture and action is highly diverse between cultures (Kendon, 1997). An example of cultural influences comes from football goal celebrations. This has progressed from a simple handshake or pat on the back in the 1960s to a highly diverse range of gestures, gymnastic feats and tactile social interactions that we see in the modern day (Turner, 2012).

The Neural Mechanisms of Empathic Learning

Much has been made of the 'theory of mind' framework of false belief understanding, and the associated role of medial frontal cortex of the brain and temporoparietal junction (Gallagher & Frith, 2003). As discussed above, there has been a long-standing notion that there is a specific cognitive capacity for belief attribution that could underlie empathy. An action-based perspective takes a different approach. In confining ourselves only to the way this is managed at the level of the cerebral cortex, we can consider three different components: action perception, sensory interoception and action-evaluation.

Action Perception

Back in 1989, David Perrett and colleagues at the University of St Andrews published a paper reporting neurons in the superior temporal sulcus, which were specifically responsive to the intentional actions of others (Perrett et al., 1989). These neurons fired specifically when they saw intentional actions, irrespective of the perspective. Over the next ten years, further cells were identified in parietal and premotor cortex, which coded not only for the observation of specific actions but also for their execution (di Pellegrino, Fadiga, Fogassi, Gallese, & Rizzolatti, 1992; Gallese, Fadiga, Fogassi, & Rizzolatti, 1996; Rizzolatti, Fadiga, Gallese, & Fogassi, 1996). These were called 'mirror neurons' and were considered particularly remarkable, because part of the brain that had previously been considered to be active only during action execution (the premotor cortex) was also found to be active during action perception. The network of brain areas that encodes the perception of motor actions has come to be recognised as the action-observation network (AON) (Caspers, Zilles, Laird, & Eickhoff, 2010). This network of brain areas can also be considered that part of the brain that encodes action configurations and some parts also hold the instructions on how to perform any action at the level of a whole action and its relationship with its meaning.

Sensory Interoception

Another component is the feedback from bodily sensors. This is visceral and skin sensory information that conveys information about such things as pain, temperature, nausea and heart rate. Then there is kinaesthetic information about body and joint-position in space, necessary for coordination of movement. Kinaesthetic information is fed back through the thalamus to the parietal cortex, whilst sensory information goes to the insula and then the somatosensory cortex. These two components show quite a lot of overlap in their anatomy as somatosensory cortex and insula are important in perceiving emotion in action.

Evaluation and Learning

One of the most phylogenetically conserved parts of the human brain is the orbitofrontal cortex (Kringelbach & Rolls, 2004). This serves the role of associative learning. It is the part of the brain that encodes the associations between experience and behavioural response. Behaviours generally go one of two ways—increase or decrease. A negative valence means punishment and a reduced likelihood of repeating a behaviour, whilst positive valence means that it is rewarded, and increases the chance of recurrence. If we think of the pigeon that learns to peck the red spot to get a sweet drink but finds that the green spot provides a bitter taste, these associations are encoded in the orbitofrontal cortex. The orbitofrontal cortex is closely connected to motor planning, so that the pigeon quickly learns to associate red with one motor action, and green with another. Unfortunately, life for humans is not so simple that the same action always serves the same function. Our versatility requires that the value of an action depends upon its context. And furthermore that value is constantly changing according to the culture. To deal with this, part of the brain has evolved to vary the value assigned to actions. This part of the brain is located in the anterior cingulate gyrus. It has very close connectivity with the action-observation network, and the insula and the medial frontal cortex (Apps, Rushworth, & Chang, 2016).

What is particularly interesting is that one part of this area of the brain appears to assign an action-value to someone else's action, not in terms of its perceived benefit to the individual perceiving it, but in terms of its perceived benefit to the other person. There are two possibly important functions for this part of the brain. Firstly, it may serve to value altruism. By reinforcing actions that are considered beneficial to others, the value of a relationship is reinforced and cooperation ensues that is fundamental to success as a member of a society. A second function is illustrated by a recent experiment in South African monkeys (van de Waal, Borgeaud, & Whiten, 2013). In this experiment, parental monkeys were provided red and yellow foodstuffs, tasting bitter and sweet, respectively. When the teaching element was removed (i.e. red and yellow foods tasted the same), there remained a preference for the yellow foods in the offspring monkeys and this preference remained as a cultural variant. The infant monkeys must have observed parental reaction to the foods and so associated observed behaviour with differential emotional value which they then incorporated into their behaviour. The idea here is that when we see someone doing something, we generally figure that they are doing it because they are finding it good for themselves. Therefore, it follows that if we copy it, we will find it good for ourselves too. Of course, we do not do this blindly, we only make the judgement that 'if it is good for them, it is good for me' in certain circumstances, when we identify with that person in some way, such as if the person is in authority over us or is one of the 'in-crowd' or 'like-me'. Therefore, empathy is critical component of social learning. When we see another person enacting a behaviour, a part of our brain computes a value of that action *to that other person*. This fundamental aspect of action perception is also a basic form of empathy. We will then utilise that computational value to determine whether we will imitate that action. An important feature of this system is the willingness to learn actions with a negative valence. If an individual observes another person carrying out an action that is apparently punishing, whether to themselves, or others, if that action is somehow judged to be of positive value to the person enacting it, it is likely to be imitated. This may help to explain the apparently paradoxical nature of martyrdom, why physical abuse is perpetuated across generations, or why self-harming behaviours may be spread by social media. In each case an action that is harmful to the individual is held in some way to be of benefit to them.

The Actions and Feelings Questionnaire (AFQ)

One hypothesis that follows if one argues that empathy is based on learned socially communicative behaviour is that the people who are the best at expressing and communicating social behaviours and emotional states will also be the best at understanding other people's feelings. Perhaps this is self-evident to some people but do we have evidence for it? Certainly, in the case of autism, we see that the diagnostic features of autism include a constellation of impaired empathy and problems with expressing and communicating feelings through gesture, voice tone, facial expression and modulated gaze, which constitute the mainstay of the diagnostic features of the condition. One notable observation here is that people with autism are not necessarily impervious to emotional contagion. Some people with autism report being acutely sensitive to other people's feelings and especially their anxiety (Rogers, Dziobek, Hassenstab, Wolf, & Convit, 2007). Indeed, some would suggest that their high sensitivity is a cause for their social withdrawal. This brings us back to the question of how the perceived emotion has to be placed within a goal-directed context. In doing so, the means of setting it within an action hierarchy occurs, and with that comes the potential of it obtaining a place in 'ordered' awareness and the means of controlling it.

The Actions and Feelings Questionnaire (AFQ) was designed to examine the idea that there would be a pattern of thought and behaviour related to individual variability in the functioning of the action-observation network and that this variability could be captured by a self-report questionnaire (Williams, Cameron, Ross, Braadbaart, & Waiter, 2015). Furthermore, this variability would predict empathic ability. A set of questions was devised which sought to ask people to report on the degree that they depended upon their AON in everyday life. The questions asked people to reflect on how much they imagined actions, read other people's behaviour by observing their actions, imitated other people, were susceptible to emotional contagion, and expressed thoughts and feelings through gesture, facial expression and body posture. We started with 30 questions and then selected 18 of these which had correlations with the total of ≥0.3. As can be seen from Table 2.1, the final questions cover a variety of issues, and yet the questionnaire showed strong internal coherence (a measure of whether the questions are all asking about a common underlying factor).

We also asked people to complete a 15-item self-report empathy scale (EQ) and showed that the totals on the EQ and the AFQ correlated strongly with one another. Next, we looked to find out if our questionnaire total correlated with brain activity, recorded whilst people were carrying out our facial imitation task. We found that activity in the somatosensory cortex during facial imitation was correlated with the score on the

Table 2.1 The 18-item AFQ. Chi-squared values illustrate magnitude of group effect (ASD vs Control) on ratings for individual items

Item		Factor	Chi-squared
1	I tend to pick up on people's body language	Feelings	588
2	To understand someone, I rely on his or her words rather than his or her expression or gesture[a]	Feelings	440
3	To make sense of what someone else is doing, I might copy his or her actions	Imagery	76.7
4	Music that I like makes me want to dance	Animation	116
5	In my mind's eye, I often see myself doing things	Imagery	21.7
6	If talking on the phone, I am sensitive to someone's feelings by the tone of their voice	Feelings	514
7	If others are dancing, I want to join in	Animation	265
8	My body movements do not tend to reflect the way I feel[a]	Feelings	322
9	I often imagine myself performing common actions	Imagery	17.1
10	I would consider myself to be a 'touchy-feely' person	Animation	171
11	When I recall what someone said to me, I have to think hard to remember their facial expression at the time[a]	Feelings	425
12	I rely on seeing how a person looks me in the eye to gauge what they really feel	Feelings	274
13	I wouldn't tend to know what someone was feeling like if they did not say[a]	Feelings	469
14	I move my hands a lot when I speak	Animation	44.6
15	I get animated when I am enthusiastic in conversation	Animation	28.8
16	I can easily bring to mind the look on someone's face when I remember telling them something	Feelings	384
17	Acting things out helps me to understand them	Imagery	27.4
18	Watching someone's body language is not a good way to judge their feelings[a]	Feelings	299

[a]Negatively scored item

questionnaire. Interestingly, the area identified corresponded to an area associated with action awareness in another study. Considering that our questionnaire was concerned with asking people to report on their self-awareness of the role of action in their everyday thoughts and feelings, this made a lot of sense, and led us to suggest that our measure was actually tapping into action awareness.

Our next study with the AFQ was to administer it to a larger population including people with autism in order to obtain a better measure of its psychometric properties and find if it had any diagnostic value (Williams & Cameron, 2017). Almost 1400 people completed the questionnaire and the 15-item empathy scale, including over 300 with an autism diagnosis. The number of responses allowed us to carry out a reliable factor analysis, which divided our questions into three factors: the feelings factor, an imagery factor and an animation factor. We found that the total score strongly discriminated between autism and control groups. However, one of the factors in the questionnaire, the 'feelings' factor, consisting of nine items was stronger, showing 86% for sensitivity and 87% for specificity at the optimal cut-off point.

These simple questionnaire studies provide evidence for the importance of action awareness and motor cognition in generating individual differences in empathy and autism spectrum disorder. The idea here is not that people can or can't do something but will have different ways of dealing with things in daily life. In communication especially, one can rely heavily on verbal aspects, or one can place more weight on the non-verbal aspects. One of the more discriminative questions is 'to understand someone I rely on his or her words rather than their expression or gesture'. This was designed on the premise that people often give mixed messages. They say one thing but their body language conveys something else. If put in the situation, and asked explicitly, then most people could probably recognise this. The question is more subtle in asking what you place most weight on, or which would you attend to the most—actions or words. People with autism show little problem naming and recognising emotional expressions but, in general, seem to place little weight on non-verbal expression, either in judging others or expressing their own feeling states.

Imitation and Empathy

If empathy is grounded in socially learned behaviours, there should be a relationship between imitation accuracy and empathic traits. However, we and others had not been able to find this. This may be because we had been looking at manual imitation rather than emotional expression. An indication that imitation of actions with a purely emotionally communicative function may be different to those that have a physically based goal comes from an observation that they are relatively rare among non-human primates. Whilst many members of the animal kingdom imitate actions designed to obtain foodstuff, there is little evidence for intentional emotional expression being imitated in any animal other than humans.

However, studying the imitation of intentional emotional expression is not as simple as it may first appear. Basic facial expressions are learned from an early age, and whilst there is much debate as to the extent that they are innate and vary across culture, they are largely similar and few individuals have any difficulty enacting the basic emotional expressions (happy, sad, surprise, disgust, fear and anger). Therefore, the task has to be more difficult than just imitating basic expressions as variance is otherwise unlikely to be informative. Secondly, there is a difficulty computing the degree of correspondence between one expression and another, since an expression is made up of multiple 'facial action units'. Any attempt to devise a measure based on measuring correspondence across all these units would be very time-consuming on the one hand and problematic to compute on the other. Our solution was in two parts (Williams, Nicolson, Clephan, de Grauw, & Perrett, 2013) and relied on the fact that the best instruments for reading human expressions are human observers. Firstly, we 'blended' basic emotional expressions to make novel expressions using computer morphing techniques. These varied in a systematic way (see figure) so that we had continua. Somebody very good at imitating would be able to imitate two slightly different expressions well enough for an observer to be able to correctly tell which expression was the model for each imitation. In contrast, a poor imitator would make a similar expression for different models and it would be more difficult to make the attribution accurately. Using this principle, we built an experiment and rated people on imitation accuracy. We then found that imitation accuracy corresponded to a self-report measure of empathy using the empathic quotient, a finding which we have since replicated another three times. This experiment therefore provides empirical evidence that the degree of motor control that an individual has over emotional expression is a strong associate of empathic traits.

Training Empathy

I am therefore suggesting that we should consider two types of sensorimotor learning. The first type is the type that is traditionally the topic of sensorimotor psychology that describes the visuomotor mechanisms underpinning the learning of most everyday actions that have physical goals, whether they are fine motor such as hand-writing, using tools and manipulating small objects, or more gross motor such as kicking a football and swimming in a straight line. Learning is coded according to emotional 'value-to-self' in orbitofrontal cortex, concerned with satisfying an appetitive motivation.

The second type is concerned with social communication and is concerned with facial expressions, body posture and manual actions that reflect an emotional state, but more importantly, an intentionally expressed and communicated emotional state. The perceived actions of others are encoded by an action-observation network and these actions have emotional values attached to them by a process we can call 'social affordance learning' in which the value of an action, as it is thought to be held by the actor, is coded in one region according to its value as it is felt to be held by the other, as well as in another area, according to its value to the self.

An important question to my mind is whether the two functions may compete with one another. Do the functional parameters which make the system best adapted for goal-directed action conflict with those that make it more suited for socioemotional communication? For example, if you are involved in sport (or in hunting during times when our brains were evolving), might you perform better if your coordination is not affected by emotion? And yet skilled social-emotional coordination means having a sensorimotor system that is closely attuned to emotional states. We might consider attentional influences or the mechanical properties of actions. Physical actions may require high levels of focus, whilst social actions require fluctuation, unpredictability and cognitive flexibility. Physical actions are rehearsed to be highly stereotyped (the same every time), whereas social-emotional actions are highly varied according to context or culture. Personally, I marvel at the ability of tennis or golf players to keep themselves cool even when the attention of millions of people is focussed upon them. But does this mean that tennis players are likely to have flat effect and no social communication skills? The answer is obviously not, because ultimately, success in any sport needs all the abilities. But perhaps there is a requirement to be able to separate emotion from action and stop it impacting upon performance, and this forms the basis of a strategy used successfully in British sports (Peters, 2012).

As well as the contrast between visuomotor skills required for sport versus socialisation, I also suggest that the overlap is equally worth considering to help us understand empathy. We can think of empathy as a motor skill which is practised in a highly social environment. The parallels with a team sport such as football are useful. At a fundamental level, footballing skill depends upon ball control; the ability to kick or head it in the right direction. However, those basic actions occur within a complex social environment and deciding when, how and where to kick the ball depends upon complex strategic decisions. We wouldn't think of separating footballing ability into two separate aspects of ball control and knowing what to do in a specific situation. Of course, you have managers who no longer have the motor abilities but have all the decision-making ability. But I have not heard of a footballer who has the ball control but not the playing skill. This is because the two aspects develop hand in hand. Similarly, empathy is a skill in coordination of emotional expression that results in cogent and coherent emotional communication. Most importantly though, it can be trained, but that training is also dependent upon the cultural environment. In countries where football is the most popular game (at least among males), boys will grow up learning to kick a ball from an early age, and perhaps spend hours each week practising the skill of kicking a ball. In the same way, socioemotional interaction can be thought about in this light. The social interactions that take up hours every day result in practice and training of a visuomotor skill. In environments where socioemotional reciprocity is central to family life, emotional responses are monitored, commented upon and trained as a fundamental part of development.

According to the mechanisms I have described, a poverty of socio-emotional interaction may be caused by an individual who innately lacks the appropriate reward mechanisms, and who pays little attention to others. This may occur in autism. But social neglect or any environment that has a poverty of social interaction will have similar effect. Consequently, we see an autism-like picture in children raised in social isolation such as those from the Romanian orphanages (Rutter et al., 1999). The other important issue is what sorts of abnormal social environment cause abnormal empathy. Borderline personality traits are now thought to involve a sort of 'hyper-empathic' pattern of responding where a person over-thinks the behaviour of another person (Carla Sharp & Vanwoerden, 2015), and these may stem from a lifetime of experiencing abuse, involving strong emotional responses coupled with a pressure to keep secrets.

Conclusion

We can think of empathy as a quality of behaviour that we can observe in the here and now, that is, a quality of a social interaction rather than an invisible function that governs the way someone thinks. Furthermore, we can think of it as something that can be trained and fostered, rather than as a fixed personality trait. Nevertheless, we should not underestimate the challenges that some individuals may face in developing their empathic skills, if their innate skills are poor or if they have experienced a lifetime of abnormal or deficient training. But training should not be hard. Like any other skill, it must be paced and adjusted to meet the trainee at his or her level and ability, and it may take a while, but this should not be complicated to deliver for anyone with reasonable empathic skills themselves. It just needs to be given the appropriate amount of space, time and will.

References

Adams, R. B., Jr., Franklin, R. G., Jr., Kveraga, K., Ambady, N., Kleck, R. E., Whalen, P. J., … Nelson, A. J. (2012). Amygdala responses to averted vs direct gaze fear vary as a function of presentation speed. *Social Cognitive and Affective Neuroscience, 7*(5), 568–577. https://doi.org/10.1093/scan/nsr038

Apps, M. A., Rushworth, M. F., & Chang, S. W. (2016). The anterior cingulate gyrus and social cognition: Tracking the motivation of others. *Neuron, 90*(4), 692–707. https://doi.org/10.1016/j.neuron.2016.04.018

Baron-Cohen, S. (1997). *Mindblindness: An essay on autism and theory of mind.* Cambridge, MA: MIT Press.

Baron-Cohen, S., & Wheelwright, S. (2004). The empathy quotient: An investigation of adults with Asperger syndrome or high functioning autism, and normal sex differences. *Journal of Autism and Developmental Disorders, 34*(2), 163–175.

Byrne, R. W., & Whiten, A. (1988). *Machiavellian intelligence: Social expertise and the evolution of intellect in monkeys, apes and humans.* Oxford: Oxford University Press.

Carla Sharp, C., & Vanwoerden, S. (2015). Hypermentalizing in borderline personality disorder: A model and data. *Journal of Infant, Child, and Adolescent Psychotherapy, 14*(1), 33–45. https://doi.org/10.1080/15289168.2015.1004890

Caspers, S., Zilles, K., Laird, A. R., & Eickhoff, S. B. (2010). ALE meta-analysis of action observation and imitation in the human brain. *NeuroImage, 50*(3), 1148–1167. https://doi.org/10.1016/j.neuroimage.2009.12.112

Coll, M. P., Viding, E., Rutgen, M., Silani, G., Lamm, C., Catmur, C., & Bird, G. (2017). Are we really measuring empathy? Proposal for a new measurement framework. *Neuroscience and Biobehavioral Reviews, 83*, 132–139.

Cuff, B. M. P., Brown, S. J., Taylor, L., & Howat, D. J. (2014). Empathy: A review of the concept. *Emotion Review, 8*(2), 144–153. https://doi.org/10.1177/1754073914558466

Danchin, E., Nobel, S., Pocheville, A., Dagaeff, A. C., Demay, L., Alphand, M., … Isabel, G. (2018). Cultural flies: Conformist social learning in fruitflies predicts long-lasting mate-choice traditions. *Science (New York, NY), 362*(6418), 1025–1030. https://doi.org/10.1126/science.aat1590

Darwin, C. (1872). *The expression of the emotions in man and animals.* London: Murray.

Darwin, C. (2009). In P. Ekman (Ed.), *The expression of the emotions in man and animals* (4th ed.). Oxford: Oxford University Press.

Davis, M. H. (1980). A multidimensional approach to individual differences in empathy. *Journal of Personality and Social Psychology, 44*, 113–126.

de Vignemont, F., & Singer, T. (2006). The empathic brain: How, when and why? *Trends in Cognitive Sciences, 10*(10), 435–441. https://doi.org/10.1016/j.tics.2006.08.008

Decety, J. (2011). Dissecting the neural mechanisms mediating empathy. *Emotion Review, 3*, 92–108.

di Pellegrino, G., Fadiga, L., Fogassi, L., Gallese, V., & Rizzolatti, G. (1992). Understanding motor events: A neurophysiological study. *Experimental Brain Research, 91*(1), 176–180.

Dunbar, R. (2003). Psychology: Evolution of the social brain. *Science (New York, NY), 302*(5648), 1160–1161. https://doi.org/10.1126/science.1092116

Flynn, E., & Whiten, A. (2008). Imitation of hierarchical structure versus component details of complex actions by 3- and 5-year-olds. *Journal of Experimental Child Psychology, 101*(4), 228–240. https://doi.org/10.1016/j.jecp.2008.05.009

Gallagher, H. L., & Frith, C. D. (2003). Functional imaging of 'theory of mind'. *Trends in Cognitive Sciences, 7*(2), 77–83.

Gallese, V., Fadiga, L., Fogassi, L., & Rizzolatti, G. (1996). Action recognition in the premotor cortex. *Brain, 119*(2), 593–609.

Hatfield, E., Cacioppo, J., & Rapson, R. (1993). Emotional contagion. *Current Directions in Psychological Science, 2*, 96–99.

Jack, R. E., Garrod, O. G., Yu, H., Caldara, R., & Schyns, P. G. (2012). Facial expressions of emotion are not culturally universal. *Proceedings of the National Academy of Sciences of the United States of America, 109*(19), 7241–7244. https://doi.org/10.1073/pnas.1200155109

Kendon, K. (1997). Gesture. *Annual Review of Anthropology, 26*, 109–128.

Kringelbach, M. L., & Rolls, E. T. (2004). The functional neuroanatomy of the human orbitofrontal cortex: Evidence from neuroimaging and neuropsychology. *Progress in Neurobiology, 72*(5), 341–372. https://doi.org/10.1016/j.pneurobio.2004.03.006

Lobmaier, J. S., & Perrett, D. I. (2011). The world smiles at me: Self-referential positivity bias when interpreting direction of attention. *Cognition & Emotion, 25*(2), 334–341. https://doi.org/10.1080/02699931003794557

Niedenthal, P. M. (2007). Embodying emotion. *Science (New York, NY), 316*(5827), 1002–1005. https://doi.org/10.1126/science.1136930

Perrett, D. I., Harries, M. H., Bevan, R., Thomas, S., Benson, P. J., Mistlin, A. J., … Ortega, J. E. (1989). Frameworks of analysis for the neural representation of animate objects and actions. *The Journal of Experimental Biology, 146*, 87–113.

Peters, S. (2012). *The chimp paradox*. London: Vermilion.

Reniers, R. L., Corcoran, R., Drake, R., Shryane, N. M., & Vollm, B. A. (2011). The QCAE: A questionnaire of cognitive and affective empathy. *Journal of Personality Assessment, 93*(1), 84–95. https://doi.org/10.1080/00223891. 2010.528484

Rizzolatti, G., Fadiga, L., Gallese, V., & Fogassi, L. (1996). Premotor cortex and the recognition of motor actions. *Brain Research Cognitive Brain Research, 3*(2), 131–141.

Rogers, K., Dziobek, I., Hassenstab, J., Wolf, O. T., & Convit, A. (2007). Who cares? Revisiting empathy in Asperger syndrome. *Journal of Autism and Developmental Disorders, 37*(4), 709–715. https://doi.org/10.1007/ s10803-006-0197-8

Rutter, M., Andersen-Wood, L., Beckett, C., Bredenkamp, D., Castle, J., Groothues, C., ... O'Connor, T. G. (1999). Quasi-autistic patterns following severe early global privation: English and Romanian Adoptees (ERA) study team. *Journal of Child Psychology and Psychiatry, and Allied Disciplines, 40*(4), 537–549.

Saxe, R. (2006). Uniquely human social cognition. *Current Opinion in Neurobiology, 16*(2), 235–239. https://doi.org/10.1016/j.conb.2006.03.001

Turner, M. (2012). From 'pats on the back' to 'dummy sucking': A critique of the changing social, cultural and political significance of football goal celebrations. *Soccer and Society, 13*(1), 1–18. https://doi.org/10.1080/14660970. 2012.627164

van de Waal, E., Borgeaud, C., & Whiten, A. (2013). Potent social learning and conformity shape a wild primate's foraging decisions. *Science (New York, NY), 340*(6131), 483–485. https://doi.org/10.1126/science.1232769

Whiten, A. (2006). The dissection of imitation and its 'cognitive kin' in comparative and developmental psychology. In S. J. Rogers & J. H. G. Williams (Eds.), *Imitation and development of the social mind: Lessons from autism and typical development* (pp. 227–250). New York: Guilford Press.

Whiten, A., & Byrne, R. W. (1997). *Machiavellian intelligence II.: Evaluations and extensions*. Cambridge: Cambridge University Press.

Whiten, A., Hinde, R. A., Laland, K. N., & Stringer, C. B. (2011). Culture evolves. *Philosophical Transactions of the Royal Society of London. Series B, Biological Sciences, 366*(1567), 938–948. https://doi.org/10.1098/ rstb.2010.0372

Williams, J. H. G., & Cameron, I. M. (2017). The actions and feelings questionnaire in autism and typically developed adults. *Journal of Autism and Developmental Disorders, 47*(11), 3418–3430. https://doi.org/10.1007/ s10803-017-3244-8

Williams, J. H., Cameron, I. M., Ross, E., Braadbaart, L., & Waiter, G. D. (2015). Perceiving and expressing feelings through actions in relation to individual differences in empathic traits: The action and feelings questionnaire (AFQ). *Cognitive, Affective, & Behavioral Neuroscience, 16*(2), 248–260. https://doi.org/10.3758/s13415-015-0386-z

Williams, J. H., Nicolson, A. T., Clephan, K. J., de Grauw, H., & Perrett, D. I. (2013). A novel method testing the ability to imitate composite emotional expressions reveals an association with empathy. *PLoS One, 8*(4), e61941. https://doi.org/10.1371/journal.pone.0061941

3

"But It Wouldn't Be Me": Exploring Empathy and Compassion for Self and Others Through Creative Processes

Melissa Cain

Introduction

As educators, we typically centre our teaching on what we want our students to know and be able to do. If we examine most curriculum documents, we are able to identify the expected knowledge and skills for particular discipline areas, as well as important capabilities such as creative thinking, interpersonal skills, and cultural understanding necessary to apply the knowledge and skills effectively. Arguably more significant are attitudes and dispositions such as empathy and compassion that underlie the core curriculum, and that work to support a peaceful world and contribute to the common good of humankind (Williams, Huong, Bui, & Lee, 2018; Jorge & Munoz Munoz, 2016). Curriculum documents and teacher education texts tend to focus on teaching skills, behaviour management, and ways to engage students; however, as Cooper (2011) notes, the importance of emotions has been "virtually absent" (p. 197) as a serious focus. The problem, suggests Gibbs (2017) is that

M. Cain (✉)
Australian Catholic University, Brisbane, QLD, Australia
e-mail: melissa.cain@acu.edu.au

© The Author(s) 2019
G. Barton, S. Garvis (eds.), *Compassion and Empathy in Educational Contexts*,
https://doi.org/10.1007/978-3-030-18925-9_3

compassion isn't very highly regarded "and it is even denigrated, in Western philosophy and in everyday life" (p. 19).

What place, therefore, do empathy and compassion have in the 'product-driven consumer service business model' of higher education (Gibbs, 2017, p. 9)? Gibbs (2017) notes that there has been little research on "cultivating compassion in educational environments specifically among undergraduate ... students" (p. 10). Noddings (2005) offers that all educators "have the responsibility to help their students develop a capacity to care" (p. 16). Empathy and compassion are innate personality dispositions but are also teachable (Jeffrey & Downie, 2016; Johnson, 1990), and it is every educator's responsibility to provide their students with opportunities to see empathy and compassion in practice, to recognise and activate these dispositions within themselves, and facilitate a range of experiences that support the emotional, aesthetic, and cognitive development of empathy and compassion. Here, empathy is considered as the ability to 'feel into' the situation of another, and compassion as the motivation to improve the wellbeing of another.

Using narrative inquiry, this chapter explores an ethnographic journey of the author through three personal and professional 'happenings'—incidents that connect to different facets of empathy and compassion—to determine the qualities, role, and place of empathy and compassion in higher education. These 'happenings' are critically reflected upon with reference to literature and aligned with the author's experiences teaching pre-service or trainee teachers in the higher education sector. This inquiry works to understand the emotional, cognitive, and aesthetic facets of empathy and suggests creative ways to develop genuine empathy in higher education students and to prompt them to move them from empathy to active compassion.

Methodology

This study is qualitative in nature. The author utilises a combination of narrative inquiry (the gathering of information for storytelling) with ethnographic reflection (descriptions and analyses of individuals, groups, and settings). Bruner (1990) offers that "the typical form of framing experience (and our memory of it) is in narrative form" (p. 56). Narrative inquiry as a research methodology centres on an open-ended investigation of a personal-professional inquiry puzzle with a set of questions to guide the investigation (Connelly & Clandinin, 1990). As such, the use of narrative inquiry was a fitting choice for the author's journey to discover the aesthetic, affective, and cognitive qualities of empathy and compassion and the role and place of such dispositions in higher education; here conceptualised as both methodology and phenomenon (Lindsay & Schwind, 2016). Ethnography has been described by Shah (2017) as potentially 'revolutionary praxis' because it "forces us to question our theoretical presuppositions about the world, produce knowledge that is new, was confined to the margins, or was silenced" (p. 45). The use of ethnography in this chapter prompts the author to consider propositions arrived at before the analysis of the stories presented, which, in turn, question dominant theoretical positions and inform future practice.

Focusing on Dewey's (1938) understanding that experience is at once relational, temporal, and situational, the three structural scaffolds of narrative inquiry—'temporality, sociality and place'—developed by Connelly and Clandinin (2006) guide the author towards the past, present, and future. Connelly and Clandinin (2006) note that narrative must "reflect the temporal unfolding of people, places, and things within the inquiry, the personal and social aspects of the inquirer's and participants' lives, and the places in the inquiry" (p. 485). Developing an empathic disposition requires the vulnerable choice to employ emotion, cognition, and reflection. In this way, this chapter reflects on the author's personal and professional experiences over *time* from childhood to present day, related through three brief *social* narratives or 'happenings' (instances that feature empathy and compassion in action). Reflection on these happenings and close connections to contemporary literature helps the author to investigate the research puzzle—*what is this thing, and is it good?*—achieved by answering the questions: (1) what is the role and place of empathy and compassion in higher education?, and (2) how can empathy and compassion be developed through teaching creatively and for creativity?

In this investigation and to reach answers, the author questions and then re-questions in a 'continual reformulation' (Clandinin & Connelly, 2000) or "spiral of possibilities and illumination as part of the research puzzle" (Cain & Nislev, 2018, p. 470). The use of narrative inquiry here is based on Lindsay and Schwind's (2016) personal, social, and practical justifications, serving to inform the author's *personal* work as an educator, to illuminate *social* practices of pre-service teachers, and to provide a series of *practical* recommendations in the higher education space. These happenings aim to provide both depth and breadth, making sense of past, present, and future events as they unfold; however, it is acknowledged that only one perspective is brought to this analysis, although the words of others play a significant role in the inquiry.

Within the chapter, the happenings are presented and reflected upon through connections to the literature. In this way, both a review of contemporary literature and the 'results' of the narrative and ethnographic inquiry are combined.

Happening: 'But It Wouldn't Be Me'

When I was young, maybe six or seven, the nightly news featured distressing images of an east African country suffering the ravages of extreme famine. The emaciated children on the television looked nothing like me and the parched countryside bared no resemblance to the Melbourne suburb in which I grew up. In my comfortable life, I couldn't imagine what famine might feel like, but it was obvious it was a pain I hadn't ever experienced. I couldn't fully comprehend the effects of severe hunger, a desperate lack of water, and the pain of losing loved ones. But I tried. I tried to put myself in this foreign place. I tried to smell, hear, and embrace something very, very different.

It was not lost on me that there was a huge discrepancy between my life and the lives of children the same age as me in this far away land. I wrestled with questions—why was I born in Australia? Why was my life a comfortable life with adequate food, an education, and safety in the family home? This was a confusing time. At some stage, I mentioned my thoughts to an adult—"we are so lucky being born here and not there. Can you imagine what that must be like?" The adult's answer stopped me in my tracks. "But I wouldn't be born there". I countered—"but you <u>could</u> have, it was just your good fortune to be born in Australia". And as resolutely the adult responded "No, that would not have happened; it wouldn't be me, I am not one of them".

This answer did not sit well with me and the confusion intensified. I truly did not understand where this reaction was coming from and it prompted so many questions about an 'abstract something' I was yet to explore. What were our personal differences in that moment? What was I expressing, and what served to jar our perspectives? As it so happened, I was involved in several '40 Hour Famines' in my teen years which aimed to replicate the intensity of hunger experienced by those afflicted by famine, and I eventually visited east Africa in my mid-20s. On foreign soil, there was a stark realisation that my imaginings, my attempts to feel into a situation foreign to me were firmly based in the negative. In placing myself in another's situation, I had not thought to also imagine the joys; the joy of communal music making, of familiar traditions, and of love shared by family and community.

Reflection: What Is This Thing and Is It Good?

Over time, moving from childhood to adulthood and into the world of work, I came to know this thing as empathy. I knew its feeling well and continued to experience empathy (which often extended to compassion), but remained on a search to identify its deeper characteristics and qualities. Reaching for answers only led to more questions: is empathy good? Do all humans feel empathy? Is empathy innate or learned, or both? I revisited these questions often, reflecting and researching; constructing and reconstructing after experiencing these 'happenings'; which served to make meaning and test my hypotheses.

The literature provides many definitions of empathy. Barnes and Thargard (1997) view empathy as 'knowing' and Bresler (2013) a type of 'tuning in' (p. 9). Empathy has its roots in the Greek word 'empatheia' which is composed of 'en' (in) and 'pathos' (feeling) (Singer & Klimecki, 2014). The term *empathy* came into use in the English language from the German notion of 'Einfühlung', or 'feeling into'. Peterson (2017) emphasises the role of imagination and our ability to take ourselves to places unseen, by describing empathy as "an imaginative reconstruction of the suffering of others" (p. 52). Margolin (2013) too describes empathy as "the capacity to imaginatively enter the life of another" (p. 86). Empathy, suggests Renck Jalongo (2014), "is the ability to identify with another living thing's emotional states, both negative and positive" (p. 6).

Someone who can explain all manner of concepts through the use of fitting analogies is Dr Brené Brown. In her audio book *The Power of Vulnerability: Teachings on Authenticity, Connection and Courage* (2012), Brown paints a picture of someone who is feeling overwhelmed and struggling; stranded at the bottom of a deep hole. To contrast sympathy and empathy, Brown describes sympathy as another person standing at the top looking down into the hole and recognising that this person is feeling distress. Empathy, however, is likened to climbing down into the hole, sitting next to the person in distress and saying, "I know what it's like down here and you're not alone". Brown asserts that empathy is 'feeling *with* people' and is a trait that fuels connection, and that in order to connect with someone empathically, firstly we need to connect with something within ourselves that knows that feeling. Here, Brown refers to Teresa Wiseman's (1996) attributes of empathy—to be able to see the world as others see it, to be nonjudgemental, to understand another person's feelings, and to communicate your understanding of that person's feelings (p. 1165). Empathy is, therefore, a choice states Brown, and it's a choice that requires vulnerability on our part.

So, in re-examining some of my initial questions, particularly in response to Brown's assertion that empathy involves a choice, I query here if we all born with feelings of empathy? Does empathy require cognition and reasoning? The answer to both of these questions is 'yes'. Demetriou (2018) notes that empathy is "a conflicting demand of intellect and evocation of feeling, a dynamic duo of cognition and emotion" (p. 43). Empathy is not confined to humans, but for humans Kramer (2013) emphasises that empathy is a complex phenomenon. It is the ability to be at once "viscerally, cognitively, imaginatively and emotionally attentive" (White, 2013, p. 101). The affective form of empathy can be described as 'vicarious emotion' and the cognitive exploration is better known as 'perspective-taking'. Every human is born with an ability to respond reflexively to the feelings of others. Babies respond to others in pain or distress as noted in neuroimaging studies using functional magnetic resonance imaging (MRI) of 'mirror neurons'. This meaningful affective link does not just extend to emotional states but to physical experiences in others such as "pain, touch, or tickling" (Gallese, 2003, p. 519) and is largely involuntary. These affective, vicarious experiences are understood instinctively and automatically without the necessity of complex cognitive input (Gallese, 2003). Meekin (2013) contests that cognition, however, is necessary "for all but the most rudimentary forms of empathy" (p. 5). More cognitive forms of empathic understanding involve a conscious intellectual drive or motivation to recognise accurately the experiences of others, and intricate capacities of imagination to re-enact another's thought processes or experiences.

Happening: Just the Other Day

One afternoon I was driving on a busy, double-carriage road thick with peak-hour traffic. Ahead I could see a figure on a motor scooter attempting to do a speedy U-turn across a double white line. This manoeuvre was undoubtedly illegal and extremely dangerous. In executing this, the driver narrowly missed being hit by a large lorry and as a result the bike skidded and the rider was thrown off into the gutter. Many other drivers witnessed this event but none stopped to assist. I pulled over and waited for a break in the traffic to cross the road by foot. The young and diminutive female driver was wearing a t-shirt, shorts, and flip flops and had injuries to her legs and arms and her helmet visor was ripped off. She appeared dazed and unable to stand after several attempts. She needed help. I realised that she was delivering take away food. Two young men sat on their balcony watching the event and waiting for their pizza. Eventually they came out onto the street and took the pizza box from her hand and went back inside the gate without a word. The rider remained in the gutter.

Reflection: The Thorn Needed to Move from Empathy to Compassion

As I experienced this happening, the predictable questions surged forward, accompanied by a sense of anger and frustration. Why did others not stop? Why were the young men not motivated to assist the rider? Is empathy therefore a prerequisite for compassion? In defining compassion, Singer and Klimecki (2014) sees empathy or feelings of "warmth, concern, and care for the other" (p. 875) as a precondition for compassion, although Gibbs (2017) sees compassion as more directly emergent from pity. When empathy is accompanied by "a strong motivation to improve the other's wellbeing" (p. 875) one is compelled to act with compassion. The link to personal morals is emphasised by Peterson (2017) who sees compassion as a 'moral virtue' stemming from an emotional response which "admits both cognitive and volitional dimensions" (p. 13). Compassion requires a "recognition and appreciation of common humanity, including humanity's fragility" (p. 157) and involves how we regard humanity and notions of what a good person would do. Just as many conceptions of empathy appear to have an emphasis on the negative, Peterson's (2017) thoughts on the nature of compassion also refer to "a feeling of recognition and sorrow in response to the suffering of others" (p. 44).

To assist me explain the seeming lack of compassion in the last happening, I turn to Peterson (2017) who suggests that compassion "is a hard virtue to practice" (p. 84) and that the challenges of alleviating suffering may seem overwhelming, leaving us with a sense of powerlessness and unable to see how we can make a difference. Peterson (2017) details several 'barriers to compassion'. Perhaps the first, the 'diffusion of responsibility', may be a reasonable explanation here. Asking 'why me'? or 'why not someone else?' may lead to inaction. Such a 'diffusion of responsibility' may occur when the potential number of helpers are many. 'Bystander apathy' (which is not a conscious decision not to assist) has been shown to occur when the responsibility for intervention is shared among all onlookers and is not unique to any one individual.

Happening: The Cloth of Dreams

The group of third-year, pre-service teachers came into the Art room with their usual loud conversations, smiles, and playful teasing. Today's lesson explored dreams. Daydreams, prophetic dreams, and our dreams for the future. We discussed how dreams could be an inspiration or a thorn for our own creativity. Focusing on the visual art elements of shape and colour, the students worked together to contribute a patchwork of individual representations of a dream, using symbols on a large calico cloth the—'Cloth of Dreams'. Over the hour, the cloth came to life and the dreams were connected through the use of lines of varying shapes and thicknesses. As important as making the cloth, the students spent another hour responding to their own work and the work of others. The invitation to talk about their own creations was taken up by everyone. A nonjudgemental ambience supported the students as they richly described their artwork, their motives and inspirations, and their use of the elements of visual art.

In those moments, the students came to know each other on a more intimate and empathic level—aesthetically as they connected with the art works, emotionally as they felt the impact of another's life's happenings, and cognitively as they analysed the symbols and analogies used to tell the creative tales. There were long moments of silence when a collective holding of breath or 'inspire-ation' took the place of words and held the room hostage. There were moments of tears, as well as brilliant laughter consociating comedic moments and stories of joy. One quiet young man had depicted a large tree using muted tones. This was the tree he and his best friend had played under throughout their childhood and he dreamt of it often. For reasons not shared his friend was no longer alive. The young man had never talked to anyone about his despair of losing his friend. An envelope of empathy was offered in response, along with recognition of comparative personal experiences of pain. Through this activity, we connected with each other as co-learners, as artists, and most importantly as humans. We found something in ourselves we recognised in each of the segments of the dreamscape and in each other. We left the room strengthened and changed.

Reflection: Empathy in the Arts

This happening demonstrates evidence of empathy as inspired by engagement with artistic and creative practices. It has been my experience both in schools and in higher education institutions that empathy and compassion are frequent outcomes of creative experiences, especially in the arts, and that students enjoy and seek to express empathy in a creative manner. Meekin (2013) too sees that it is not uncommon for artistic projects "to engender feelings and conceptions of empathy" (p. 2). Robert Bersson (1982) has witnessed arts education as "a pedagogy of sensuous aesthetic response" (p. 38) which serves to cultivate affective empathy. Indeed, posits Mayo (2013), as arts education "has a critical role to play in cultivating empathy through aesthetic consciousness" (p. 79). Ultimately, Phillips and Siegesmund (2013) contest that the arts are "the only areas in which deep personal meanings can be recognised and expressed" (p. 243). We may not be able to easily quantify or measure empathy, but like creativity, we definitely know it when we see it. The ability of visual arts, in particular, to evoke empathy and stimulate compassion is expressed so poignantly by influential educational philosopher Maxine Greene (1995):

> There are images and figures that speak directly to our indignation, to some dimension of ourselves where we connect with others. They open our eyes, they stir our flesh, they may even move us to try to repair our world. (p. 143)

The Cloth of Dreams is one example of how engagement with arts education can inculcate feelings of empathy and compassion. Kessler (2000) relates that "when students find an opportunity to express their pain and challenges through creative expression, they often undergo healing transformations" (p. 114). So too is process or educational drama. Process drama provides an opportunity for students to do more than stand in another's shoes, but to communicate the feelings of another in an empathic and genuine manner. Process drama is about taking on role; not pre-scripted role but crafting role improvisationally and creatively based on pretexts and using historical and social knowledge. It's about allowing the drama to unfold as it will—each iteration uniquely dependent "on the action, reaction and interaction of the participants" (Dunn, 2016, p. 218). Through the use of symbol and analogy, process drama provides a forceful and motivating framework for the empathic exploration of the familiar and the foreign, and of tension and coalescence. Using process drama, teachers can cover the requirements of the curriculum as well as supporting students to *feel into* what might be like to be the 'other', to express these emotions in a variety of ways, and to connect with a vulnerability in themselves.

Ultimately, it is imagination that allows us to *feel into* a situation and to take ourselves to places unseen. Maxine Greene, through her work with the arts, has no doubt of the paramount place of imagination, stating that "imagination is what, above all, makes empathy possible. It is what enables us to cross the empty spaces between ourselves and [others]" (1995, p. 3). Yaniv and Candland (2012) explain that affective empathy occurs through neural processing achieving an "automatic sharing of the emotional states of others" (p. 72). According to Meekin (2013), these new aesthetic sensations can "destabilize our habits of perception and increase aesthetic sensitivity" (p. 66). Cognitive perspective-taking then spurs a more mature form of empathic understanding, which is then followed by "realization and concretization" of what has been laid bare (p. 72). Meekin defines this experience of connecting with 'the other' as *creative empathy* (p. 73).

Dance too provides a way for humans to connect kinaesthetically to experience the human condition. Through teaching creative dance, I have witnessed some of the most intriguing displays of understanding and insight. For example, using Melbourne author Shaun Tan's (2007) graphic novel *The Arrival* as a pretext, students in groups can explore the many facets of cross-cultural migration aesthetically, emotionally, and cognitively. Through purposefully sequenced movements, students can vividly express displacement, separation, longing, fear, confusion, hope, persistence, and joy to *physically* align themselves with others. Margolin (2013) describes her incorporation of 'empathy dances' as a vehicle for her students learning to trust themselves and others through "kinaesthetic emotional attunement" (p. 89). One such dance is a 'mirror dance', where pairs stand face to face, and palm to palm, with only a small space between them. One moves slowly and the other mirrors the movements as closely as possible; fluidly "to the point of indistinguishable leadership" (p. 88). One of Margolin's students describes the impact of taking part in such empathy dances:

> Eventually I didn't even have to look at her arms anymore. I never felt that before with another person where you just know what's next. It feels like you are touching but you are not. It was the most amazing feeling ever. (p. 89)

Here, the indispensable role of 'play' is obvious. The permission to engage in play is a necessary prerequisite for being satisfactorily mindfully free to engage at the deepest levels. Through artistic play, we can achieve both affective awareness and "robust cognitive empathy" (Meekin, 2013, p. 70). Through both making and responding in the arts, we come to know more about ourselves. We are given the time, spaces, tools, and incentive to take risks and to offer up a part of ourselves to others in the hope that it will be acknowledged and valued. Through rich conversation, we can develop creative insight, artistic thinking, wonder, imagination, subjective interpretation, perception of experience, empathy, and compassion.

Reflection: Knowing Self Than Other

It would seem that higher education institutions rarely promote the importance of knowing self before knowing other. Maxine Greene refers to knowing self as 'wide-awakeness'. She observes that "[w]ithout the ability to think about yourself, to reflect on your life, there's really no awareness, no consciousness. Consciousness doesn't come automatically; it comes through being alive, awake, curious, and often furious" (2008, para 2). An essential component of cultivating an empathetic disposition is purposefully getting to know ourselves first: our emotions, our preconceptions, our biases, and our social conduct before we investigate our relationship with 'the other' (Demetriou, 2018). In fact, suggests Peterson (2017), self-regard is seen to play an essential role in the active embodiment of compassion. If one has not engaged in 'knowing self' and feels they do not have the personal capacity to cope with another's difference, their resistant response may be to avoid exposure to such difference. Here, perceived personal apathy or callousness may be seen as "a self-focused, aversive reaction to the vicarious experience of another's emotion that may manifest itself as discomfort or anxiety" (Demetriou, 2018, p. 57).

So, what of the relationship between self and others? Fenichel (1945) states that empathy consists of two acts: "(a) an identification with the other person, and (b) an awareness of one's own feelings after the identification, and in this way an awareness of the object's feelings" (1946, p. 511). Barnes and Thargard (1997) acknowledge that it may indeed be very difficult to cross-cultural boundaries and make such associations with those who differ from us. They suggest that this type of analogical transfer is not, however, reliant on specific personal experiences, but can take place via a schema we develop from multiple previous cases. We share, for example, a basic human need to be understood and valued by others, and most of us have experienced situations where "loss made us sad, betrayal made us angry, and difficult situations made us indecisive" (p. 7) and upon which we may draw for this schema.

Research on compassion suggests that care for ourselves precedes care for others, and our experience of the aesthetic is an important mode of self-understanding. Kessler (2000) emphasises the importance of moments of deep connection to self "when we really know ourselves, express our true self, feel connected to the true essence of who we are—nourish the human spirit" (p. 20). Karen Armstrong (2011), an eminent scholar in comparative religions, agrees. She argues that "before you can embrace the whole world you must focus on yourself ... become conscious of your anger, fear and anxiety. Look deeply into the seeds of rage within yourself. Bring to mind some of your past suffering and the pleasure in things we all tend to take for granted. Finally, look at yourself with even-mindedness" (p. 102).

Making Meaning of Empathy and Compassion in Higher Education

Rashedi, Plante, and Callister's (2015) research finds that "humans have a natural capacity for compassion" and that "compassion is a skill that can be taught" (p. 131). Teacher educators, suggests Conklin (2008), share responsibility for "not only working to prepare teachers who will teach in socially conscious, equitable ways, but also for helping the teachers themselves become ready for this work" (p. 665). Personality dispositions such as empathy and compassion are most frequently taught in civic, moral, social justice, community service, or religious education courses; however, this type of association (i.e. 'feel good' courses are associated with 'feel good' outcomes) neglects the wisdom and insight needed for the holistic development of dispositions that engender care, peace, and wellbeing. Noddings agrees that all teachers "have the responsibility to help their students develop a capacity to care" (2005, p. 16). In the words of His Holiness the Dalai Lama XIV (Lama, n.d.), "Compassion is not religious business, it is human business; it is not luxury, it is essential for our own peace and mental stability; it is essential for human survival". I advocate that 'pedagogy of care' should be core content and not merely a by-product of a curriculum focused on knowledge and skills.

With a view to my continuing work with pre-service teachers and their prospective futures which will impact the lives of hundreds of students, I reflect on the 'happenings' related here and the literature examining empathy and compassion to make some observations about how empathic dispositions may be nurtured in creative ways. I suggests that we give ourselves the permission to engage in what Greene calls 'social imagination' "the capacity to invent visions of what should be and what might be in our deficient society" (1995, p. 5). Let's imagine that all higher education teachers see value in the need for developing caring dispositions in their students, and that there is a commitment to this growth in *all* disciplines and a commitment to working with creative processes. What would be the guiding parameters to encourage this to happen? Here are six suggestions:

1. **Support a vulnerable choice**. It is essential that educators take care to prepare an atmosphere of acceptance, trust, and safety. Encouraging students to make a vulnerable choice to critically examine themselves, their families, value systems, norms, traditions, and biases must be scaffolded with care and with attention to possible distress and anxiety. We must ask our students to take risks but to do so in safety. Kessler (2000) wisely notes that "safety seems to be the *opposite* of risk, but it is a *pre-condition* for risk" (p. 108). With risk comes responsibility, suggests Heaton (2018), "but also belief that one can defend, instigate, disrupt and alter actions and ideologies" (p. 141).

2. **Model and practice**. As part of this, we must model the outcomes we encourage and teach towards caring empathy. Students need to see empathy and compassion in practice and know what it is to be the recipients of empathy and compassion. Teresa Wiseman's (1996) framework provides helpful guidelines to begin with: to see the world as others see it; to be nonjudgmental; to understand another person's feelings; and to communicate your understanding of that person's feelings (p. 1165). For some educators, however, this may not be an innate response. We should practice and develop the attitudes of empathy but also be aware that students have a strong radar for false and feigned empathy.

3. **Engage with people**. We must focus our work on people. Not just learning *about* people or their situations, but engaging deeply and meaningfully with a range of 'others' on a personal level. These encounters should be grounded in real, lived experience, not abstract conceptions, and about hearing stories presented with heart and courage. Maxine Greene states that by "attending to a range of human stories [young people] may be provoked to heal and to transform" (1992 p. 259). We must find ways for students to climb down into the hole, to sit with the other, hear the stories, connect with something within themselves that knows that feeling, and relate these feelings that back in empathic ways.

4. **Respond aesthetically and creatively**. We must undertake engagement with empathy and compassion by coming to know self and others in creative ways. This means responding *aesthetically* through activities that require creative thought, collaboration, rich conversations, and responding to our own work and the work of others. We must practice perspective-taking, consider ways to invoke kinesthetic attunement, and opportunities to express ourselves through the use of analogy and symbol. For accessing aesthetics empathy, suggests Kessler (2000), "can help bridge the unbridgeable" (p. 104).

5. **Value time**. To achieve quality aesthetic and creative engagement, we must value time. Time for the components of the journey to empathy and compassion to unfold. We must stimulate these with an affective arousal and provide information and personal connections to allow both conscious cognitive engagement and unconscious active incubation. In particular, and with reference to the creative process, we must provide time for the incubation of information, for memories and tenuous associations to find each other before coming back to relate the illumination and test our thoughts and findings.

6. **Care for self**. Finally, we must care for ourselves, and be aware that empathy and compassion are ultimately prosocial behaviours, but can be hard work. It is possible that engaging empathically and compassionately may lead to empathic distress, negative feelings, or withdrawal (Decety, 2011). We must notice if we become compassion weary, or perhaps become cynical over time and through interaction.

Conclusions

In this chapter, the use of narrative inquiry has facilitated the undertaking of an open-ended investigation of a personal-professional inquiry puzzle with reference to temporarily, sociality, and place. This has been achieved through reflection over time on three personal and professional happenings and engagement with a wide range of literature on empathy, compassion, and the arts. Returning to the research question, what has become evident is that the dispositions of empathy and compassion are both innate and teachable. Empathy and compassion play an essential role in higher education and should be part of the core curriculum and not be relegated to a limited number of subjects such as religious or ethics education. Educators need to employ empathy and compassion in their work and prepare their students to care. As expected, this inquiry has answered some questions and spurred many others for future investigation. With Australian universities becoming more culturally diverse and with greater numbers of international students, further inquiry might address culturally specific perspectives of empathy and compassion, and how they might impact a pedagogy of care with adult learners. This investigation has also revealed a close association between the components empathy and compassion and the creative process. Further investigation of the potential alignment between the tenets of empathy and compassion, the creative process, and the attitudes of creative people is warranted. Finally, ways of working with higher education students to overcome 'bystander apathy' is essential, so that 'but it wouldn't be me' becomes 'it should, and will be me'.

References

Armstrong, K. (2011). *Twelve steps to a compassionate life*. New York: Alfred A. Knopf.

Barnes, A., & Thargard, P. (1997). *Empathy and analogy*. Ontario: University of Waterloo. Retrieved from http://cogsci.uwaterloo.ca/Articles/Pages/Empathy.html

Bersson, R. (1982). Against feeling: Aesthetic experience in technocratic society. *Art Education, 35*(4), 34–39.

Bresler, L. (2013). The spectrum of distance: Empathic understanding and the pedagogical power of the arts. In B. White & T. Constantino (Eds.), *Aesthetics, empathy and education* (pp. 7–28). New York, NY: Peter Lang Publishing.

Brown, B. (2012). *The power of vulnerability: Teachings on authenticity, connection and courage*. Boulder, CO: Sounds True.

Bruner, J. (1990). *Acts of meaning*. Cambridge, MA: Harvard University Press.

Cain, M., & Nislev, E. (2018). Art as transformative education. Starting the conversation. *Australian Art Education, 39*(3), 468–491.

Clandinin, D. J., & Connelly, F. M. (2000). *Narrative inquiry: Experience and story in qualitative research*. San Francisco, CA: Jossey-Bass.

Conklin, H. (2008). Modeling compassion in critical, justice-oriented teacher education. *Harvard Educational Review, 78*(4), 652–674.

Connelly, F. M., & Clandinin, D. J. (1990). Stories of experience and narrative inquiry. *Educational Researcher, 19*(5), 2–15.

Connelly, F. M., & Clandinin, D. J. (2006). Narrative inquiry. In J. L. Green, G. Camilli, & P. Elmore (Eds.), *Handbook of complementary methods in education research* (pp. 477–487). Mahwah, NJ: Lawrence Erlbaum.

Cooper, B. (2011). *Empathy in education: Engagement, values and achievement*. London: Continuum.

Decety, J. (2011). Dissecting the neural mechanisms mediating empathy. *Emotion Review, 3*(1), 92–108.

Demetriou, H. (2018). *Empathy, emotion and education*. London: Palgrave Macmillan.

Dewey, J. (1938). *Experience and education*. New York, NY: Macmillan.

Dunn, J. (2016). Demystifying process drama: Exploring the why, what, and how. *Drama Australia Journal, 40*(2), 127–140. https://doi.org/10.1080/144 52294.2016.1276738

Fenichel, O. (1945). *The psychoanalytic theory of neurosis*. New York, NY: W W Norton.

Gallese, V. (2003). The manifold nature of interpersonal relations: The quest for a common mechanism. *Philosophical Transactions: Biological Sciences, 358*(1431), 517–528.

Gibbs, P. (2017). *The pedagogy of compassion at the heart of higher education*. London: Springer.

Greene, M. (1992). The passions of pluralism. *Journal of Negro Education, 61*(3), 250–261.

Greene, M. (1995). *Releasing the imagination*. San Francisco, CA: Jossey-Bass.

Greene, M. (2008, October 14). *Wide-awakedness*. Retrieved from http://teachingwideawake.wordpress.com/tag/maxine-greene/

Heaton, R. (2018). Artist teacher cognition: Connecting 'self' with 'other'. *Australian Art Education, 39*(1), 139–145.

Jeffrey, D., & Downie, R. (2016). Empathy-can it be taught? *Journal of the Royal College of Physicians of Edinburgh, 46*(2), 107–112.

Johnson, J. (1990). Empathy as a personality disposition. In R. Mackay, J. Hughes, & E. Carver (Eds.), *Empathy in the helping relationship*. New York, NY: Springer.

Jorge, M., & Munoz Munoz, F. (2016). Uncovering the virtues of peace within visual culture: The case for nonviolence and imperfect peace in the western tradition. *Peace & Change, 41*(3), 329–353.

Kessler, R. (2000). *Soul of education: Helping students find connection, compassion, and character at school*. Alexandria, VA: Association for Supervision & Curriculum Development.

Kramer, J. (2013). Multisensory aesthetic experiences and the development of empathy: The big bad wolf's not so bad after all. In B. White & T. Constantino (Eds.), *Aesthetics, empathy and education* (pp. 167–184). New York, NY: Peter Lang Publishing.

Lama, D. (n.d.). A quote by Dalai Lama XIV. *Goodreads*. Retrieved from https://www.goodreads.com/quotes/161864-compassion-is-not-religious-business-it-is-human-business-it

Lindsay, G., & Schwind, J. (2016). Narrative inquiry: Experience matters. *Canadian Journal of Nursing Research, 48*(1), 14–20.

Margolin, I. (2013). Expanding empathy through dance. In B. White & T. Constantino (Eds.), *Aesthetics, empathy and education* (pp. 83–98). New York, NY: Peter Lang Publishing.

Mayo, S. (2013). Art in the expanded field: Notions of empathy, aesthetic consciousness, and implications for education. In B. White & T. Constantino (Eds.), *Aesthetics, empathy and education* (pp. 61–82). New York, NY: Peter Lang Publishing.

Meekin, L. (2013). *Art education and the encouragement of affective and cognitive empathy in early childhood*. Doctoral dissertation. Virginia Commonwealth University: Richmond, Virginia, USA.

Noddings, N. (2005). *The challenge to care in schools: An alternative approach to education* (2nd ed.). New York, NY: Teachers College Press.

Peterson, A. (2017). *Compassion and education cultivating compassionate children, schools and communities*. London: Palgrave Macmillan.

Phillips, L., & Siegesmund, R. (2013). Teaching what we value: Care as an outcome of aesthetic education. In B. White & T. Constantino (Eds.), *Aesthetics, empathy and education* (pp. 221–234). New York, NY: Peter Lang Publishing.

Rashedi, R., Plante, T., & Callister, E. (2015). Compassion development in higher education. *Journal of Psychology and Theology, 43*(2), 131–139.

Renck Jalongo, M. (2014). Humane education and the development of empathy in early childhood: Definitions, rationale, and outcomes. In M. Renck Jalongo (Ed.), *Teaching compassion: Humane education in early childhood* (pp. 3–16). London: Springer.

Shah, A. (2017). Ethnography? *HAU: Journal of Ethnographic Theory, 7*(1), 45–59.

Singer, T., & Klimecki, O. (2014). Empathy and compassion. *Current Biology, 24*(18), 875–878.

Tan, S. (2007). *The arrival.* New York: Arthur Lavine Books.

White, B. (2013). Pay attention, pay attention, pay attention. In B. White & T. Constantino (Eds.), *Aesthetics, empathy and education* (pp. 99–116). New York, NY: Peter Lang Publishing.

Williams, C., Huong, T., Bui, K. Y., & Lee, H. (2018). Art as peace education at "dark" museums and sites in the United Kingdom, Europe, and Southeast Asia. *Asian Journal of Peacebuilding, 6*(1), 157–198.

Wiseman, T. (1996). A concept analysis of empathy. *Journal of Advanced Nursing, 23*(6), 1162–1167.

Yaniv, D., & Candland, D. (2012). Dynamics of creativity and empathy in role reversal: Contributions from neuroscience. *Review of General Psychology, 16*(1), 70–77.

Part II

The Importance of Compassion and Empathy for Children and Young People

Part II

4

Towards a Test-Driven Early Childhood Education: Alternative Practices to Testing Children

Susanne Garvis, Heidi Harju-Luukkainen, and Tina Yngvesson

Introduction

In 2016 the Organisation for Economic Co-operation and Development (OECD) invited bids to develop and pilot what has been referred to as 'baby PISA.' The study was called 'International Early Learning and Child Well-Being Study' (or IELS). While many people are familiar with PISA aimed at 15-year-olds on various assessment domains that among other information rank countries by performance, a similar concept was

S. Garvis (✉)
Department of Education, University of Gothenburg and Stockholm University, Göteborg and Stockholm, Sweden
e-mail: susanne.garvis@gu.se

H. Harju-Luukkainen
University of Helsinki, Helsinki, Finland
e-mail: heidi.harju@helsinki.fi

T. Yngvesson
Gothenburg University, Gothenburg, Sweden
e-mail: tina.yngvesson@gu.se

© The Author(s) 2019
G. Barton, S. Garvis (eds.), *Compassion and Empathy in Educational Contexts*,
https://doi.org/10.1007/978-3-030-18925-9_4

proposed for early childhood education with five-year-olds. The proposal was to create a 'PISA' for five-year-olds that looked at a variety of inputs related to child development and learning.

Alarm bells began to ring for some academics, governments and educational organisations around the world with the announcement of an international testing regime for five-year-olds. In particular, questions were raised about the foundation of well-being and compassion within early childhood contexts and if we truly are taking children's perspective and including children's opinion into the discussions connected to international assessments (see, for instance, Karlsson, Hohti, Tammi, Olli & Hakomäki, 2014). What has been seen with international PISA assessment is that policy makers and opinion leaders have made problematic interpretations of the results which have had its impact on education systems across the world. Further, the development conducted on the basis of these PISA results have in some cases had an unexpected outcome, and they have not necessarily been all positive considering children's further learning prospects. This was, for instance, the case in Portugal (see Feytor Pinto & Kouki, 2015). The limitations of PISA are fairly well known, however not necessarily among the public. According to Kivinen and Hedman (2017), PISA has not been designed to assess how well students master the contents of the school curricula, yet opinion leaders in Finland keep reading PISA results as schools' report cards indicating the excellence of education policy in a country. They argue further, that every three years PISA produces masses of standardised numerical information, which unfortunately does not redeem the strict requirements of policy based on scientific facts. There has also been other critical voices internationally, especially towards the methodology (Fernandez-Cano, 2016; Feniger & Lefstein, 2014) and towards the translation of the instrument (Arffman, 2007).

This chapter will provide three perspectives to explore some of the current debates around the so-called baby PISA and provide an overview of current research around children's well-being in early childhood education. A teacher perspective will be shared. The researcher perspective has already been shown in academic literature and featured strongly in academic debate. The perspectives will consist of narratives blended with research literature to show the importance of contextual and cultural understanding. In the final section, alternate pathways for supporting children's well-being will be made to provide different possibilities for the future.

International Early Learning and Child Well-Being Study (IELS)

Before taking a look at IELS, we need to put it into context and consider the Organisation for Economic Co-operation and Development's (OECD's) first international assessment called PISA (Programme for International Student Assessment), which has been known as the "world's premier yardstick for evaluating the quality, equality and efficiency of school systems" (OECD, 2018, 2). After the first PISA 2000 execution, we have witnessed a rapid development of many international assessments in different domains and for various target groups. Examples of these are TIMSS (mathematics and science study) and PIRLS (reading literacy study), but also surveys directed towards adults like PIAAC or towards teachers like TALIS.

According to OECD (2018, 3), PISA assesses the extent to which 15-year-old students have acquired key knowledge and skills that are essential for full participation in modern societies. Further, it argues that the assessment does not just ascertain whether students can reproduce knowledge; it also examines how well students can extrapolate from what they have learned and can apply that knowledge in unfamiliar settings, both in and outside of school. PISA measures students' proficiency in five main domains: reading literacy, mathematical literacy, scientific literacy, collaborative problem-solving skills and financial literacy. However, in the first PISA, the main domains were only three, excluding collaborative problem-solving skills (added to PISA 2009) and financial literacy (added to PISA 2015). Additionally to PISA 2018, an assessment domain of global competencies was presented. The latest PISA 2015 assessment covered 72 participating countries and economic areas across the world where approximately 540,000 students completed the two-hour assessment (OECD, 2018). This makes PISA one of the largest international educational assessments. PISA is conducted every three years with an alternating main domain. Alternating main domains gives OECD as well as the participating countries an opportunity to monitor changes more reliably in the main domains every nine years. In addition to the assessment in domains, PISA consists of a questionnaire for schools and for students as well. It gives moves detailed information of family socioeconomic and cultural background, students' interests and motivation towards different aspects of the assessed domains, as well as information on different aspects of the schools.

The IELS collects, similarly as PISA assessment information from different domains as well as information about the early childhood education context and homes as following. According to OECD (2018 home pages), the IELS study is an international survey that assesses children at age five across three countries, identifying key factors that drive or hinder the development of early learning. The purpose of the study is to provide countries with a common language and framework, encompassing a collection of robust empirical information and in-depth insights on children's learning development at a critical age. With this information, countries will be able to share best practices, working towards the ultimate goal of improving children's early learning outcomes and overall well-being. The International Early Learning and Child Well-Being Study will:

Provide robust empirical data on children's early learning through a broad scope of domains that comprise cognitive and social and emotional development.

Identify factors that foster and hinder children's early learning, both at home and in early childhood education programmes.

Provide findings that will allow parents and caregivers to learn about interactions and learning activities that are most conducive to child development.

Inform early childhood education centres and schools about skill levels of children at this age as well as contextual factors related to them that they could use to make more informed decisions about curriculums and pedagogical methods.

Provide researchers and educators in the field of early education with valid and comparable information on children's early learning, and characteristics obtained from a range of sources and accompanied by a broad scope of contextual variables.

Three countries taking part are England, the United States and Estonia. The four early learning domains that will be measured are as follows:

1. Emerging literacy skills: oral language and listening comprehension, vocabulary, phonological awareness
2. Emerging numeracy skills: working with numbers, numbers and counting, shape and space, measurement, pattern
3. Self-regulation: working memory, mental flexibility/adaptability, self-control
4. Social and emotional skills: trust, empathy, prosocial behaviours

While some information has been available to the public about the project, some researchers have also reported secrecy about the overall process and test (see Moss & Urban, 2017). Moss and Urban (2017, p. 255) describes the OECD's actions around IELS as a form of "secrecy and dismissal of concerns." They argue that rather than having an "opening for debate and contestation, the OECD has chosen to dismiss the concerns that have been expressed about the IELS by simply ignoring them" (Moss & Urban, 2017, p. 255).

The connection between PISA for 15-year-olds and 5-year-olds was made in the call for tender with:

> *In time, the information (from the IELS) can also provide information on the trajectory between early learning outcomes and those at age 15, as measured by PISA. In this way, countries can have an earlier and more specific indication of how to lift the skills and other capabilities of its young people.* (OECD, 2016, p. 9)

The experience with PISA therefore provides a warning for IELS, as Morris (2016, p. 26) states:

> [T]he simplest way to improve PISA scores is for nations to align their curricula more closely to what is measured by PISA ... If countries do this and improve their scores, we will enter into a closed and self-fulfilling system in which nations teach according to test requirements and better scores create an illusion of improvement.

It is known that the contractor for the project consists of the Australian Council for Educational Research, the International Association for the Evaluation of Educational Achievement, and cAp-StAn. Which countries are involved however is unknown. What is known is the list of countries that have chosen to not participate including Belgium, Canada, Denmark, Germany, Norway and Sweden. Within these countries, numerous articles and statements have appeared in national magazines about criticisms towards the OECD's project and possible outcomes. This has also lead to claims about the need for cultural and contextual understanding within early childhood contexts as well as some focus on the overall importance of well-being in early childhood education: in particular, why the project has decided to include child well-being in the title and how this is actually explored within the testing region.

The behaviour by the OECD is described by Moss and team as follows:

> The Organisation adopts a particular paradigmatic position which might be described as hyper-positivistic … The OECD is free to choose its position. However, it should be aware that it has made a choice and taken a particular perspective. It should also be aware that there are other choices and other perspectives. Yet on both counts it shows a total lack of self-awareness. (Moss et al., 2016, p. 346)

In particular the authors question the concept of child participation and the child perspective in the project. Moss and Urban (2017) make it clear that while the project includes the child perspective, there is no indication of how a child's consent to participate will be conducted. Again this leads to the earlier suggestions of secrecy over implementation and intention.

One important consideration is the cultural and contextual understanding within each country's landscape. While comparative assessments can be useful to provide snapshots of current points in time, we must also remember they are bound within a cultural and contextual lens. This means that everything that a child experiences in preschools is unique and understood best in that context. As Alexander (2012, p. 5) notes:

National education systems are embedded in national culture ... no educational policy or practice can be properly understood except by reference to the web of interested ideas and values habits and customs, institutions and world views, that make one country distinct from another.

If we look within the different understanding of early childhood curriculum, we can notice many immediate differences. Some countries have cultures of play; other countries may have cultures of intentional teaching. Some countries may value certain aesthetic and creative ways of working in early childhood classrooms while others may not. Some countries also have different starting ages for compulsory schooling (some countries have five years others have later or earlier starting ages). Even the concept of a classroom varies across countries. For example, in Sweden, the word 'classroom' is not commonly used when talking about preschool. Rather it is a learning environment to support the development of children. The term 'classroom' is reserved for the formal schooling context. It is only understanding the culture and context that important differences can be known.

Focus of Chapter

Against the backdrop of baby PISA, it is important to share our narrative understanding of the possibilities of an international test for early childhood education. As Swedish researchers, we have had many encounters with researching and learning about PISA. Our concern about baby PISA stems from the positioning of early childhood education as a technical practice within discourses of industrial benchmarking and neo-liberalism. From this perspective, early childhood education and the proposed study are viewed as a technical practice, where comparative education is:

A technical process modelled on industrial benchmarking, in which the outcomes have been determined, and the aim is simply to engage in the global war for talent by learning enough from competitors to beat them at their own game. (Auld & Morris, 2016, p. 226)

In this chapter we share our combined teacher perspectives to explore the possibilities associated with baby PISA and try to seek the place of compassion and well-being within each. We have experience working across the globe and have worked at the 'coalface' with a number of educational issues across multiple countries. We are also within the Swedish paradigm of education that places the child's perspective, well-being and human rights as the pillar for Swedish education. Part of taking a stance in this chapter includes sharing personal stories as a teacher to share our perspective. As yet, this perspective has not been present in reflections about baby PISA. Our particular focus is the placement of well-being and compassion within the agenda of baby PISA. Our stories are constructed from "a metaphorical three-dimensional inquiry space" and is an engagement with my "story as data". It enables us as authors, to capture and communicate the emotional nature of our lived experience as well as capturing the dynamic nature of these lived experiences in relation to baby PISA.

The strength in our perspective is that we are three authors who all come from different countries and currently live in countries different to our nationality. Striking a balance is difficult but it is hoped that our story of the lived reality of being a teacher provides important insights into the positioning of well-being and compassion within the baby PISA regime.

Swedish Teacher Reflections

'*Good morning!' My voice fills the quiet corridor as I greet the first arrival of the day, a five-year-old girl and her mother. It's dark outside, the sun is still two hours away from rising and the ground is hard from ice and frozen earth. Inside the corridor is lit and there are rows of colourful children's rain clothes and coveralls, winter boots and sneakers lining the floor and walls. The mother nods a shy smile at me and continues to help her daughter take off her boots, coat and gloves. The girl turns to me and says in perfect Swedish, 'I'm wearing my new leggings today, see?' She quickly pulls off her thermal trousers and proudly shows off her bright pink leggings, the seam on the outside of the leg lined with silver sequin. 'I chose them myself. Do you like them?' I smile and reply that I do. I tell her they look comfortable and soft. I suggest they might be good for playing and dancing in. She smiles. Her mother smiles and says something to the girl in Polish. The girl quickly switches language and explains the exchange to her mother, her mother smiles at me and says something with a slight laugh. I don't understand, but I smile back. It's 5:50 am on a Monday and this particular girl has a 55-hour week ahead.*

One by one they start dropping in, all of her 16 five-year-old preschool mates, until they are all there, collected in the small front room where they all huddle together on the sofa and on the soft round mat on floor. Here we have our morning chat. Here we talk together and wish each other a good morning before dividing ourselves into themed playgroups (build, crafts, bard games, storytelling and so on) which we will rotate until 8 am when breakfast is served.

The preschool has several departments, like most Swedish preschools do. However, this particular department cater only to five-year-olds; these are the children being prepped to start primary school the following year. Many of the children are bi- or trilingual and most of the immigrant parents of these children do not speak Swedish or English. The children have long days as the parents work full-time, are engaged in studies and/or have several younger children or babies at home to look after. The majority of the children arrive before 7 am and finish around 5 pm, thus their days are long.

The children's ethnic backgrounds vary greatly; there is no homogeneity among them and in many cases no cultural similarities at all. This is a common example of a Swedish preschool group today. However, in the preschool setting, the children share one common culture, namely, the one that they create *together*. We know from research that young children demonstrate prosocial behaviour such as compassion and empathy in many preschools. In high-quality preschool programmes, this includes actions such as sharing toys, negotiating disagreements peacefully, comforting others in distress, giving others a chance to play, giving and receiving compliments graciously, warning others of danger and seeking adult assistance if another child is in trouble (Hyson & Taylor, 2011). The children are able to understand others' thoughts and feelings, regulate their own behaviour and learn socially acceptable ways for dealing with emotions (Pizzolongo & Hunter, 2011). This type of social and emotional development allows a strong sense of togetherness amongst the children. It is demonstrated when the children come together during group time and sit together on the sofa or on the soft mat.

Within the diverse group, there is the potential for conflict; however, this rarely occurs as the children develop prosocial skills based on compassion and empathy. Despite different value systems, home cultures, language skills and personality differences, the children manage their time together to be rewarding and enjoyable. The time spent learning about one another through dialogue, play and meals create a valuable foundation upon which they can later build their repertoire of social skills and understanding, a foundation that will allow them to easier adjust to compulsory school and the academic learning climate when the time comes. The International Early Learning and Child Well-Being Study as conducted by the OECD states that "there is growing interest in enhancing the quality of early childhood education programmes and children's home environments in order to give every child a strong start early on" and that "empirical research however, is limited on how children's competences are interconnected at an early age." This indicates that a potential need for change has been identified, but more importantly that the knowledge as to how to collect the information (from the children) needed in order to carry out the changes is currently not identified. So what does this mean for the children? Can there be an ethical path in the quest to collect information from the children? What about this sense of togetherness that is already demonstrated within Swedish preschools?

As teachers we know the importance of early childhood education for building a child's social and emotional well-being. The Center on the Social and Emotional Foundations for Early Learning (CSEFEL) lists key skills that support children's success in school and in the community:

- Confidence
- Capacity to develop relationships with peers and adults
- Concentration and persistence on challenging tasks
- Ability to effectively communicate emotions
- Ability to listen to instructions and be attentive
- Ability to solve problems (Hemmeter, Ostrosky, Santos, & Joseph, 2006)

These key skills are implemented within the Swedish Preschool Curriculum (Swedish National Agency for Education, 2018). As the Swedish preschool curriculum encompasses the whole child—meaning it takes a holistic view of the child (Swedish National Agency for Education, 2018)—the children learn through play and there are no compulsory academic requirements for the child to meet. A large part of the day is spent outdoors on the playground or in the forest, playing in the mud kitchen or racing on tricycles—on average the children spend four or more hours outdoors every day, no matter the weather. The notion that this time of play, exploration and togetherness in close symbiosis with nature should be replaced by time spent striving to achieve certain goals that better would meet the 'baby PISA' requirements, provoke thoughts of potentially shortened or, worse, *lost* childhood. Social learning theory propose that children learn by observing the behaviour of those around them and that their real-life experiences shape their behaviour as well as their practice in communication and engagement (Akers & Sellers, 2011; Gardner, Burton, & Klimes, 2006; Hood & Eyberg, 2003; Kazdin, 2005; Patterson, DeBaryshe, & Ramsey, 1989; Scaramella & Leve, 2004; Stormshak, Bierman, McMahon, & Lengua, 2000; Wahler & Meginnis, 1997). These real-life experiences compute into knowledge and "are carried forward across setting and time" (O'Connor, Matias, Futh, Tantam, & Scott, 2013).

When the foundations of children's learning and the expectations of children's learning shift, how then are the children affected? In Sweden, for instance, compulsory schooling starts with 'Förskoleklass' the year the child turns six years old—during this year the child will learn how to adjust to the academic setting where he or she will be enrolled for a total of ten years (Swedish national Agency for Education, 2018). Hence, there are no learning requirements in preschool when the child is five years old. All learning is done through play, and there are no assessments other than a parent-teacher meeting twice annually where the child's well-being and social adaptation are discussed. Were the child to officially be assessed on a scale according with the PISA requirements, the learning environment and pedagogy would need to change in order to answer to the demands created by the political and economic driving forces that motivate the PISA assessment. At which point do we begin to value assessment results more than childhood itself and the importance of social and emotional development? Do we value that which we can measure, or measure that which we value (Biesta, 2009)? The empathetic perspective of childhood and children is in its very essence dependent of children learning how to think and what to think. As teachers we also ask ourselves 'at what point do we justify teaching children *what* to think instead of *how* to think?' Can a PISA assessment for five-year-olds be beneficial to their personal growth and well-being? Will the foundation of children learning about each other and developing a sense of compassion change because of a changing political agenda? Can we not look at alternative ways for exploring quality early childhood settings and a different set of outcomes?

Alternate Ways Forward

The assessment domains in literacy and numeracy skills as well as self-regulation are important and somewhat streamlined with the PISA assessment. These domains give us undoubtedly interesting information about children's knowledge and skills across countries. However, there is also the converse to assessing skills and competencies. We have seen previously that international assessments, PISA included, have faced challenges when it comes, among others, to the interpretation of the results (Feytor Pinto & Kouki, 2015; Kivinen & Hedman, 2017), methodology (Fernandez-Cano, 2016; Feniger & Lefstein, 2014), translations (Arffman, 2007) and in integrating children's perspective (Karlsson et al., 2014). But also questions have been raised if we can consider these assessment results as scientific facts (Kivinen & Hedman, 2017). With no doubt, these weaknesses should be taken into consideration in the development of the instrument, execution as well as publication of the results in order for the scientific community to be taking these assessments seriously but even more importantly to hinder development based on false or exaggerated facts.

The assessment of the fifth domain, social and emotional skills, is challenging from many perspectives. It also does not have a clear overlapping with PISA assessment. Firstly, compassion and empathy are important for the well-being of all children. However, how 'baby PISA' assesses and further contributes to the support and development of compassion and empathy in early childhood across the different countries is unclear.

We also argue that so far many international assessments have failed in considering and/or including children's voices and further, there are no clear evidence that the new 'baby PISA' would be developed further on this aspect. Therefore, we suggest a stronger recognition of children's voices across international assessments but also a broader discussion of what are children's rights when it comes to being assessed and graded (here reference from ethics in child research). For instance, argues that "within social science research, in particular, research ethics guidelines, including those guidelines specific to child research, lack direct reference to human rights principles such as those articulated within the UN Convention on the Rights of the Child (UNCRC)." She argues further that "child researchers do not stand apart from their obligations to protect and promote children's rights, research ethics guidelines relied upon by child researchers need to be informed by human rights principles and that those researchers may draw upon the UNCRC, in particular, to inform their consideration of inevitable ethical dilemmas arising within child research."

As teachers we want children who are happy, healthy and able to develop values that allow an understanding and acceptance of others. We also want to support the moral and ethical development of young children to help create a better world for all. As educators and as parents, we advocate that this begins with young children.

Rather than a focus on a testing regime for young children, we ask for understanding about the moral and ethical development of young children and call on policy makers and stakeholders to consider alternate pathways. This could start with a discussion within countries about the importance of compassion and empathy in early years curriculum/frameworks and the importance of implementing tools in the classroom for social and emotional well-being.

Also rather than testing children for what they do and don't know, we suggest that a better way forward would be to assess the quality of the learning environment that children experience within early childhood settings. An international comparison could be made about the quality of learning environments that support children's learning and development that does not directly require child assessment. There are already a number of environmental rating scales in early childhood that have been trialled in a number of countries. An alternative testing regime may also collect information from teachers who can provide information about what the skills and knowledge of children. Some countries already collect information from teachers in large-scale studies in the early years.

As parents and researchers living in different contexts as expats, we can see in our everyday lives the differences in interpretations, for instance, on quality connected to ECEC. It is also difficult or even impossible to define different aspects of ECEC and to rank or value them. Therefore, within international comparisons it is important to also recognise cultural and contextual differences that exist within and between countries. When viewing countries considerations are necessary of variation in pedagogy, didactics and structural features (ratios, qualified staff, space, time in early childhood settings). Early childhood education acts in different ways in different countries, and any comparison must be taken with an understanding of cultural difference.

Conclusion

The future of 'baby PISA' is unknown and we must wait for what will happen from the initial study. We do not know the influence of 'baby PISA' on a child's social and emotional development, or where aspects of ideas such as compassion fit within an international comparative study agenda. Moss and Urban (2017, p. 256) urge people to start to consider what will happen after the initial study with:

> But it is not too late to think about what should follow after the conclusion of the initial study. With this in mind, we call on the early childhood community to develop and sustain a critical engagement with the IELS; and we call upon OECD and its member-state governments to enter into open discussion with the early childhood community about the future direction of comparative work on ECEC, and to do so now, rather than in 2020. (Moss & Urban, 2017, p. 256)

Their words provide a call for advocacy for people to discuss future possibilities with their communities and politicians now to ensure that their voices and concerns are heard and understood by key stakeholders. By talking now about possible concerns, key stakeholders are also made aware of how many people in the community are passionate about providing the best outcomes for children in the early years of education. Possible futures and outcomes need to be discussed to ensure as many different scenarios as possible are explored.

As we wait to learn more about 'baby PISA,' we also need to reflect on what is the purpose of early childhood education and why is there a current focus on comparing different early childhood contexts across the world. How does compassion and well-being fit within current models of thinking in relation to child development? What do we want children in the early years to experience? While there are more questions than answers, 'baby PISA' does also allow countries to stop and reflect on what they want as a focus for early childhood education.

It is important that we also reflect on previous ideas of what we want for changes in society. As Archbishop Desmond M. Tutu (Castle, 2000) states "We can each make a difference if we are vigilant to create a new kind of society, more compassionate, more caring, more sharing where human rights, where children's rights are respected and protected."

From this reflection we must always think of the future, especially around the rights of the child and creating a more compassionate world for children. It is hoped that the discussions continue to shed light on the actual project but also bring to the forefront the importance of children's well-being.

References

Akers, R., & Sellers, C. (2011). Social learning theory. In D. M. Bishop & B. C. Feld (Eds.), *The Oxford Handbook of Juvenile Crime and Juvenile Justice* (Part IV). USA: Oxford University Press. https://doi.org/10.1093/oxfordhb/9780195385106.013.0014

Alexander, R. J. (2012). Moral panic, miracle cures and educational policy: What can we really learn from international comparisons? *Scottish Education Review, 44*(1), 4–21.

Arffman, I. (2007). Kansainvälisten lukukokeiden kääntämiseen liittyviä ongelmia (The problem of equivalence in translating international reading literacy studies). *Kasvatus, 38*(4), 348–353.

Auld, E., & Morris, P. (2016). PISA, policy and persuasion: Translating complex conditions into education 'best practice'. *Comparative Education, 52*(2), 202–229.

Biesta, G. (2009). Good education in an age of measurement: On the need to reconnect with the question of purpose in education. *Educational Assessment Evaluation and Accountability, 21*(1), 33–46. https://doi.org/10.1007/s11092-008-9064-9

Castle, C. (2000). *For every child: The UN convention on the rights of the child in words and pictures*. Hong Kong: Midas Printing.

Feniger, Y., & Lefstein, A. (2014). How not to reason with PISA data: An ironic investigation. *Journal of Education Policy, 29*(6), 845–855.

Fernandez-Cano, A. (2016). A methodological critique of the PISA evaluations. *Revista Electrónica de Investigación y Evaluación Educativa, 22*, 1, art. M15. https://doi.org/10.7203/relieve.22.1.8806

Feytor Pinto, P., & Kouki, E. (2015). PISAn vaikutus opetuskäytäntöihin ja yliopistomenestykseen (PISA's effect on educational practices and success at university). Puheenvuoroja. *Kasvatus, 1*, 85–90.

Gardner, F., Burton, J., & Klimes, I. (2006). Randomised controlled trial of a parenting intervention in the voluntary sector for reducing child conduct problems: Outcomes and mechanisms of change. *Journal of Child Psychology and Psychiatry, 47*, 1123–1132. https://doi.org/10.1111/j.1469-7610.2006.01668.x

Hemmeter, M. L., Ostrosky, M. M., Santos, R. M., & Joseph, G. (2006). *Promoting children's success: Building relationships and creating supportive environments*. Presenters Scripts, Module 1 http://csefel.vanderbilt.edu/modules-archive/module1script.pdf

Hood, K. K., & Eyberg, S. M. (2003). Outcomes of parent–child interaction therapy: Mothers' reports of maintenance three to six years after treatment. *Journal of Clinical Child and Adolescent Psychology, 32*, 419–429. https://doi.org/10.1207/S15374424JCCP3203_10

Hyson, M., & Taylor, J. L. (2011). Caring about caring: What adults can do to promote young children's social skills. *Young Children, 66*(4), 74–83.

Karlsson, L., Hohti, R., Tammi, T., Olli, J., & Hakomäki, H. (2014). *Päättäjä, kuuntele lasta! (Policy maker, listen to the child!)* (Vol. 1, pp. 65–66). Kasvatus.

Kazdin, A. (2005). *Parent management training*. New York, NY: Oxford University Press.

Kivinen, O., & Hedman, J. (2017). Moniselitteiset PISA-tulokset ja niiden ongelmalliset koulutuspoliittiset tulkinnat (Ambiguous PISA-results and its problematic political interpretations). *Politiikka, 59*(4), 250–263.

Morris, P. (2016). *Education policy, cross-national tests of pupil achievement, and the pursuit of world-class schooling.* London: UCL Institute of Education Press.

Moss, P., Dahlberg, G., Grieshaber, S., Mantovani, S., May, H., Pence, A., ... Vandenbroeck, M. (2016). The organisation for economic co-operation and development's international early learning study: Opening for debate and contestation. *Contemporary Issues in Early Childhood, 17*(3), 343–351.

Moss, P., & Urban, M. (2017). The organisation for economic co-operation and development's international early learning study: What happened next. *Contemporary Issues in Early Childhood, 18*(2), 250–258.

O'Connor, T., Matias, C., Futh, A., Tantam, G., & Scott, S. (2013). Social learning theory parenting intervention promotes attachment-based caregiving in young children: Randomized clinical trial. *Journal of Clinical Child & Adolescent Psychology, 42*(3), 358–370.

Organisation for Economic Co-operation and Development (OECD). (2018). *PISA 2015: Results in focus.* http://www.oecd.org/pisa/pisa-2015-results-in-focus.pdf

Patterson, G. R., DeBaryshe, B. D., & Ramsey, E. (1989). A developmental perspective on antisocial behavior. *American Psychology, 44,* 329–335.

Pizzolongo, P. J., & Hunter, A. (2011). I am safe and secure: Promoting resilience in young children. *Young Children, 66*(2), 67–69.

Scaramella, L. V., & Leve, L. D. (2004). Clarifying parent-child reciprocities during early childhood: The early childhood coercion model. *Clinical Child and Family Psychology Review, 7,* 89–107.

Stormshak, E. A., Bierman, K. L., McMahon, R. J., & Lengua, L. J. (2000). Parenting practices and child disruptive behavior problems in early elementary school. Conduct Problems Prevention Research Group. *Journal of Clinical and Child Psychology, 29,* 17–29. https://doi.org/10.1207/S15374424jccp2901_3

Swedish National Agency for Education. (2018). *Lpfö 18.* Translated-curriculum for the preschool. https://www.skolverket.se/undervisning/forskolan/laroplan-for-forskolan/reviderad-laroplan-for-forskolan

Wahler, R. G., & Meginnis, K. L. (1997). Strengthening child compliance through positive parenting practices: What works? *Journal of Clinical and Child Psychology, 26,* 433–440. https://doi.org/10.1207/s15374424jccp2604_12

5

Compassion in Children's Peer Cultures

Jaakko Antero Hilppö, Antti Rajala,
and Lasse Lipponen

Introduction

Research on compassion has shown that children, even as young as toddlers, are capable of displaying concern for the wellbeing of others and acting with compassion (Spinrad & Eisenberg, 2017). Research has pointed to a range of biological and social influences on children's capability for compassion. Firstly, children's competence for compassion increases with age (Eisenberg, Spinrad, & Knafo-Noam, 2015), with older children being better at discerning the concerns of others as well as finding appropriate responses to others' plight. Secondly, it has been argued that parenting practices (such as modeling or perspective-taking emphasizing induction as well as children's participation in adult practices such as helping with family chores) have an impact on how and to whom children learn to show compassion (Eisenberg et al., 2015; Kirby, 2017; Lopez, Najafi, Rogoff, & Mejía-Arauz, 2012). Likewise, research

J. A. Hilppö (✉) • A. Rajala • L. Lipponen
Department of Educational Sciences, University of Helsinki, Helsinki, Finland
e-mail: jaakko.hilppo@helsinki.fi; antti.rajala@helsinki.fi; lasse.lipponen@
helsinki.fi

© The Author(s) 2019
G. Barton, S. Garvis (eds.), *Compassion and Empathy in Educational Contexts*,
https://doi.org/10.1007/978-3-030-18925-9_5

conducted in early childhood educational contexts has shown that teachers' warmth (e.g., emotional closeness, fewer conflicts between teacher and student) can be conducive to children's compassion (Luckner & Pianta, 2011). Regarding peer interaction, Eisenberg et al. (2015) note that existing research offers suggestive evidence of the possible impact of peer interactions on children's compassion, or more broadly pro-sociality, and propose that peer interactions possibly offer unique opportunities for compassion.

Despite this growing body of research on compassion, Eisenberg et al. (2015) note that the literature is currently thin on situational analysis on compassion in action, especially regarding research on children's peer interaction. In other words, while much is known about compassion in children, to a large extent, our knowledge of it relies on experimental investigations and parental (or teacher) reports and interviews (e.g., Volling, Kolak, & Kennedy, 2009). Less empirical work has been done analyzing how compassion manifests in children's everyday interactions.

In our own work, we have begun to address this research gap by taking an ethnographic research approach to study compassion in Finnish kindergartens (e.g., Lipponen, 2018; Rajala & Lipponen, 2018). Our studies have revealed that compassion can be embedded as part of the culture and social relations of a kindergarten. For example, Lipponen (2018) discovered that the local early education and care curriculum of a kindergarten encompassed many rules related to compassion that everyone should be included. In practice, the rule was not explicitly referenced in interaction, but it contributed to the creation of inclusive practices through which everybody could feel welcomed and recognized. Rajala, Lipponen, Kontiola, and Hilppö (submitted) analyzed a kindergarten's interactional practices in relation to compassion. The findings pointed to an implicit division of labor between the adults and children. Adults were mainly expected to show compassion. While children were also present in situations in which their peers displayed distress, in most of their observations, the adults were the only ones showing compassion and the children acted as the audience. In some cases, children could even be forbidden from showing compassion. For example, when a child was hurt, and a peer would approach him with the intent of helping, an adult would tell the peer to turn away and take sole responsibility of consoling the crying child. Furthermore, when the children did show compassion, such as by helping their peers or consoling a crying friend, they were not always able to act in a way that would alleviate the concerns or plight of their peers, unless helped by an adult.

However, the existing research on compassion has not shed light on how children orient to and address the worries, concerns, or suffering of their peers between themselves, namely, how compassion is enacted in children's peer interaction. Considering the impact that peers can have on children's learning and development (e.g., Rubin, Bukowski, & Bowker, 2015), analyzing the interactional nuances and dynamics of children's compassionate peer interactions is an important step if we want to understand how children learn to show compassion and what their ways of acting compassionately toward their peers are. To this end, in this chapter we will present our cultures of compassion approach (Lipponen, Rajala, & Hilppö, 2018) to studying compassion in children's peer interactions in a Finnish kindergarten and share an example of our video ethnographic work and interaction analysis on compassion. We will conclude our chapter by discussing how it is possible to foster compassionate peer cultures in early childhood education and care settings.

Conceptualizing Compassion in Children's Peer Interactions

The *Oxford English Dictionary* defines compassion as *"Suffering together with another, participation in suffering; fellow-feeling, sympathy"* and *"The feeling or emotion when a person is moved by the suffering or distress of another, and by the desire to relieve it"* (OED, 1989). In this chapter, we approach compassion from a sociocultural perspective and conceptualize it as a culturally mediated and distributed phenomenon (Lipponen et al., 2018). In contrast to dominant research approaches that focus on compassion as an individual skill or trait, and hence as internal property of an individual child (e.g., Goetz, Keltner, & Simon-Thomas, 2010), we understand compassion as an aspect of the children's engagement in joint activities, as something that children do and show in different situations and in varied ways. Furthermore, we emphasize that compassion is substantially constituted by the cultural tools employed in these acts as well as the social organization of the joint activity. That is, in order to understand compassion in any of its forms, we argue that it is important to understand the cultural means of achieving compassion and the social organization of the joint activity that constitute the local cultures of compassion. In the case of our investigation, this means looking at how the joint activities are accomplished and how duties regarding them are divided and shared between adults and children, what the material and cultural tools, artifacts and spaces used in these activities are, as well as how the local rules and values come to play in the way compassion is enacted in Finnish kindergartens.

Our approach to compassion builds on sociocultural and cultural-historical theories of human functioning. Accordingly, the core argument of this chapter is that human cognitive capabilities, emotions, and actions are mediated by cultural tools and activities and their cultural-historical development (e.g., Vygotsky, 1987). Importantly, mediation not only accounts for the structure and content of our actions and experiences, but also for their emergence in the first place. Moreover, human actions are always encompassed within larger activity systems that also take part in establishing the actions, for example, through how the work is distributed between other people (e.g., Engeström, 1987). In this sense, the cultural means and the people using them form a distributed cognitive and affective system that together constitute and shape whatever actions are taken (Valsiner, 2001). For example, when a child falls down and hurts him or herself, the words, expressions, tones of voice, objects, and embodied actions others use to comfort him or her and the way they distribute this work are culturally mediated through and through. In different cultural settings, what is seen as an appropriate response to a similar situation might be different and elicit a different set of cultural tools and practices that are used to comfort the child, if it is responded to at all (e.g., Rogoff, 2003).

Important to our perspective is also the process through which children come to learn how to show compassion. Building on other sociocultural perspectives (e.g., Gutiérrez & Rogoff, 2003; Lave & Wenger, 1991), we argue that central to this process is children's participation in cultural practices. By seeing how adults help others, by being recipients of adults' care themselves or taking care of younger siblings and by doing charity or communal work with their family, children learn how to console, help, and alleviate the plight of others (e.g., Lopez et al., 2012). Over time, children gradually come to take more central positions in these activities and also learn that showing compassion is an important value for their community. Moreover, learning compassion is also an aspect of formal educational settings. In the same way as in children's families, the social practices of an early childhood education and care (ECEC) setting also encompass different ways to show compassion. In ECEC settings, one of the first extrafamilial communities that children spend a significant part of their everyday life, young children can encounter and interact with people (children and adults) who might significantly differ from the children's families and other communities in terms of ethnicity, social status, and cultural background. If we think of education not merely as transmission of qualifications but as also involving processes of enculturation and subjectification (Biesta, 2010), the question of how compassion is enacted within such diversity is crucial.

However, this learning process is not solely one-way socialization. Rather, in addition to children sustaining the cultural practices of their communities by learning them, children also contribute to the change of these practices. From our perspective, people do not just passively occupy their cultural settings and their practices of compassion are not given, static or eternal. Instead, people actively create and maintain the cultures they live in and their practices (e.g., Varenne & McDermott, 1999). In this sense, what is seen as suffering and the ways to alleviate it exist only through the active upkeep of the people living within that culture. As such, these practices are open to change through collective effort (Engeström, 1987) and children can be part of this process. For example, children can extend the range of people who a family helps or and even large-scale child-led compassionate projects can emerge through children's efforts (Hilppö, 2017). In this sense, children are not just passive recipients of adult culture and its ways of showing compassion, but active agents who have an impact on how compassion is shown, when and to who.

Moreover, children, through their agency, can also contribute to the development of new cultural practices. Importantly, children's creative uptake of the activities, values, norms, routines, and materials around them can create distinct peer cultures between children within their everyday lives (Corsaro & Eder, 1990; Corsaro & Johannesen, 2007). For example, children interpretively reproduce shared routines through play and, through this, create new activities with their own goals. In Corsaro and Molinari's (2005) ethnography of an Italian daycare center, they observed the recreation of the familiar disappearance-reappearance play routine in the form of a hide-and-seek play in which children hid from their peers behind the curtains of the center. This interpretative reproduction not only concerns activities that children come up with, but also the way in which they relate to their own community and the broader culture around them. In relation to compassion, this raises the question of what practices of compassion children's peer cultures encompass.

A Micro-ethnographic Approach to Researching Peer Compassion

As part of our ongoing research project to study compassion in early childhood education, we engaged in a micro-ethnography (e.g., Erickson, 1992) that focused on how compassion was enacted as part of the flow of everyday life in kindergarten. Our study took place in a public kindergarten located in Helsinki, Finland. The kindergarten is situated near the town center. Three groups of children and their educators participated in the study. In two of the groups, the ages of the children varied between one and three years, and in the third group, the ages were between two and four years. All groups had adults working as kindergarten teachers or nurses. Some of the adults had several years' work experience, while others were in their first position since graduation. This type of multi-professional work community, with a varying combination of professional qualifications and job descriptions, is characteristic of Finnish ECEC. The minimum requirement for a kindergarten teacher is a bachelor's degree in education or in social science. Other staff at ECEC centers are expected to have at least a vocational upper-secondary qualification in the fields of social welfare or health care.

The curricula of the kindergarten highlight that children would be learning to express and verbalize emotions in the kindergarten. The kindergarten also aimed to create an inclusive and just environment for the children, and they took active measures to prevent bullying, for example. According to our observations, the daily activities of the kindergarten exemplified the culture of Finnish early childhood education, which can be characterized in terms of a holistic approach that encourages play, relationship, and curiosity. The daily practices also included adult-initiated activities, such as reading to children and presenting hands-on activities. Activities such as eating lunch, dressing for outdoor activities, and taking naps were also considered to be educationally valuable, and educators played an important role in these activities by guiding and helping the children.

To understand in detail how compassion was embedded in the kindergarten's practices, we video recorded the everyday activities of the three groups intermittently over the course of three weeks. We collected 51 hours of video over nine separate days. Our video-based research was informed by the interaction analysis tradition (Jordan & Henderson, 1995). Two researchers (Rekar Abdulhamed and Annukka Pursi) recorded the events with a handheld video camera, sometimes using an additional camera on a camera stand. We recorded the audio with either the camera microphone or a wireless microphone worn by either a child or an adult. We used the principle of maximum variation (Patton, 1990) across different situations (varying persons, locations, and types of activity) when selecting which events to record. The guardians of all the participating children and the kindergarten staff gave informed consent to conduct the research. We also paid careful attention to how the children reacted to the presence of the camera with the intention of stopping the recording if we noticed that they were hesitant about the camera. However, this did not happen.

We started our analysis by taking a rough overview of all the videos and made content logs—time indexed lists of topics and events—of each video (Jordan & Henderson, 1995). We then watched the videos several times and identified episodes in which someone expressed distress or physical or emotional pain (Lilius, Worline, Dutton, Kanov, & Maitlis, 2011). In addition, we identified episodes in which suffering was not expressed but implicit or explicit references were made to someone's distress or pain. We identified 15 episodes from the video corpus.

"You Called Me Stupid": An Example of Compassion in Children's Peer Interaction

The following episode is an illuminating example of our cultures of compassion perspective and how children can show compassion toward each other when together. The episode took place during lunch time between Aino, Ilmari, and Veikko (age 2–3 years) while they waited to get lunch (Fig. 5.1). Armas, a fourth child, also sat at the table but engaged only minimally in the interaction. What is important to know is that just a moment before the interaction in the example took place, Veikko had called Aino stupid. The adult, Kirsi, who had been present, had asked Veikko to apologize to Aino by saying he was sorry and hugging Aino, which was a common apology practice in the kindergarten. Kirsi had also had a short one-to-one discussion with Veikko during which she had told him that calling other children names will "make others feel bad and you too" and that they don't call anyone stupid in the kindergarten. After they had sat down and Kirsi had left to get their lunch, the following interaction ensued.[1]

Turn	Speaker	Verbal and non-verbal action
1	Aino	You both called me stupid a moment ago was here (looks at Veikko)
2	Ilmari	(unclear)
3	Aino	Yes you called me stupid (looks at both Ilmari and Veikko)
4	Ilmari	Are you so like feeling bad?
5		(Ilmari looks at Aino. Aino looks at Ilmari, but also elsewhere)
6	Ilmari	Are you feeling bad?
7	Aino	Yeah (nods her head)
8	Ilmari	(turns his head slightly to one side, presses lower lip to upper lip and nods his head. See Fig. 5.2)
9	Aino	You called me badly (looks at Ilmari with a sideway glance)
10	Ilmari	How did you get boo-boo? (looks down to Aino's hands where Aino has a band-aid on her finger)

(continued)

---

[1] In the following transcript, we have used parentheses to indicate nonverbal action and also describe prosodic aspects of the children's talk. We have also simplified the transcript for better readability.

Turn	Speaker	Verbal and non-verbal action
11	Aino	I scratched it (Raises her hand from lap. Taps on her finger. Looks at Ilmari)
12	Ilmari	Ho- at home?
13	Aino	Yeah, during the night you slept
14	Veikko	Burn night but I burn finger already I got li direction when the finger got
15	Aino	(Lifts finger in front of Veikko)
16	Veikko	Mmm aa like this finger better already
17	Aino	My back burned in the evening it took
18	Veikko	There was fire from my finger
19	Aino	And my back burned in the sun
20	Ilmari	Look I got hurt here too (shows his finger to Aino, grins and laughs. See Fig. 5.3)
21	Aino	My back burned (emphasis on last two words)
22	Ilmari	Boo-boo (said with rising intonation)
23	Aino	The sun can be really strong
24	Armas	From there
25	Ilmari	Boo-boo (said with rising intonation, moves finger from right to left to show how the sun hurt his finger, looks at Aino)
26	Aino	Ee th the sun is really strong that it can burn back yes yeah and then it is very strong it can and the strong sun. I'm three years old (shows three fingers)

Fig. 5.1 Aino, Ilmari, Veikko and Armas sitting at the table

Fig. 5.2 Ilmari expressing his awareness of Aino's feelings

Fig. 5.3 Ilmari grinning to Aino in a friendly manner

Interpreting "You Called Me Stupid"

What took place in the episode was a discussion in which Ilmari and Veikko showed compassion to Aino by addressing Aino's concerns and her wellbeing. The conversation started with Aino returning to Veikko's recent name-calling. Apparently, the apology that Veikko had given her did not suffice, and she wanted to continue addressing the issue. Aino also directed her claim to Ilmari, possibly because he had been involved in a previous name-calling incident earlier the same day and had then not apologized in the same way as Veikko had. After talking about the name-calling, the conversation gradually evolved to other issues related to Aino's wellbeing, from a cut on Aino's finger to her sunburnt back. The episode ended when Aino changed the topic to her age at the end of her last turn.

In the following, we will unpack our analysis of how compassion manifests itself in children's peer interaction. We show how Ilmari and Veikko address Aino's concerns with compassion. Based on our analysis, we argue that the episode represents an example of the array of interactional strategies children have to show compassion toward their peers. In our analysis, we will draw attention to three significant aspects of the interaction. Firstly, how Ilmari and Veikko verbalized Aino's experiences and expressed their intersubjective understanding of them (lines 4, 8, and 14). Secondly, how Ilmari invited Aino to talk about her concerns (lines 4 and 10), both of which reflect strategies also used by adults when responding to peer concerns compassionately (e.g., Kuroshima & Iwata, 2016; Pudlinski, 2005). In our video data, we could observe that this strategy was also used by the adults of this kindergarten. Thirdly, we will draw attention to an aspect which most shows children's peer culture in action and their own endogenous strategies for showing compassion, namely, how Ilmari oriented playfully to Aino's concerns (lines 20 and 22).

The episode started with Aino topicalizing her first concern, that she was called stupid (line 1). By this she treated Veikko's apology and Ilmari's previous actions as insufficient and something that still needed to be addressed. After Aino had repeated her claim (line 3), Ilmari responded by asking if she was feeling bad (line 4). Ilmari's response here verbalized Aino's possible emotional state, sought confirmation of it, and created an opportunity for Aino to further elaborate on this. Ilmari's response also showed that he was aware of Aino's possible emotional reaction to the name-calling. Aino did not answer Ilmari's question at first, but after Ilmari had asked again, she confirmed how she felt. Ilmari then responded (line 8) by further expressing his awareness of Aino's feelings and his alignment with her through his facial expression (Fig. 5.2).

Ilmari's display of concern for Aino's wellbeing in response to the name-calling can be interpreted as an act of compassion. However, Aino did not accept Ilmari's response as satisfactory and she repeated her accusation (line 9). Ilmari responded to this by changing the topic of the conversation to the band-aid on Aino's finger (line 10). Ilmari's action here could arguably be interpreted as a continuation of his previous strategy of creating opportunities for Aino to talk about her feelings and wellbeing. Here, Ilmari offered Aino another opportunity to verbalize her feelings and also showed his concern for her wellbeing. This time, Ilmari succeeded in alleviating the tension as Aino and he engaged in a short discussion about her finger (lines 11–13).

Importantly, Aino's story about her finger evoked a compassionate response from Veikko, who up to this point had stayed silent and not shown any concern for Aino's accusations. In his turn, Veikko shared a story about how he had burned his finger (line 14) and how it had healed (line 16). Through the topical connection (hurt fingers), Veikko showed that he understood Aino's position and also attempted to console her by telling that her finger will heal, like his did. Veikko's story prompts Aino to explain how her back had been sunburnt (line 17). After Veikko's attempt to continue talking about his finger, Aino reiterated her concern (line 19).

At this moment in the interaction, Ilmari responded to Aino's concern in a new way. In his next three turns (20, 22, and 24), Ilmari makes a series of attempts to elicit a playful response to him from Aino and change the mood of the discussion. Ilmari first pretends that his finger is also hurt, grins to Aino in a friendly manner (Fig. 5.2), and laughs (line 20). Then his rising intonation (line 22) and acting out the sun beam hurting his finger (line 25) can be read as invitations to engage in play. However, Aino turns down Ilmari's invitations and indicates that she is more serious about the matter. She does this by emphasizing with her intonation the fact that her back got hurt (line 21) and that the sun can be dangerous at times (in her words: "strong", lines 23 and 26). However, Ilmari, Veikko, and Armas don't engage in the discussion with her, and Aino then changes the topic of the discussion (end of turn 26).

Fostering Compassionate Peer Cultures

In this chapter, we have presented an episode that illuminates children's own ways of addressing each other's worries and showing compassion.

Situations like the one in the episode are common place in Finnish kindergartens, and presumably in other early childhood education and care settings as well. Children hurt themselves while playing, pine after their parents, or get into arguments with each other almost on a daily basis, and adults, despite their best efforts, cannot always be around to provide them with care, help, or consolation. In those moments, children have the opportunity to act with compassion toward their peers, and like Aino, Ilmari, and Veikko showed that they have the skills and the will to do so.

With the analysis of this episode, we have illuminated our cultures of compassion perspective. We showed how in the situation, children took up and reproduced the compassionate practices that are endemic to that particular community and participate in maintaining that culture. Specifically, we could observe Ilmari and Veikko help Aino to verbalize and elaborate her negative feelings using strategies similar to those used by the adults in this kindergarten community. Paraphrasing Vygotsky (1987), in these situations, children could be seen as doing independently today what they did cooperatively and with guidance yesterday. In addition, we have also argued the interaction visible in the episode could be understood as indicating children's unique ways of showing compassion. That is, the playful orientation at the end of the episode can arguably be seen as a way to alleviate or deal with Aino's concern that is inherent to children's peer cultures. Furthermore, given the different creative ways in which children can create their own peer cultures (Corsaro and Johannesen 2007), our observation here is most likely not the only unique way in which children show compassion to each other. If so, our observation points toward an interesting and possibly fruitful avenue of further research. In addition to undercovering other possible means by which children show compassion, these studies could explore what local children's cultures of compassion are constituted by such means, if any at all. Such research could illuminate, in interactions such as the ones between Aino, Ilmari, and Veikko above, how children establish the norms of their peer culture in relation to others' concerns, distress, or suffering and practices to alleviate it. Understanding these moments in depth would advance our knowledge not only of how children act compassionately but also of how children through their agency can take part in building compassionate communities.

This emphasis on children's agency in relation to the compassionate practices of their kindergartens' culture or their home cultures possibly highlights an important avenue in relation to how early childhood education and care professionals can foster compassion in kindergartens or other early childhood settings. It is important to create space for children to appropriate the values promoting compassion in their own ways. It has been argued that suppressing children's agency and imposing mechanical rules for their conduct lead children to only pay lip service to the rules and hide their creative ways of resisting the adults' imposition (Matusov & Marjanovic-Shane, 2018; Rajala & Sannino, 2015). If the children also reproduce compassionate practices creatively, these renewed practices can offer insights to how children see compassion, who they offer it to, in what ways, and what kind of situations. That is, children's peer cultures can bring to fore their interactional strategies for showing compassion, and when recognized, these methods can be taken as grounds for developing the culture of compassion of that particular early childhood education and care setting. In this sense, moments of peer compassion can encompass one potential future, a concrete utopia (Bloch, 1986) for cultures of compassion in early childhood education.

However, the way in which these grassroot-level acts of compassion could be encouraged in children's peer culture or fostered as more widely adopted and sustained practices in the kindergarten might not be a straightforward process. Efforts to spread practices, whether ones relating to compassion or ways of acting, can often face obstacles and even resistance in workplaces, and early childhood settings are not immune to this. Instead, as we have previously suggested (Lipponen et al., 2018), employing methods like formative interventions (Engeström, 2011) and social design experiments (Gutiérrez & Jurow, 2016) might offer a more fruitful guidance for this. As part of such efforts, observations and documents about how and when children act compassionately among themselves would act as materials for reflection between early childhood education and care professionals, the children and the researchers facilitating the change process. Importantly, this way the practices would then also be under critical collective scrutiny which would open up the possibility for seeing what the "politics of compassion" (Ure & Frost, 2014) of the community are. That is, joint reflection, if carefully done, could reveal where and to whom acts of compassion are directed to and if all persons of the community are included.

Acknowledgments We wish to thank the kindergarten staff and the children and their parents for opening their lives to us by participating in this study. We also wish to thank Annukka Pursi for her insightful comments on the episode analyzed in this chapter and Rekar Abdulhamed for his efforts in collecting the dataset from which the episode is from. The research reported in this chapter was funded by the Academy of Finland, project no. 299191.

References

Biesta, G. (2010). *What is education for? Good education in an age of measurement: Ethics, politics, democracy.* Boulder, CO: Paradigm Publishers.

Bloch, E. (1986). *The principle of hope.* Cambridge, MA: MIT Press.

Compassion. (1989). *The Oxford English dictionary* (2nd ed.).

Corsaro, W. A., & Eder, D. (1990). Children's peer cultures. *Annual Review of Sociology, 16*(1), 197–220.

Corsaro, W. A., & Johannesen, B. O. (2007). The creation of new cultures in peer interaction. In J. Valsiner & A. Rosa (Eds.), *The Cambridge handbook of sociocultural psychology* (pp. 444–459). Cambridge: Cambridge University Press.

Corsaro, W. A., & Molinari, L. (2005). *I Compagni: Understanding children's transition from preschool to elementary school.* New York, NY: Teachers College Press.

Eisenberg, N., Spinrad, T. L., & Knafo-Noam, A. (2015). Prosocial development. In M. Lamb & R. Lerner (Eds.), *Handbook of child psychology and developmental science. Volume 3: Socioemotional processes* (pp. 610–656). Hoboken, NJ: Wiley.

Engeström, Y. (1987). *Learning by expanding: An activity-theoretical approach to developmental research.* Orienta-Konsultit: Helsinki.

Engeström, Y. (2011). From design experiments to formative interventions. *Theory & Psychology, 21*, 598–628.

Erickson, F. (1992). Ethnographic microanalysis of interaction. In M. LeCompte, W. Millroy, & J. Preissle (Eds.), *The handbook of qualitative research in education* (pp. 201–225). New York: Academic Press.

Goetz, L., Keltner, D., & Simon-Thomas, E. (2010). Compassion: An evolutionary analysis and empirical review. *Psychological Bulletin, 36*, 351–374.

Gutiérrez, K. D., & Rogoff, B. (2003). Cultural ways of learning: Individual traits or repertoires of practice. *Educational Researcher, 32*(5), 19–25.

Gutiérrez, K. D., & Jurow, A. S. (2016). Social design experiments: Toward equity by design. *Journal of the Learning Sciences, 25*(4), 565–598.

Hilppö, J. (2017). *Children's projects. A proposal for a research agenda.* Poster presented at the 5th International Congress of the International Society for Cultural-historical Activity Research (ISCAR) Quebec, August 30.

Jordan, B., & Henderson, A. (1995). Interaction analysis: Foundations and practice. *The Journal of the Learning Sciences, 4*(1), 39–103.

Kirby, J. N. (2017). Compassion-focused parenting. In E. Seppälä, E. Simon-Thomas, S. Brown, M. Worline, C. Cameron, & J. Dory (Eds.), *The Oxford handbook of compassion science* (p. 91). Oxford: Oxford University Press.

Kuroshima, S., & Iwata, N. (2016). On displaying empathy: Dilemma, category, and experience. *Research on Language and Social Interaction, 49*(2), 92–110.

Lave, J., & Wenger, E. (1991). *Situated learning: Legitimate peripheral participation.* Cambridge: Cambridge University Press.

Lilius, J., Worline, M., Dutton, J., Kanov, J., & Maitlis, S. (2011). Understanding compassion capability. *Human Relations, 64*, 873–899.

Lipponen, L. (2018). Constituting cultures of compassion in early childhood educational settings. In S. Garvis & H. Harju-Luukkainen (Eds.), *Nordic dialogues on children and families* (pp. 39–50). New York: Routledge.

Lipponen, L., Rajala, A., & Hilppö, J. (2018). Compassion and emotional worlds in early childhood education. In C. Pascal, A. Bertram, & M. Veisson (Eds.), *Pedagogic innovations in early childhood education in cross-cultural contexts.* New York: Routledge.

Lopez, A., Najafi, B., Rogoff, B., & Mejía-Arauz, R. (2012). Collaboration and helping as cultural practices. In J. Valsiner (Ed.), *The Oxford handbook of culture and psychology* (pp. 869–884). New York, NY: Oxford University Press.

Luckner, A. E., & Pianta, R. C. (2011). Teacher-student interactions in fifth grade classrooms: Relations with children's peer behavior. *Journal of Applied Developmental Psychology, 32*(5), 257–266.

Matusov, E., & Marjanovic-Shane, A. (2018). Beyond equality and inequality in education: Bakhtinian dialogic ethics approach of human uniqueness to educational justice. *Dialogic Pedagogy: An International Online Journal, 6.*

Varenne, H., & McDermott, R. (1999). *Successful failure: The School America Builds.* Boulder, CO: Westview Press.

Patton, M. Q. (1990). *Qualitative evaluation and research methods.* London: Sage.

Pudlinski, C. (2005). Doing empathy and sympathy: Caring responses to troubles tellings on a peer support line. *Discourse Studies, 7*(3), 267–288.

Rajala, A., & Sannino, A. (2015). Students' deviations from a learning task: An activity-theoretical analysis. *International Journal of Educational Research, 70*, 31–46.

Rajala, A., & Lipponen, L. (2018). Compassion in narrations of early childhood education student teachers in Finland. In S. Garvis, S. Phillipson, & H. Harju Luukkainen (Eds.), *International perspectives on early childhood education and care. Early childhood education in the 21st century* (Vol. 1). New York: Routledge.

Rajala, A., Lipponen, L., Kontiola, H., & Hilppö, J. (submitted). Päiväkodin myötätuntoteot ja myötätuntokulttuuri alle kolmivuotiaiden ryhmässä. *Kasvatus.* [Title in English: Compassionate acts and culture of compassion in the everyday conduct of a kindergarten].

Rogoff, B. (2003). *The cultural mature of human development.* Oxford: Oxford University Press.

Rubin, K. H., Bukowski, W. M., & Bowker, J. C. (2015). Children in peer groups. In M. Bornstein, T. Leventhal, & R. Lerner (Eds.), *Handbook of child psychology and developmental science. Vol. 4: Ecological settings and processes* (pp. 175–222). Hoboken, NJ: Wiley.

Sawyer, K. (Ed.). (2015). *The Cambridge handbook of the learning sciences.* Cambridge: Cambridge University Press.

Spinrad, T. L., & Eisenberg, N. (2017). Compassion in children. In E. Seppälä, E. Simon-Thomas, S. Brown, M. Worline, C. Cameron, & J. Dory (Eds.), *The Oxford handbook of compassion science* (p. 53). Oxford: Oxford University Press.

Ure, M., & Frost, M. (Eds.). (2014). *The politics of compassion.* New York: Routledge.

Valsiner, J. (2001). Process structure of semiotic mediation in human development. *Human Development, 44*(2–3), 84–97.

Volling, B. L., Kolak, A. M., & Kennedy, D. E. (2009). Empathy and compassionate love in early childhood: Development and family influence. In B. Fehr, S. Sprecher, & L. Underwood (Eds.), *The science of compassionate love: Theory, research, and applications* (pp. 159–200). London: Wiley-Blackwell.

Vygotsky, L. S. (1987). Thinking and speech (N. Minick, Trans.). In R. W. Rieber & A. S. Carton (Eds.), *The collected works of L. S. Vygotsky: Vol. 1. Problems of general psychology* (pp. 39–285). New York: Plenum Press. (Original work published 1934).

6

Fostering Students' Psychological Well-Being Amidst the Threat of Bullying: Emotional Intelligence May Hold the Key

Neha Kulkarni and Sairaj M. Patki

Introduction

School emerges as a significant social institution immediately after family and home, during the formative years of childhood and adolescence. Besides being a centre for imparting knowledge, the school acts as an environment for fostering the process of learning, developing, practising, and enhancing various life skills. With its complex dynamics characterized by a rigid framework of discipline, paired with numerous and unbound opportunities for development through interpersonal relationships at various levels, school presents the developing individual the necessary raw material to explore, identify, and attempt to fulfil their potentials. This is the period when the child's self-concept too is taking shape. The nature of

N. Kulkarni (✉)
Centre for Mental Health Law and Policy, Indian Law Society, Pune, India

S. M. Patki
Department of Social Sciences, School of Liberal Education, FLAME University, Pune, India
e-mail: sairaj.patki@flame.edu.in

© The Author(s) 2019
G. Barton, S. Garvis (eds.), *Compassion and Empathy in Educational Contexts*,
https://doi.org/10.1007/978-3-030-18925-9_6

the school environment significantly contributes to this moulding process. Like every complex system, the school environment too comes with its set of challenges, which, if left unattended to or unmet, may lead to detrimental consequences. While some of these consequences would have a momentary and marginal impact on the development process, some others may scar the student for life. This chapter explores the phenomenon of bullying in schools, the impact of bullying, and suggests how instilling emotional intelligence skills, such as compassion and empathy, in schools can function as a preventive as well as curative measure to deal with the phenomenon of bullying, and consequently improving psychological well-being.

Bullying: A Global Phenomenon

A meta-analysis of 82 studies revealed that 53% of the youth were involved in bullying, either as bullies, victims, or both bullies and victims (Cook, Williams, & Guerra, 2010). More recently, a global status report revealed that each year, a staggering 246 million children and adolescents experience some or the other form of bullying (UNESCO, 2017). These statistics are based on the data of reported cases, leaving one to wonder what the actual number of cases could be.

One reason for this increase in the number of cases could be the fact that the way experts define bullying too has undergone changes. A more traditional definition of bullying would include aggressive acts that are carried out with the intention of harming a defenceless individual by a group (Menesini & Salmivalli, 2017). Over time, the definitions of bullying and the list of acts that account for bullying have evolved drastically. Today bullying is not restricted to overt tangible harm caused to the victim. Bullying could comprise verbal and physical violence, threats, language, ridiculing or teasing, insulting behaviour, or using facial expressions to demean the individual (Jan & Husain, 2015). Moving beyond body shaming and attacking peculiar behaviours, bullying now may be based even on sexual orientation of the victim. The other forms of bullying may include verbal abuse, sexual harassment, or dating violence (Berger, 2007). Secondly, the statutes and laws that are in place to curb acts of bullying seem to have been unsuccessful to some extent in effectively reducing this phenomenon. The reason for this could be the nature of these statutes and laws. Duncan (2011) pointed out that most anti-bullying statutes fail to include restorative justice—a process wherein all stakeholders come together to discuss bullying and its aftermath.

A new menace that has plagued the mental health of adolescents and teenagers is cyberbullying. Willard (2006) has identified that cyberbullying may comprise flaming (sending angry, rude, and vulgar message via email or text messaging or other electronic means), online harassment (sending offensive messages online), denigration (sending or posting gossip about someone online in order to ruin their reputation), impersonation (pretending to be someone to get that person in trouble or to ruin his/her reputation), outing (sharing an embarrassing information about someone online, in the form of images or videos), trickery (talking someone into revealing private information, then revealing it online), exclusion (intentionally and maliciously not including someone in their group), and cyberstalking (repeated harassment and denigration). Moreover, as these behaviours take place in a virtual space and as anonymity of the perpetuator is higher in this form of bullying compared to in traditional bullying, conventional methods of penalizing the guilty may not be easily applicable. This means that it is important for parents and educators to be aware of this recent challenge and to be equipped in dealing with it effectively. More importantly, it is necessary that students be taught appropriate socio-emotional skills to protect themselves from either being victimized in the cyberspace or from indulging in cyberbullying themselves.

Gender Differences in Bullying: Reality or a Myth

The stereotype stating that boys are more aggressive than girls and thus bullying is more prevalent in boys than in girls was supported by literature in the past (Block, 1983; Parke & Slaby, 1983). Since just over a decade, there seems to have been a slight shift in this perspective. For instance, a study across 14 countries by Smith and colleagues used stick figure cartoons to study the perceptions of students with reference to identifying bullying behaviours. The results showed no significant gender differences in the understanding of behaviours that are considered as acts of bullying. Thus though boys may directly experience more physical bullying as compared to girls, there is significant overlap in the experience of bullying (Smith, Cowie, Olafsson, & Liefooghe, 2002). Studies showing that gender differences in the prevalence rates of bullying aren't straightforward and that they depend on several factors (Hanish, Ryan, Martin, & Fabes, 2005).

It appears that the gender differences may not be significant with reference to the absolute rate of bullying but rather with reference to the nature, type, and location of bullying. It was found that hitting or pushing other students is the most widespread form of bullying used by adolescent male bullies, whereas calling other students bad names is the most frequent form of bullying used by adolescent female bullies (Kareem & Jaradat, 2017).

In the context of cyberbullying it was seen that boys are more likely to be the bullies, whereas girls are more likely to be the victims (Wang, Iannotti, & Nansel, 2009). The location of bullying must also be taken into consideration when it comes to differences in bullying between genders. For boys, bullying most often takes place on the way home from school, while for girls bullying often exists in the classrooms (Kareem & Jaradat, 2017).

While these factors have been well researched, some other less investigated factors too may contribute to reported gender differences in bullying. For instance, response of the teachers, which may change across cultural expectations and biases, too is crucial when attempting to understand bully behaviour in boys and girls. In a study by Costley, Han, and Lee (2013), it was found that teachers were less likely to intervene in bullying incidents involving girls as compared to boys. Teachers were also less likely to intervene in relational bullying than in physical bullying. This could pose a serious risk especially to female students as relational bullying is the most prevalent type of bullying that they are exposed to (Chee, 2006; Koo, 2007; Koo, Kwak, & Smith, 2008). Such lack of timely and unbiased intervention by school authorities may lead to differential reporting of bullying incidents by victims, thus leading to differences in the number of reported cases across the genders.

Another factor that has been found to be relevant in the context of gender and bullying is the manner in which boys and girls differently react to and cope with bullying. Girls for instance are more likely to be affected by indirect forms of bullying such as teasing, whereas physical bullying seems to affect boys more (Carbone-Lopez, Esbensen, & Brick, 2010). Even within girls, it was reported that high school girls experienced more bullying and sexual harassment as compared to their middle school counterparts, though the impact of these experiences was less among them. These differences in outcomes could be ascribed to better support systems and coping mechanisms (Gruber & Fineran, 2007). It is important to note that peer support with respect to coping with bullying is crucial, and research has concluded that peer support is generally beneficial for both victims and the peer supporters themselves. Unfortunately boys are usually underrepresented as peer supporters, which may dissuade male victims from reporting bullying victimization to their male peers (Cowie, 2000).

Bullying and Well-Being

It has been seen that childhood bullying has serious implications on health, resulting in significant costs on health for the victims and their families (Schroeder et al., 2012). In the UK alone, over 16,000 adolescents are said to be absent from state school to prevent being victims of bullying (Brown, Low, Smith, & Haggerty, 2011). What is more disturbing is that the issue could be more severe as about half of the students who participated in a survey said that they would never talk about their suffering to their parents, while a third of them stated that they would never report being bullied to their teacher (Radford, Corral, Bradley, & Fisher, 2013). A survey comprising of 20,406 high school students in MetroWest Massachusetts showed that irrespective of the type of bullying, victims were more likely than non-victims to demonstrate distress, depressive symptoms, and suicidal attempts requiring medical attention (Schneider, O'Donnell, Stueve, & Coulter, 2012). Depressive symptoms are known to be precursors to suicidal attempts or ideations (Guyer, Caouette, Lee, & Ruiz, 2014) and thus, in some serious cases, the victims may end up taking the extreme step. The relatively less severe symptoms include feeling sad, preferring to stay alone, poor academic performance, and so on. Bullied children are usually more likely to report symptoms such as school phobia, vomiting, and sleep disturbances (Kshirsagar, Agarwal, & Bavdekar, 2007).

An additional issue that can hinder timely intervention in incidences of bullying is the trivialization of certain acts of bullying. Some authorities consider minor acts of bullying like teasing as less severe and may intervene more promptly only when physical violence is involved. Results of a study that looked into teachers' perceptions about cyberbullying showed that almost one fourth of the teachers believed that the effects of cyberbullying do not last long and that in fact cyberbullying may prepare the children for a 'harsher' reality of the real world outside school. The study also revealed that many teachers did not deem the implementing of a formal cyberbully prevention programme necessary. According to them, the issue can be better tackled by including parents in the process, by warning students about it, and by taking more punitive actions (Stauffer, Heath, Coyne, & Ferrin, 2012). However, much contrary to the earlier belief that only the severe (especially physical) acts of bullying are harmful, findings of recent studies reveal that the impact of bullying on psychological well-being can be seen irrespective of the type of bullying. It was found in fact that indirect forms of bullying like social exclusion had the strongest relation with psychological distress and reduced mental well-being (Thomas et al., 2016).

Besides these immediate and direct effects of bullying, we must look at the long-term effect of bullying as well. Violence against self and a range of other psychosomatic illnesses may emerge in adulthood as a consequence of childhood victimization, and thus it is necessary for health practitioners to address the aftereffects of bullying (Lereya, Copeland, Costello, & Wolke, 2015). Victims are seen to be suffering not only from emotional distress but also from social marginalization, owing to their reduced social status in the eyes of their classmates (Juvonen, Graham, & Schuster, 2003). Longitudinal research has also shown evidence that victimization in childhood might be a marker of later psychopathology rather than a cause of long-term adverse outcome (Klomek et al., 2008).

Beyond Victims: The Story Less Told

Earlier bullying was assumed to be an act of oppression in the power equation of groups wherein the oppressor was assumed to be strong and dominating and the victim, a weak, helpless, and passive recipient. However, as our understanding of this phenomenon is increasing, we are in a slightly better position to look at the complexities involved in it. While a large number of studies earlier focussed on the victims of bullying, researchers later turned their focus on understanding the bullies as well. In order to be able to intervene effectively and pro-actively rather than in retrospect, we need to understand what leads to bullying in the first place. A study revealed that about 67% of the armed students that opened fire against teachers and classmates in schools were themselves victims of bullying in the past. They are thought to have resorted to violence to combat the power that had once dominated them. This behaviour did not have a specific target, but it was later disclosed that they wanted to bring down the place where everyone saw them suffering yet did not help or protect them (Lopes Neto, 2005).

Most experts agree that adolescents who indulge in bullying do share many characteristics of generally more aggressive adolescents, like a hot temperament, a less fortunate family background, and an interpersonal style comprising of aggression and bullying as a means of achieving power and influence in a competitive peer environment (Olweus, Limber, & Mihalic, 1999). Studies also point out towards lower empathy among those who indulge in bullying. For instance, a study by Jolliffe and Farrington (2006) revealed that irrespective of gender and the type of bullying, those students who indulged in bullying frequently scored significantly lower on affective and total empathy as compared to those who rarely indulged in it or did not indulge in bullying at all. A study of 2070 secondary school students by Steffgen and colleagues showed that, like in the case of individuals indulging in antisocial behaviours, students indulging in acts of cyberbullying demonstrated lower empathy than those who didn't (Steffgen, König, Pfetsch, & Melzer, 2011). There are mixed reviews however on whether bullies have low self-esteem. While some studies suggest that they do have poor self-esteem (e.g. O'Moore, 2000), others indicate the contrary (e.g. Olweus, 1997), and still others that there is no difference between bullies and victims in terms of level of self-esteem (e.g. Seals & Young, 2003). Taking a different perspective to answer this vagueness, Frisén and her colleagues conducted a study to understand the perspective of adolescents themselves on bullying (rather than on an adult perception of the adolescents' issues). The study thus gave an 'insider's perspective' on the issue based on firsthand experiences. According to the findings, 28% participants believed that bullies indulge in those acts as they have low self-esteem. On the other hand, 26% felt that what motivates bullies is the belief that it makes them look 'cool'. That the bullies themselves have problems was the explanation given by 15% of the participants. Peer pressure came next with 9% participants claiming that the cause of bullying is influence of peers, while other factors contributed marginally (Frisén, Jonsson, & Persson, 2007). This points out to the vulnerability that may underlie the behaviours of the bullies themselves.

Another category of individuals related to the phenomenon of bullying is being studied lately—the 'bully-victims'. These individuals, who both bully others and also get bullied themselves, are especially the most troubled ones. These bully-victims end up being the most ostracized by their peers as they are looked down upon by their aggressors and avoided and hated by their victims. This category of students is most likely to display conduct problems, is usually least engaged in academics, and also reports higher levels of depression and loneliness (Juvonen et al., 2003).

Insights from an Indian Study

This section presents the reader with some major findings of a study that we conducted to explore experienced bullying, emotional intelligence, and psychological well-being among secondary school students exclusively from boarding schools (Kulkarni & Patki, 2016). The setup of boarding schools was chosen as bullying was expected to be a more serious problem (in spite of strict laws put in place), as the setup is a residential one. Gender differences in experienced bullying, emotional intelligence, and psychological well-being too were explored along with the relationships between frequency of experienced bullying, emotional intelligence, and psychological well-being.

The sample for the study was selected from two boarding schools, through convenience sampling technique. It comprised 84 students (47 male students and 37 female students), in the age range of 12–16 years. Based upon the inclusion criteria, only those students who had studied in that particular school for at least three years participated in the study. Experience of bullying victimization was assessed using the Multidimensional Peer Victimization Scale (Mynard & Joseph, 2000). It includes statements on negative physical actions (e.g. punching and kicking), negative verbal actions (e.g. making fun, abusing), social manipulation (e.g. trying to turn one's friends against him/her), and attacks on property (e.g. breaking one's belongings) and uses a three-point Likert-type response pattern based on the frequency of experienced bullying. Emotional intelligence of the students was assessed using the Emotional Intelligence Test by Sharma (2011) that comprises the five sub-scales—self-awareness, managing emotions, motivating oneself, empathy, and handling relationships. Well-being of the students was measured using the Psychological General Well-being Index (PGWBI) (Chassany, Dimenäs, Dubois, Wu, & Dupuy, 2004). It measures six dimensions—anxiety, depressed mood, positive well-being, self-control, general health, and vitality.

Contrary to the majority of earlier literature, it was found that both the genders experienced similar amount of bullying, with no significant differences in bullying victimization between boys and girls, even across sub-scales, including the physical victimization sub-scale on which one expect boys to score higher than girls. This could be attributed to the changes in ascribed social norms and existing social systems (Talbani & Hasanali, 2000). Results also showed that psychological well-being was negatively correlated with experienced bullying while emotional intelligence was positively correlated with psychological well-being. Besides re-establishing the ill effects of bullying on well-being and the importance of emotional intelligence in fostering well-being, these findings also suggest that studying gender differences in prevalence statistics may be less relevant in contemporary times.

Emotional Intelligence: Medicine to the Rescue

Emotional intelligence, as seen through the lens of the ability model (Mayer, Caruso, & Salovey, 2016), is a capacity and system of mental abilities. Applying reasoning skills to emotions thus helps emotionally intelligent people to perceive emotions accurately, to use emotions to facilitate thought, to understand emotions and emotional meanings, and finally to manage emotions in themselves and others (Mayer & Salovey, 1997). According to this perspective, emotional intelligence can be looked upon as the ability to solve problems just like in the case of cognitive problems, but in the emotional context. The moment one considers emotional intelligence as ability and a set of skills that can be taught and learnt, and not as an innate tendency, it opens up the opportunity to intervene.

The usual curriculum, while focussing on the academic competencies and growth of the students, may end up paying lesser attention to building the child's socio-emotional competencies. Unfortunately, these competencies are not always taught consciously even in the family setup. A traditional family environment favours expression of 'positive' emotions, while 'negative' emotions are to be avoided, hidden, or at least controlled, thus drawing a clear black and white divide between 'good' and 'bad' emotions. As a result, the child enters the school environment ill-prepared to face the challenges posed at the emo-socio level. Schools could become an ideal centre for teaching emotional and social skills like empathy that are needed throughout life to build and sustain interpersonal relationships. They help the students to be more resilient in the face of adversity, feel more connected with those around them, and aim higher in their aspirations for the future (UNESCO, 2017). Organizing interventions through the school is also the most viable and practical option in terms of the infrastructure and resources necessary for their execution and the wide reach possible.

It has been suggested that the influence of social interactions in adolescents at school, including bullying and peer victimization, can be better understood when considered in terms of the construct of emotional intelligence (Mayer & Cobb, 2000). There is evidence that emo-social skills can indeed be enhanced through school-based interventions. For instance, a meta-analysis of over 300 studies established the effectiveness of programmes designed to enhance social and emotional learning in significantly improving social and emotional competencies as well as academic performance of students (Durlak & Weissberg, 2005). A study conducted on college students (aged 18–20 years) by Kaur (2011) too revealed a statistically significant increase in emotional intelligence scores after a three-month emotional development intervention programme. A recent study (Oke, Kelkar, Kapre, & Patki, 2018) conducted across two cities in India involving 430 students (258 boys and 172 girls) from seventh grade to ninth grade tested the efficacy of school-based emotional intelligence interventions. This study too reported a significant increase in emotional intelligence for both boys and girls after the intervention.

Schools that teach emotional intelligence skills tend to report not only an increase in academic success in the long run, but also better teacher-student relationships and a decrease in problem behaviours, including bullying. A meta-analysis of 213 school-based social-emotional skills training programmes, involving over 2,70,000 students, revealed an 11% point gain in academic achievement in schools with well-implemented social-emotional learning programmes (Durlak, Weissberg, Dymnicki, Taylor, & Schellinger, 2011). In addition, students who participated in these programmes were at significantly reduced risk for substance abuse, absenteeism, and other problem behaviours. Students were shown to exhibit more pro-social behaviour and less emotional stress. Enhanced social-emotional skills lead to improved self-concept, positive classroom behaviour, reduced conduct problems, decreased aggressive behaviour, and lowering of emotional distress.

There could be two primary explanations for why emotional intelligence education turns out to be an effective way of dealing with bullying. Firstly, the self-related skills of emotional intelligence help students identify their own emotions, label them, and then understand the dynamics of the complete range of emotions—even the so-called negative ones. With reference to the victims of bullying, this would translate into the empowerment of the victims to accept their emotional state and deal with it more effectively. Secondly, the acceptance of the negative emotions associated with bullying victimization (like depression and anxiety) encourages victims to report the incidence and seek timely help—both for resolving the actual problem of bullying and for dealing with the emotional distress associated with it. This newly developed emo-socio skill set would work towards healing of any mental scars that were caused by the traumatic experience of being victimized by peers. Moreover, as these skills would also promote the building of assertiveness and better socialization in the victims, they would transform and start being perceived as likable and valuable by their peers rather than as meek and vulnerable targets.

Emotional intelligence training is appropriate for all ages—from preschoolers to high schoolers. Intervening at the stage of high schools could have some benefits though. Firstly, younger children would still be in the phase of developing their cognitive abilities and abilities to fully express their emotions. Thus while the self-related skills may be absorbed by them through interventions, the people-related skills may be slightly more complex for them to practice. This age group also experiences less instances of bullying as revealed in several surveys. As far as intervening after high school is concerned, one would point out rather instantly, that it would be an intervention 'too little, too late'. The age group lying in between—the adolescents—thus seems to be appropriate for executing emotional intelligence skills-based programmes through the school.

The EI Vaccine

While teaching emotional intelligence skills would equip victims with dealing with the trauma of bullying, it would only be a post hoc intervention. As discussed earlier, if bullying is to be prevented, the focus needs to be placed on the source of bullying—the bully. The bully is usually struggling to cope with his/her internal conflicts to begin with. An easy target in a peer environment then sets the perfect stage for displacement of personal internal conflicts, while receiving a certain level of status among the peers in the bargain. The victim therefore not only becomes a medium of catharsis for the bully, but also provides the bully with the steps to climb the complex social ladder at school. Interventions based on imparting the necessary emo-social skills thus must be directed towards the bullies, in fact with even more concentrated efforts. This section discusses how emotional intelligence can aid in preventing the 'making of the bully' and thus prevent incidences of bullying as a natural consequence. We present some possibilities of intervening at different stages in the victim-bully-victim cycle.

As revealed earlier, bullies are sometimes born out of victimization experiences that they themselves endured. This victim-bully segment of the cycle can be dealt with in the way discussed in the earlier section—by using emo-social skills as a medicine to heal the psychological wounds of the victims. This would help them to cope with their victimization experience better, thus helping them to 'forgive and forget'. This stage is crucial as negative emotions like depression, helplessness, fear, and anger may combine to make room for feelings of hatred and vengeance. Moreover, as hatred and vengeance could be predominantly expressed through passive-aggressive behavioural acts rather than overt aggressive acts, the associated intentions may remain dormant and unnoticed by others around. Under such circumstances, not only would the chances of timely reporting of acts of bullying be compromised, but also the chances of timely intervention for helping the victim-bully would be poor. Once left unchecked, the victim-bully's disruptive acts may get reinforced, leading to repeated offences, which may culminate into more serious acts of violence against others.

The second stage of intervention would be targeted at the bullies who indulge in acts of bullying not with the aim of seeking revenge for past victimization, but owing to aggressive tendencies. These adolescents can be expected to lack empathy and compassion as they seek to harm peers out of the sadistic satisfaction derived and do not usually show any guilt or remorse. A preventive measure in such cases can involve identifying students scoring low on a standardized measure of emotional intelligence, who can then be put through training of emo-social skills related to others, especially empathy. Studies have shown that emotional intelligence education definitely contributes towards building empathy and compassion (McKenna & Webb, 2013). In classrooms that use the emotional intelligence approach, students become more likely to show empathy to others, to choose kind actions instead of cruel ones, and to acknowledge others' emotions. Students trained in emotional intelligence skills learn to navigate their complex social and emotional worlds with insight, empathy, and kindness.

Bringing Emotional Intelligence to the Classroom

The identification of factors relating to bullying behaviours may give an opportunity to improve anti-bullying programmes in the educational setting. Teachers can be encouraged to move beyond the 'policing' role to inhibit the antisocial behaviours of bullies and work towards fostering pro-social behaviours (Whitted & Dupper, 2005). As emotional intelligence skills are linked not just to reduction in antisocial behaviours at school, but also to success in many areas of life (Goleman, 1995), a proactive rather than corrective approach would work better towards building a healthy learning environment. The Missing Piece Report in fact warns that the more we ignore the importance of teaching social-emotional skills in schools, the more we are disengaging both teachers and students from learning and from contributing to a thriving learning community (Bridgeland, Bruce, & Hariharan, 2013). The specific skills that may be emphasized during such positive interventions at schools may include identifying and understanding of one's own emotions; recognizing one's strengths; making responsible decisions; caring for others by developing respect, empathy, and appreciation for diversity; effectively communicating (e.g. being assertive but not aggressive); building relationships; negotiating fairly; seeking help when needed without hesitation; avoiding provocations; and acting ethically (Elias, 2006). Teachers can be trained, who can then impart these skills to students through school-wide approaches that simultaneously create supportive and caring climate for learning and focus on emotional skill development, to consequently foster a mutually supportive student community. As an ongoing extension of the efforts to build a healthy environment, parents too can be involved in the training process.

Furthermore, these interventions need to be merged with the formal teaching-learning-evaluation process with emotional intelligence skills being made an integral part of the regular school curriculum. This would provide a structure to the efforts of imparting these skills, guarantee participation and involvement, and assure sustained effectiveness. Efforts in this direction have already begun and are seeing a significant increase. One such programme that is now recognized globally is the social-emotional learning (SEL) programme. SEL programmes are being run across the UK and over a dozen other European countries and in the USA. In the past few years, the endeavour has reached Canada, Latin America, Africa, Australia, New Zealand, and even Korea, Singapore, Malaysia, Hong Kong, and Japan. A quantitative analysis of over 300 research studies on SEL revealed that students enrolled in an SEL programme scored about ten percentile points higher on achievement tests than those students who did not participate in it, had better grade point averages, had significantly better attendance records, displayed more constructive versus disruptive classroom behaviour, reported liking school more, were less likely to be suspended, and were less likely to be involved in any disciplinary issues (Weissberg & Durlak, 2005). The Roots of Empathy (ROE) programme developed in Canada by Mary Gordon is another well-known initiative now. It is primarily a preventive programme for social-emotional learning that has been designed to promote emotional and social understanding among children. Between 2006 and 2007, the ROE programme was implemented in over 2000 kindergarten classrooms to grade 8 classrooms across Canada, involving more than 50,000 children. The programme is being implemented in Japan, Australia, and New Zealand, and findings from ROE research have been encouraging. Students who participated in the programme experienced significant improvement in emotional knowledge and pro-social behaviours and displayed reduction in forms of aggression associated with bullying (UNESCO, 2017).

Conclusion

To summarize, it may be said that emotional intelligence-based interventions would surely be the answer to tackle the growing menace of bullying and its repercussions. Secondly, the focus would have to be multi-pronged with an equal emphasis on helping the victims, victim-bullies as well as bullies. Also, a pro-active and preventive skill-building-based approach of developing the emo-social skills of students through interventions at school would be needed as much as the usual post hoc healing approach that focusses primarily on helping the victim and punishing the aggressor.

Schools where emotional intelligence interventions are effectively implemented would help ensure the following:

- students with the necessary knowledge of vocabulary and understanding of grammar of emotions (just like languages they learn as part of their academic courses)
- students who can place their own emotions and those of others under a conscious microscope and understand their complex nature (something they would do in their biology labs)
- students who can mentally calculate the consequences of their actions and deeds on people around them, and thus choose the socially and mutually most appropriate behaviour (just like they would do while solving mathematical problems)
- students who can apply emotional first aid to their wounds and to those of their peers (as they would during a Scouts and Guides camp)
- students who can understand the present better based upon the past wrongdoings of themselves and others, and therefore opt for a better future (like they would learn from their history class)
- students who can place their socio-emotional priorities in the larger scheme of the societal map (like they would for an assignment given by their geography teacher)

All we need to do is to educate ourselves and our students in a subject that has always been an integral part of our lives but, unfortunately, was almost never formally a part of our curriculum. Like other societal issues, bullying too would take time to be eradicated, but an empathetic, compassionate, socially sensitive, and responsible community would soon evolve through widespread collective efforts across the globe.

References

Berger, K. S. (2007). Update on bullying at school: Science forgotten? *Developmental Review, 27*, 91–92.

Block, J. H. (1983). Differential premises arising from differential socialization of the sexes: Some conjectures. *Child Development, 54*, 1335–1354.

Bridgeland, J., Bruce, M., & Hariharan, A. (2013). *The missing piece: A national teacher survey on how social and emotional learning can empower children and transform schools.* Collaborative for Academic, Social, and Emotional Learning. Retrieved from http://www.casel.org/library/the-missing-piece

Brown, E. C., Low, S., Smith, B. H., & Haggerty, K. P. (2011). Outcomes from a school randomized trial of steps to respect. *School Psychology Review, 40,* 423–443.

Carbone-Lopez, K., Esbensen, F. A., & Brick, B. T. (2010). Correlates and consequences of peer victimization: Gender differences in direct and indirect forms of bullying. *Youth Violence and Juvenile Justice, 8,* 332–350.

Chassany, O., Dimenäs, E., Dubois, D., Wu, A., & Dupuy, H. (2004). *The psychological general well-being index (PGWBI) user manual.* Lyon: Mapi Research Institute.

Chee, F. (2006). The games we play online and offline: Making wang-tta in Korea. *Popular Communication, 4*(3), 225–239.

Cook, C. R., Williams, K. R., & Guerra, N. G. (2010). Predictors of bullying and victimization in childhood and adolescence: A meta-analytic investigation. *School Psychology Quarterly, 25,* 65–82.

Costley, J. H. M., Han, S. L., & Lee, J. E. (2013). Pre-service teachers' response to bullying vignettes: The effect of bullying type and gender. *International Journal of Secondary Education, 1*(6), 45–52.

Cowie, H. (2000). Bystanding or standing by: Gender issues in coping with bullying in English schools. *Aggressive Behaviour, 26,* 85–97.

Duncan, S. H. (2011). Restorative justice and bullying: A missing solution in the anti-bullying laws. *New England Journal on Criminal and Civil Confinement, 37,* 267–298.

Durlak, J. A., & Weissberg, R. P. (2005, August). *A major meta-analysis of positive youth development programs.* Presentation at the Annual Meeting of the American Psychological Association, Washington, DC.

Durlak, J. A., Weissberg, R. P., Dymnicki, A. B., Taylor, R. D., & Schellinger, K. B. (2011). The impact of enhancing students' social and emotional learning: A meta-analysis of school-based universal interventions. *Child Development, 82*(1), 405–432.

Elias, M. J. (2006). The connection between academic and social-emotional learning. In M. J. Elias & H. Arnold (Eds.), *The educator's guide to emotional intelligence and academic achievement* (pp. 4–14). Thousand Oaks, CA: Corwin Press.

Frisén, A., Jonsson, A. K., & Persson, C. (2007). Adolescents' perception of bullying: Who is the victim? Who is the bully? What can be done to stop bullying? *Adolescence, 42*(168), 749–761.

Goleman, D. (1995). *Emotional intelligence.* New York: Bantam Books.

Gruber, J. E., & Fineran, S. (2007). The impact of bullying and sexual harassment on middle and high school girls. *Violence Against Women, 13*, 627–643.

Guyer, A. E., Caouette, J. D., Lee, C. C., & Ruiz, S. K. (2014). Will they like me? Adolescents' emotional responses to peer evaluation. *International Journal of Behavioural Development, 38*, 155–163.

Hanish, L. D., Ryan, P., Martin, C. L., & Fabes, R. A. (2005). The social context of young children's peer victimization. *Social Development, 14*, 2–19.

Jan, A., & Husain, S. (2015). Bullying in elementary schools: Its causes and effects on students. *Journal of Education and Practice, 6*(19), 43–56.

Jolliffe, D., & Farrington, D. P. (2006). Examining the relationship between low empathy and bullying. *Aggressive Behavior, 32*(6), 540–550.

Juvonen, J., Graham, S., & Schuster, B. (2003). Bullying among young adolescents: The strong, weak, and troubled. *Pediatrics, 112*, 1231–1237.

Kareem, M., & Jaradat, A. (2017). Gender differences in bullying and victimization among early adolescents in Jordan. *People: International Journal of Social Sciences, 3*(3), 440–451.

Kaur, T. D. (2011). A study of impact of life skills intervention training on emotional intelligence of college adolescents. *Indian Journal of Psychological Science, 2*(2), 112–125.

Klomek, A. B., Sourander, A., Kumpulainen, K., Piha, J., Tamminen, T., Moilanen, I., … Gould, M. S. (2008). Childhood bullying as a risk for later depression and suicidal ideation among Finnish males. *Journal of Affective Disorders, 109*(1–2), 47–55.

Koo, H. (2007). A time line of the evolution of school bullying in differing social contexts. *Asia Pacific Education Review, 8*(1), 107–116.

Koo, H., Kwak, K., & Smith, P. K. (2008). Victimization in Korean schools: The nature, incidence, and distinctive features of Korean bullying or wang-ta. *Journal of School Violence, 7*(4), 119–139.

Kshirsagar, V. Y., Agarwal, R., & Bavdekar, S. B. (2007). Bullying in schools: Prevalence and short-term impact. *Indian Pediatrics, 44*(1), 25–28.

Kulkarni, N., & Patki, S. (2016). A study of emotional intelligence, experienced bullying and psychological well-being among secondary school students from boarding schools. *International Journal of Indian Psychology, 3*(4), 12–27.

Lereya, S. T., Copeland, W. E., Costello, E. J., & Wolke, D. (2015). Adult mental health consequences of peer bullying and maltreatment in childhood: Two cohorts in two countries. *Lancet Psychiatry, 2*, 524–531.

Lopes Neto, A. A. (2005). Bullying: Aggressive behaviour among students. *Jornal de Pediatria, 81*(5), 164–172.

Mayer, J. D., Caruso, D. R., & Salovey, P. (2016). The ability model of emotional intelligence: Principles and updates. *Emotion Review*, 1–11. https://doi.org/10.1177/1754073916639667

Mayer, J. D., & Cobb, C. D. (2000). Educational policy on emotional intelligence: Does it make sense? *Educational Psychology Review, 12*, 163–183.

Mayer, J. D., & Salovey, P. (1997). What is emotional intelligence? In D. J. Sluyter (Ed.), *Emotional development and emotional intelligence: Educational implications* (pp. 3–34). New York, NY: Basic Books.

McKenna, J., & Webb, J. A. (2013). Emotional intelligence. *British Journal of Occupational Therapy, 76*(12), 560–561.

Menesini, E., & Salmivalli, C. (2017). Bullying in schools: The state of knowledge and effective interventions. *Psychology, Health & Medicine, 22*(1), 240–253.

Mynard, H., & Joseph, S. (2000). Development of the multidimensional peer-victimization scale. *Aggressive Behavior: Official Journal of the International Society for Research on Aggression, 26*(2), 169–178.

Olweus, D. (1997). Bully/victim problems in school: Facts and intervention. *European Journal of Psychology of Education, 12*(4), 495.

Olweus, D., Limber, S., & Mihalic, S. F. (1999). *Blueprints for violence prevention, book nine: Bullying prevention program*. Boulder, CO: Center for the Study and Prevention of Violence.

O'Moore, M. (2000). Critical issues for teacher training to counter bullying and victimisation in Ireland. *Aggressive Behaviour: Official Journal of the International Society for Research on Aggression, 26*(1), 99–111.

Oke, A., Kelkar, S., Kapre, P., & Patki, S. (2018). *Emotional intelligence among adolescents: Tool development and enhancement through training and study of correlates*. ICSSR Sponsored Research Project, Modern College of Arts, Science and Commerce, Pune.

Parke, R. D., & Slaby, R. G. (1983). The development of aggression. In E. M. Hetherington (Ed.), P. H. Mussen (Series Ed.), *Handbook of child psychology: Vol. 4. Socialization, personality and social development* (4th ed., pp. 547–642). New York: Wiley.

Radford, L., Corral, S., Bradley, S., & Fisher, H. (2013). The prevalence and impact of child maltreatment and other types of victimization in the UK: Findings from a population survey of caregivers, children and young people and young adults. *Child Abuse & Negligence, 37*, 801–813.

Schroeder, B. A., Messina, A., Schroeder, D., Good, K., Barto, S., Saylor, J., & Masiello, M. (2012). The implementation of a state-wide bullying prevention program: Preliminary findings from the field and the importance of coalitions. *Health Promotion Practice, 13*(4), 489–495.

Seals, D., & Young, J. (2003). Bullying and victimization: Prevalence and relationship to gender, grade level, ethnicity, self-esteem, and depression. *Adolescence, 38*(152), 735–747.

Schneider, S. K., O'Donnell, L., Stueve, A., & Coulter, R. W. (2012). Cyberbullying, school bullying, and psychological distress: A regional census of high school students. *American Journal of Public Health, 102*(1), 171–177.

Sharma, E. (2011). *Emotional intelligence test (EIT)*. New Delhi, India: Prasad Psycho Corporation.

Smith, P. K., Cowie, H., Olafsson, R. F., & Liefooghe, A. P. (2002). Definitions of bullying: A comparison of terms used, and age and gender differences, in a fourteen-country international comparison. *Child Development, 73*(4), 1119–1133.

Stauffer, S., Heath, M. A., Coyne, S. M., & Ferrin, S. (2012). High school teachers' perceptions of cyberbullying prevention and intervention strategies. *Psychology in the Schools, 49*(4), 352–367.

Steffgen, G., König, A., Pfetsch, J., & Melzer, A. (2011). Are cyberbullies less empathic? Adolescents' cyberbullying behavior and empathic responsiveness. *Cyberpsychology, Behavior and Social Networking, 14*(11), 643–648.

Talbani, A., & Hasanali, P. (2000). Adolescent females between tradition and modernity: Gender role socialization in South Asian immigrant culture. *Journal of Adolescence, 23*(5), 615–627.

Thomas, H. J., Chan, G. C., Scott, J. G., Connor, J. P., Kelly, A. B., & Williams, J. (2016). Association of different forms of bullying victimisation with adolescents' psychological distress and reduced emotional wellbeing. *Australian & New Zealand Journal of Psychiatry, 50*(4), 371–379.

UNESCO. (2017). *School violence and bullying: Global status report*. Retrieved January 17 from unesdoc.unesco.org

Wang, J., Iannotti, R. J., & Nansel, T. R. (2009). School bullying among adolescents in the United States: Physical, verbal, relational, and cyber. *Journal of Adolescent Health, 48*, 415–417.

Weissberg, R. P., & Durlak, J. (2005). *Social and emotional learning for school and life success*. Invited address for the Society for Community Research and Action (APA Division Distinguished Contribution to Theory and Research Award) at the Annual Meeting of the American Psychological Association, Washington, DC.

Whitted, K. S., & Dupper, D. R. (2005). Best practices for preventing or reducing bullying in schools. *Children and Schools, 27,* 167–175.

Willard, N. E. (2006). *Educators guide to cyberbullying: Addressing the harm caused by online social cruelty.* Retrieved April 4, 2009, from http://clubtnt.org/safeOnline/printResources/EducatorsGuideToCyberbullyingAddressingTheHarm.pdf

Part III

Compassion and Empathy in the Curriculum

7

When Caring Counts: Fostering Empathy and Compassion Through the Arts Using Animation

Susan N. Chapman

Introduction

In Australia, our family has a tradition of hosting Fair Trade Markets in our home, featuring beautiful handmade craft items from artisans in "developing" countries. The warm-hearted creativity of the Australian lady who coordinates these community projects has shaped our children's view of the world over the last 30 years. We told our children that their voice matters, that not all people in the world are as resource rich as we are in Australia, and that our support for Fair Trade allows other families the dignity of being able to support those they love. I remember handing out flyers for our market to a trader at the local shopping centre in suburban Brisbane, explaining the concept of Fair Trade, and being shocked by her reply, "Oh, I try to protect my children from things like that". I was, and continue to be, dumbfounded at the choice to "protect" children from the opportunity to develop empathy and compassion.

S. N. Chapman (✉)
Queensland University of Technology, Brisbane, QLD, Australia
e-mail: s23.chapman@qut.edu.au

© The Author(s) 2019
G. Barton, S. Garvis (eds.), *Compassion and Empathy in Educational Contexts*,
https://doi.org/10.1007/978-3-030-18925-9_7

Constraints on Developing Empathy and Compassion

The Over-Protection of Children

As a parent and educator, I am concerned that the over-protection of children, in some homes and educational institutions, may constrain their ability to develop empathy and compassion. The objective driving this approach is to ensure that children's lives are free from any form of suffering, anxiety or discomfort. This is often achieved by seeking to shield children from negative experiences and from the suffering of others. There is much talk of building the attribute of resilience in students (Clayton, 2015; Lukianoff & Haidt, 2015; Parker & Folkman, 2015). However, the over-protection of children may disempower them by suggesting that they can only tolerate cloudless skies and temperate weather, and all else must be banished from their horizon (Lukianoff & Haidt, 2015). There have been "tensions between two conceptualisations of children: as active, knowing, autonomous individuals…and as passive, innocent, dependents" (Scott, Jackson, & Backett-Milburn, 1998, p. 689). Lukianoff and Haidt (2015) respond to the latter of these conceptualisations, by noting the loss of "free range" childhood in homes and schools.

In *The Coddling of the American Mind*, Lukianoff and Haidt (2015) describe two terms: *microaggressions*, which are "small actions or word choices that seem on their face to have no malicious intent but that are thought of as a kind of violence nonetheless" (p. 1), and *trigger warnings*, which are educator alerts to potentially strong emotional responses to course content. While I acknowledge that these descriptions seem reasonable and would certainly aid students with current or past experience of genuine trauma, the examples provided indicate increasingly vehement restrictions on what can be said in the classroom. Lukianoff and Haidt (2015) contend that patterns of over-protection which have begun in childhood may persist throughout all educational sectors, elevating "the goal of protecting students from psychological harm" (p. 2), shielding young adults "from words and ideas that make some uncomfortable" (p. 2), and contributing to "vindictive protectiveness" (p. 2) in which those who speak up "may face charges of insensitivity, aggression, or worse" (p. 2). These patterns may have adverse repercussions.

Vindictive protectiveness is considered likely to contribute to: inadequately preparing students for future professional life by avoiding people and ideas which challenge their own perspectives and opinions; engendering patterns of thought that may lead to depression and anxiety; and encouraging students to think pathologically (Lukianoff & Haidt, 2015). In my opinion, it is crucial to differentiate between discomfort and the triggering of past or current genuine trauma. To my mind, the elevation of all forms of discomfort to a pathological level of trauma on the grounds of subjective experience can demean the experience of those whose suffering needs to be urgently addressed to prevent significant long-term harm. If the assumption that student discomfort cannot be beneficial had pervaded earlier educational systems, I question whether students would have advocated for social justice after experiencing discomfort when confronted with misogyny, child exploitation, the slave trade or environmental degradation. I would argue that just as aural tension may propel music towards a resolution, the tension created by a developing awareness of suffering and injustice can act as a catalyst for positive change. In my view, political inertia and the silencing of voices who are prepared to stand for the voiceless in our societies are surely not models for children who wish to advocate for a better world.

The Rise of Virtual Online Experiences

Fuller and Söderlund (2002) express concern that developments in technology and technology-driven learning are sometimes being presented as the panacea to solve all educational ills, which "may result in auto-responsive 'robosapiens'" (p. 745). Similarly, Twenge (2013) suggests that youth who spend more time online are less likely to help others.

> Social media build shallow, "weak" ties, increase self-focus (including narcissism), and may lead to mental health issues for some individuals. Over the time social media became popular, young people's empathy for others, civic engagement, and political involvement declined. (p. 11)

Dunbar (2018) points out that the single factor that best predicts human health and well-being is the number and quality of a person's friendships. He worries that the obsession with online experiences attributed to current and future younger generations will prevent them from developing skills and negotiating strategies which are learned in the "sandpit of life" (p. 3). According to Dunbar (2018), the major issue associated with the whole of technology is that "the distance that it places on us from those we interact with has serious mal-consequences" (p. 4). I have found that the rise of virtual online experiences, while offering the benefits of participating in an online community, may therefore exacerbate the disconnection that is fostered by a spectator culture whose participants are to some extent removed from real-life experiences. As Dunbar (2018) says, "I think there's nothing like seeing the whites of people's eyes to make a difference" (p. 4). The question I would ask educators is how do we help our students to do this? The difference Dunbar (2018) refers to is not merely seeing, but caring about what is seen.

The Commodification of Education

In the commodification of education, students are viewed as consumers, and teachers and educational institutions are regarded as educational product providers, developing skills for the market place (Altbach, 2002; Fanelli & Evans, 2015). Hardy (2015) criticises the growing obsession with risk management in which education is regarded as "an increasingly 'risky business' that employs a myriad of products and tests to manage perceived and actual risks" (p. 375). When education is commodified, "the primacy of human relationships in the production of value is denied. Beliefs and values are no longer important. It is output that counts" (Yang, 2006, p. 1). Walzer's (1984) warning of the "collapse of moral spheres and a total subordination of moral obligations to economic ones" (in Yang, 2006, p. 2) indicates that this is not only a recent phenomenon. Notions of the public good, character development and education as a collective endeavour have no place in this system (Daviet, 2016; Schwartzman, 2013). These emphases fundamentally change the nature of education in institutions and classrooms, shifting the emphasis from preparation for citizenship to a business model measured by perceived market value.

Serious concerns have been expressed regarding the adverse effects of the commodification of education on learning, teaching, education systems and the creation of knowledge (Ewing, 2012a; Karpov, 2013; Williams, 2011). In Australia, there is evidence that individual, school-based and state-based competition has emerged in a battle for supremacy that conflicts with best educational practice (Ewing, 2012a). In their examination of the perverse systemic effects of audit and accountability in Australian schooling, Lingard and Sellar (2013) explain "how States seek to protect their 'reputational capital' and as such, 'game' the system" (p. 634). Karpov (2013) highlights the urgency of this situation by warning of the destruction of "the deeper formative, essential nature of spiritual and intellectual disciplines" (p. 76). Rowan Williams (2011), previously Archbishop of Canterbury, speaks of the need to build virtue, character and citizenship for the purpose of educating citizens rather than consumers. If William's (2011) concept of education as the development of skills, attitudes and values is replaced by the notion of education as a product to be consumed, I find it unlikely that empathy and compassion will find a place in learning and teaching.

Entitlement Versus Gratitude

Consumer mentality may also drive student entitlement behaviour, which expresses their belief that they deserve better immediately (Lippman, Bulanda, & Wagenaar, 2009). There are reports that increasingly, students do not exhibit the traits they expect from their educators and are often not truly present during classroom learning (Schaefer, Barta, Whitely, & Stogsdill, 2013). To address this issue, Howells et al. (2012) proposes that teachers change student attitudes by modelling gratitude to overcome toxic environments characterised by "resentment, victim mentality, envy or a sense of entitlement" (p. 6). She recommends developing the practice of gratitude, through action, to discover embodied understandings and lived experiences that are heart-felt and not just intellectual, and notes that gratitude, unlike positivity, is essentially interpersonal.

However, I would contend that the development of positive attributes may also be influenced by educational systems which determine classroom priorities.

The Impact of High-Stakes Testing Programmes

International literature includes reports of the adverse effects of high-stakes testing programmes on children's well-being, on the breadth of children's learning experiences and on the structure and nature of the curriculum (Polesel, Dulfer, & Turnbull, 2012). The predominance of these programmes has sometimes resulted in a test-based curriculum and narrowed pedagogical approaches (Caldwell, 2013; Comber, 2012; Cormack & Comber, 2013; Jones, 2007; Kohn, 2000; Ladd, 2017; Minarechová, 2012; Munro, 2010; Northam, 2017; West, 2012; Wu, 2010) which focus on "memorisation and simple factual recall" (Gibson & Ewing, 2011, p. 7). Hardy and Boyle (2011) argue that in attempting to reduce educational practice to numbers, the Australian MySchool website has ignored a moral philosophical account of educational practices and lost sight of "the internal goods of education" (p. 211) which can't be codified. In my opinion, the issue is not that empathy and compassion should be somehow included in high-stakes testing programmes, but that the pervasive influence of this assessment system has sidelined the development of these attributes within learning and teaching.

Spoon-Feeding Students

It is my view that narrow pedagogical models, such as "spoon-feeding" information to students, do not place high importance on the development of empathy and compassion. Dehler and Welsh (2014) argue that teachers need to build reflexive practice and develop students as "more sophisticated 'knowers'" (p. 875). McKay and Kember (1997) reveal that while students regurgitate information that is "spoon-fed" to them, they actually prefer more meaningful independent learning and student-centred approaches, even when it requires more work. Despite evidence to the contrary, some educators still experience strong pressure to conform to long-standing beliefs and traditions that "spoon-feeding" students is an effective approach to learning and teaching (Raelin, 2009). Through my professional contacts, I have seen that when student tasks are exhaustively scaffolded and information is delivered by the teacher-as-instructor approach, the consequent emphasis on rigid teacher accountability may be less likely to engage students in creative risk taking.

Overcrowded Curriculum

These constraints may be compounded by an increasingly crowded curriculum in which the traditional curriculum separates knowledge into a hierarchy of subjects (Russell-Bowie, 2009). Decontextualised and fragmented learning may emerge from "teacher-centred pedagogy and formal competitive assessment" (Gibson & Ewing, 2011, p. 15) as teachers wonder what to emphasise in a content-heavy curriculum (Daggett, 2000). I believe that teachers will need to find alternative strategies for managing an overcrowded curriculum.

Cultivating Empathy and Compassion in Schools

Despite these constraining factors, empathy and compassion are viewed as desirable human virtues in curricular documents. Since my own educational experiences have primarily occurred in Australia, I will use that context to frame my views on this topic. While this is an Australian project, I believe the underpinning concepts may hold resonance and relevance for other communities of learning. In the Australian Curriculum (Australian Curriculum Assessment and Reporting Authority, 2010) compassion is explored as a value through Civics and citizenship and included in the General Capability of Ethical understanding (in Peterson, 2017). In the Australian Curriculum: The Arts, Foundation to Year 10—Version 8 (ACARA, 2015) empathy for multiple viewpoints is included in the aims. However, as Peterson (2017) notes, valuing these human virtues is very different from providing curricula in which they are explicitly cultivated. Peterson (2017) advocates for a "virtue-centred (or character-based) approach to moral education in school" (pp. 113–114), describing the virtues of empathy and compassion as practical wisdom common to all humanity and developed through engagement and reflection like a skill. This requires "a 'general blueprint' of the good life that can be conveyed through teaching" (Peterson, 2017, p. 115). In his opinion, empathy plays a key role in helping students engage with and understand human fragility and suffering. Peterson (2017) recommends two specific pedagogical approaches to foster and cultivate these virtues: engaging with narratives which "reconstruct the mental experience of another" (p. 122); and intersubjective communication in which students develop critical inquiry skills to build relationships with characters in the text. He contends that this allows us to engage with the motivation, ideas and emotions of others while exploring our own responses. To explain the explicit building of empathy and compassion, I have chosen an arts-based project.

Fostering Empathy and Compassion Through the Arts

Arts Embodying Interconnecting Stories and Co-constructing Knowledge

In the Australian Curriculum: The Arts, Foundation to Year 10—Version 8 (ACARA, 2015), students communicate ideas, thoughts, opinions and cultural knowledge through the Arts to make meaning of their world and understand themselves. Barton (2014) describes literacy in the Arts as "[i]nterpretive and expressive fluency through symbolic form, whether aural/sonic, embodied, textual, visual, written or a combination of these within the context of a particular art form" (p. 3). The Arts provide students with an opportunity to share their emotions, observations and experiences through comprehending and manipulating "the distinct and related languages, symbols, techniques, processes and skills of the Arts subjects" (ACARA, 2015, para 2).

I have found that the Arts help us to tell our stories and acknowledge the interwoven narratives that extend across times, places and cultures, thereby opening us to the possibility of developing empathy and compassion. According to Hsu (2008), this is because storytelling is a universal human trait in which "the emotional and cognitive effects of a narrative influence our beliefs and real-world decisions" (p. 46). The Arts provide spaces in which we can practice interacting within real and imagined contexts through the power of storytelling which can "appeal to our emotions and capacity for empathy" (Hsu, 2008, p. 46). Manney (2008) focuses on the ways storytelling creates social empathy by functioning as "the engine of social/cultural liberalization and change" (p. 51). I have seen that the unique languages of the Arts can evoke stories that may be beyond the power of words to portray.

The Arts represent unique ways of knowing (Eisner, 2003, 2005), bringing to education, "the ability to deal with conflicting messages, to make judgements in the absence of rule, to cope with ambiguity, and to frame imaginative solutions to the problems we face" (Eisner, 2004, p. 9). As a storehouse of huge potential, the Arts are essential in helping us negotiate the complexity of the twenty-first century.

> Learning in the Arts is based on cognitive, affective and sensory/kinaes-thetic response to arts practices as students revisit increasingly complex content, skills and processes with developing confidence and sophistication across their years of learning. (ACARA, 2015, para 3)

This view demonstrates that the Arts evoke responses in us which reach across all aspects of our humanity, helping us to accept that life is often messy and cannot be safely packaged in codified transactions. I am confident that the Arts encourage us to embrace complexity.

It is my contention that the Arts are ideally positioned to support a constructivist view of education as they can offer individual and collective opportunities to draw on a cumulative history of cultural experiences, create meaning through activity and personal interactions, and reveal a world of multiple perspectives (Jonassen, Peck, & Wilson, 2001). The Arts provide cognitive, social, affective and curricular benefits by deepening cognition and facilitating knowledge retention, building respectful and diverse learning communities, enhancing well-being and building confidence, as well as fostering equity in the classroom by broadening pedagogy and developing reflexive practice (Barton, 2014; Barton

& Baguley, 2017; Caldwell & Vaughan, 2012; Catterall, 2009; Chapman, 2015; Cole, 2011; Deasy, 2002; Donovan & Pascale, 2013; Ewing, 2010, 2012b; Goldberg, 2012; Greene, 2011; McArdle & Wright, 2014; McDonald & Fisher, 2006; Russell-Bowie, 2011; Wright, 2012). Importantly, the Arts are not only valuable for their contribution to the curriculum, but because of the value they bring to our formation as persons living in community.

> The Arts entertain, challenge, provoke responses and enrich our knowledge of self, communities, world cultures and histories. The Arts contribute to the development of confident and creative individuals, nurturing and challenging active and informed citizens. (ACARA, 2015, para 3)

In my experience, the Arts can encourage us to remain open to challenge and discomfort, recognising that we are capable of contributing to the well-being of others. These experiences can lay the ground work for fostering empathy and compassion.

Transformational Learning Through Arts Immersion

Transformative learning has been defined as "significant, systematic and sustained change that secures success for all students in all settings" (Caldwell & Vaughan, 2012, p. 46); and as "a curriculum that enables learning that challenges our traditional stereotypes and saturated consciousness to help us become more open, inclusive, reflective and ready to change" (Ewing, 2012b, p. 8). The Arts have the capacity to transform our understanding of the world (Caldwell & Vaughan, 2012), to transform the practice of education (Eisner, 2004), and to transform "brains into minds" (Eisner, 2003, p. 341). Reports suggest that an integrated or interdisciplinary approach fosters transformative learning as this more accurately reflects the holistic view of knowledge that operates in the real world (Gibson & Ewing, 2011), allows the transfer of knowledge across disciplinary boundaries (Russell-Bowie, 2009), and addresses the problem of an overcrowded curriculum by encouraging enhanced learning across two or more Learning Areas at the same time (Chapman, 2015)— in this case the Arts and SOSE (Study of Society and Environment).

This transformation process can spread across the curriculum through an *Arts Immersion* approach to learning and teaching. *Arts Immersion* refers to "the process of using the Arts as the purposeful medium through which enhanced learning occurs across disciplines to inform mutual understandings" (Chapman, 2015, p. 93). In this process, the Arts are used as a set of unique languages which constitute both a domain of learning and a vehicle for accessing other learning areas. Eisner acknowledges the multi-modal nature of language by defining it as "the use of any form of representation in which meaning is conveyed or construed" (Eisner, 2005, p. 342). The potential for transformational learning through unique arts languages opens up a greater range of experiences to develop empathy and compassion. As an arts educator, I am always looking for opportunities to foster transformational learning by accessing the Arts as a unique set of languages. Through the Arts, students can be brought closer and deeper into the narratives of others, reframing the world as they know it, and awakening in them the potential to become citizens whose character demonstrates human virtues.

The Study: Maristely's Story

Background

In 2014, the primary school in which I taught was buzzing with news about the World Cup in Sao Paolo. At the same time, our students were viewing online video clips including *A Flower in the Favelas* (Project Compassion, 2014), about an 18-year-old girl, Maristely, growing up in a favela (slum) in Sao Paolo. The Year 6 students reviewed this story as part of the social justice component of the curriculum which drew on these words of Pope Francis: "Men and women of all times and all places desire a full and beautiful life...a life that is not threatened by death but that can mature and grow to its fullness" (Project Compassion, 2014). I decided to explore the role of compassion in developing students' awareness of social justice, and to use the Arts languages to foster empathy in the students. In my role as the performing arts teacher, I collaborated with the visual art teacher to foster a closer connection between our Year 6 students and a community that they were not likely to meet in person.

Strategies

We created a story with two sections: the first section depicting the challenges of life in a favela, and the second section using the "fairy houses" students had made earlier as aspirational symbols based on the "I have a dream" speech by Martin Luther King Jr. Both Year 6 classes had a one-hour visual art class and a one-hour performing arts class each week. During one school term, students worked on this project during these classes as well as some lunch hours.

Just as favela communities were built from recycled materials and paint that had been discarded, the students recycled scraps of materials to cobble together the favela urban landscape. Students had to consider the materials and methods used to construct a favela, the use of physical space, the way paint was used, the presence of human waste and rubbish, the absence of waste management and other utilities, and the pervading sense of disrepair. They used a variety of mismatched recycled materials which were painted in random blocks of colour and constructed in a cramped, haphazard manner around narrow walkways. The base was painted in mottled neutral colours to represent waste matter and express the ever-present smell of the favela. Students considered the challenges of everyday life in the favelas, creating characters with backstories that represented these issues. These characters represented an amalgam of experiences portrayed through a compilation of connected stories. The characters were physically constructed by noting how their life roles and experience shaped their physical appearance and facial expressions. For the second part of the Claymation, based on an aspirational view of the same community, the "fairy houses" became "dream houses" with multi-level positions featuring uplifting colours, gardens and more open spaces.

Discussion

Through this project, *Maristely's Story*, students were explicitly encouraged to develop the human virtues of empathy and compassion (Peterson, 2017; Williams, 2011) through being thoughtfully exposed to the suffering of a favela community (Dunbar, 2018). Far from being traumatised, students were empowered to make a difference in the world (Lukianoff & Haidt, 2015) by becoming advocates of social justice, and demonstrated this by initiating a student-driven campaign to raise money for favela communities. This real-world decision emanated from students' experience of listening to and creating stories which shaped their belief that all persons deserve to be valued (Hsu, 2008). Through engaging in the narratives of this favela community, students participated in intersubjective communication with the compilation characters that emerged from the media arts text (Peterson, 2017).

Their verbal responses to these stories during class discussion demonstrated the awakenings of social empathy (Manney, 2008), enabling them to make informed artistic choices, based on their emerging understanding of new cultural experiences (Jonassen et al., 2001). An opportunity was created to observe life in the favelas, to understand the issues involved in this daily struggle, and to form reasons for wanting improved outcomes for these people so that students could gain insights into the thoughts and feelings of those in the favelas (Hsu, 2008; Manney, 2008). An effective connection was made between a real-life example and an artistic representation as both created the cramped space and the lopsided buildings that were literally made from other peoples' rubbish. Similarly, as they were inspired by the courage of Maristely, students used "dream houses" as artistic representations of what 'the good life' might look like (Peterson, 2017). The creation of the aspirational utopia of "dream houses" (see Appendix 2) encouraged students to consider what changes would need to be made for the favela people to flourish and to acknowledge that this is a human right for all people. To create a wider platform for their voice to be heard (Hsu, 2008; Manney, 2008), this claymation was shown to the school, featured at an arts exhibition, and became an award-winning entry in several national media arts competitions.

Key to this whole process was the *Arts Immersion* approach (Chapman, 2015) which positioned the Arts at the centre of the curriculum as a set of unique Drama, Media Arts, Music and Visual Arts languages (ACARA, 2015), operating beyond the power of words (Eisner, 2005). Students were able to communicate through these art forms as they used arts languages to making meaning of Maristely's world (ACARA, 2015). The arts languages gave students opportunities to think more extensively about poverty in Sao Paolo's favelas (Eisner, 2003), to transfer this emerging knowledge across disciplinary boundaries (Russell-Bowie, 2009), and to experience a holistic view of knowledge and understanding that more closely mirrors the mental and emotional experiences of real life (Gibson & Ewing, 2011). Activity, in the form of artistic process and personal interactions with their peers (Jonassen et al., 2001), provided opportunities to develop arts-based skills and enhance students' interpretive and expressive fluency (Barton, 2014). Students expressed concern for Maristely's community through their developing skills in vocal expression, photography and editing by creating three layers of meaning-making through photos, recorded voice overs and music.

As unique ways of knowing, arts languages enabled students to make sense of the conflicting messages of poverty and World Cup euphoria that coexisted in Sao Paolo, to make artistic judgements that would best tell *Maristely's Story*, and to engage in the creative problem-solving—which is a necessary part of the artistic process—by exploring imaginative solutions (Eisner, 2003, 2005). This awakening understanding was reflected in the quality of their discussions, the forming of the narrative, the accuracy of the favela construction, and the poignant creation of clay and peg characters to express the toll that daily challenges take on the people of the favelas. Despite the physical distance between the student and favela communities, the artistic process enabled students to engage meaningfully with multiple perspectives (Jonassen et al., 2001) by encouraging them to ask questions such as: "What does it look like, feel like, smell like and sound like, to live in a favela?". In other words, what does it *mean* to live in a favela? Through the recreation of *Maristely's Story* as an animation, students learned to be aware of the actual details of individual lives, began to realise the consequences of these interacting circumstances and came to care about the suffering of those in the story.

As students sat around the model of the favelas to think about who might live in the houses they constructed, the issues involved became more accessible (see Appendix 1). The tactile experience of holding those characters in their hands and shaping them according to the agreed backstories brought the students closer to understanding a favela community, and caring about what happened to them. The recreative artistic process of immersing the students in *Maristely's Story* through the arts languages led to transformative learning as students came to change the frameworks through which they perceived the world and themselves (Caldwell & Vaughan, 2012; Ewing, 2012b).

Conclusion

By allowing students to be thoughtfully made aware of the suffering in the favelas of Sao Paolo, students became immersed in a larger narrative with multiple perspectives, and were invited to take a participatory rather than a spectator role. Their emerging understanding and recreation of *Maristely's Story* through claymation contributed to reducing the distance between the students and the favela culture, and encouraged a sense of gratitude. The Arts languages were unique in their capacity to allow students to express their discomfort and concern, and to be moved by the plight of others, since they avoided the extremes of engendering high distress or promoting disinterest. Indeed, students were empowered and inspired by this project. Year 6 primary school students responded very positively and productively when allowed the freedom of creative risk taking and the opportunity to co-construct knowledge through imaginative arts-based exploration, rather than being heavily scaffolded through every step of the process. Using *Arts Immersion* as an interdisciplinary approach to learning and teaching eased the pressure of the overcrowded curriculum, allowing time to highlight the role of human relationships and explicitly cultivate the development of human virtues such as empathy and compassion. When the Arts were placed at the centre of the curriculum as the vehicle for critical thinking, students were offered a rich and diverse means of meaning-making. The act of artistic representation clarified students emotional and cognitive responses and their call for justice was depicted with compassion and empathically expressed through the Arts (see Appendix 2). Through the Arts, students drew on the experiences of those in *Maristely's Story*, they came to see the "whites of their eyes" and to care enough about what they saw to want to make a difference.

Acknowledgement I wish to acknowledge Mrs Faye Graham for her excellent visual art guidance in this project and her great support of the students involved in *Maristely's Story.*

Appendices

Appendix 1: Photo Selection from the Favela in *Maristely's Story*

Appendix 2: Aspirational Utopia of "Dream Houses" in *Maristely's Story*

References

Altbach, P. G. (2002). Knowledge and education as international commodities: The collapse of the common good. *International Higher Education, 4*, 2–5.

Australian Curriculum Assessment and Reporting Authority. (2010). *Australian curriculum.* Retrieved February 1, 2019, from https://www.australiancurriculum.edu.au/

Australian Curriculum Assessment and Reporting Authority. (2015). *Australian curriculum: The arts foundation to Year 10*—version 8.3. Retrieved November 10, 2017, from https://www.australiancurriculum.edu.au/f-10-curriculum/the-arts/

Barton, G. (2014). Literacy and the arts: Interpretation and expression of symbolic form. In G. Barton (Ed.), *Literacy in the arts: Retheorising learning and teaching* (pp. 3–19). Dordrecht: Springer.

Barton, G., & Baguley, M. (2017). Editors' introduction: The world alliance for arts education: Forging forward in and through the arts. In G. Barton & M. Baguley (Eds.), *The Palgrave handbook of global arts education* (pp. 1–16). London: Palgrave Macmillan. https://doi.org/10.1057/978-1-137-55585-4_1

Caldwell, B. J. (2013, February). *Common causes in arts education.* Invited keynote presented at Arts Up Front: ACT Arts Education Conference, Canberra, ACT.

Caldwell, B., & Vaughan, T. (2012). *Transforming education through the arts.* Hoboken, NJ: Routledge.

Catterall, J. (2009). *Doing well and doing good by doing arts: The long term effects of sustained involvement in the visual and performing arts during high school.* Los Angeles, CA: Los Angeles Imagination.

Chapman, S. N. (2015). Arts Immersion: Using the arts as a language across the primary school curriculum. *Australian Journal of Teacher Education, 40*(40), 85–101. https://doi.org/10.14221/ajte.2015v40n9.5

Clayton, I. (2015). *Actions of master teachers in building student resilience framed within Ginsburg's crucial Cs.* Doctoral dissertation, Lamar University, Beaumont, United States. Available from ProQuest Dissertations and Thesis database. UMI 3721242.

Cole, K. (2011). Professional notes: Brain-based-research music advocacy. *Music Educators Journal, 98*(1), 26–30. https://doi.org/10.1177/0027432111416574

Comber, B. (2012). Mandated literacy assessment and the reorganisation of teachers' work: Federal policy, local effects. *Critical Studies in Education, 53*(2), 119–136. https://doi.org/10.1080/17508487.2012.672331

Cormack, P., & Comber, B. (2013). *High-stakes literacy tests and local effects in a rural school.* Retrieved from http://eprints.qut.edu.au/59272/

Daggett, W. (2000). Moving from standards to instructional practice. *National Association of Secondary School Principals Bulletin, 84*(620), 66–72. https://doi.org/10.1177/019263650008462008

Daviet, B. (2016). Revisiting the principle of education as a public good. *Education Research and Foresight Series*, No. 17. Paris: UNESCO. Available from http://www.unesco.org/new/en/education/themes/leading-theinternational-agenda/rethinking-education/erf-papers/

Deasy, R. (2002). *Critical links learning in the arts and student academic and social development.* Washington: Arts Education Partnership.

Dehler, G. E., & Welsh, M. A. (2014). Against spoon-feeding. For learning. Reflections on students' claims to knowledge. *Journal of Management Education, 38*(6), 875–893. https://doi.org/10.1177/1052562913511436

Donovan, L., & Pascale, L. (2013). *Integrating the arts across the content areas.* Huntington Beach, CA: Shell Educational Publishing.

Dunbar, R. (2018). *Communications skills diminished by excessive screen time.* Retrieved from https://www.abc.net.au/radionational/programs/science-show/communications-skills-diminished-by-excessive-screen-time/10548116#transcript

Eisner, E. (2003). The arts and the creation of mind. *Language Arts, 80*(5), 340–344.

Eisner, E. (2004). What can education learn from the arts about the practice of education? *International Journal of Education and the Arts, 5*(4), 1–12.

Eisner, E. (2005). Opening a Shuttered Window: An introduction to a special section on the arts and the intellect. *The Phi Delta Kappan, 87*(1), 8–10.

Ewing, R. (2010). The arts and Australian education: Realising potential. *Australian Educational Review*, No. 58. Camberwell: Australian Council for Educational Research Press. Retrieved from http://research.acer.edu.au/aer/11/

Ewing, R. (2012a). Competing issues in Australian primary curriculum: Learning from international experiences. *Education 3–13, 40*(1), 97–111. https://doi.org/10.1080/03004279.2012.635059

Ewing, R. (2012b). The imperative of an arts-led curriculum: Lessons from research. *Drama Australia Journal, 36*, 7–14.

Fanelli, C., & Evans, B. (2015). Capitalism in the classroom: The commodification of education. *Alternate Routes: A Journal of Critical Social Research, 26*, 11–22.

Fuller, T., & Söderlund, S. (2002). Academic practices of virtual learning by interaction. *Futures, 34*(8), 745–760. https://doi.org/10.1016/S0016-3287 (02)00018-6

Gibson, R., & Ewing, R. (2011). *Transforming the curriculum through the arts.* Melbourne: Palgrave Macmillan.

Goldberg, M. (2012). *Arts integration: Teaching subject matter through the arts in multicultural settings* (4th ed.). Boston, MA: Pearson/Allyn and Bacon.

Greene, M. (2011). Releasing the imagination. *Drama Australia Journal, 34,* 1–9.

Hardy, I. (2015). Education as a "risky business": Theorising student and teacher learning in complex times. *British Journal of Sociology of Education, 36*(3), 375–394. https://doi.org/10.1080/01425692.2013.829746

Hardy, I., & Boyle, C. (2011). My School? Critiquing the abstraction and quantification of Education. *Asia-Pacific Journal of Teacher Education, 39*(3), 211–222. https://doi.org/10.1080/1359866X.2011.588312

Howells, K. ProQuest Ebooks, & ebrary, I. (2012). *Gratitude in education: A radical view* (1. Aufl.ed.) Rotterdam: Sense Publishers. https://doi.org/ 10.1007/978-94-6091-814-8

Hsu, J. (2008). The secrets of storytelling: Our love for telling tales reveals the workings of the mind. *Scientific American Mind, 19*(4), 46–51.

Jonassen, D. H., Peck, K. L., & Wilson, B. G. (2001). *Learning with technology: A constructivist perspective.* Upper Saddle River, NJ: Merrill.

Jones, B. (2007). The unintended outcomes of high-stakes testing. *Journal of Applied School Psychology, 23*(2), 65–86.

Karpov, A. O. (2013). The commodification of education. *Russian Education & Society, 55*(5), 75–90. https://doi.org/10.2753/RES1060-9393550506

Kohn, A. (2000). Burnt at the high stakes. *Journal of Teacher Education, 51*(4), 315–327. https://doi.org/10.1177/0022487100051004007

Ladd, H. (2017). No child left behind: A deeply flawed federal policy. *Journal of Policy Analysis and Management, 36*(2), 461–469. https://doi.org/10.1002/ pam.21978

Lingard, B., & Sellar, S. (2013). "Catalyst data": Perverse systemic effects of audit and accountability in Australian schooling. *Journal of Education Policy, 28*(5), 634–656. https://doi.org/10.1080/02680939.2012.758815

Lippman, S., Bulanda, R. E., & Wagenaar, T. C. (2009). Student entitlement: Issues and strategies for confronting entitlement in the classroom and beyond. *College Teaching, 57*(4), 197–204. https://doi.org/10.3200/CTCH.57. 4.197-204

Lukianoff, G., & Haidt, J. (2015). The coddling of the American mind. *The Atlantic, 316*(2), 42–52.

Manney, P. (2008). Empathy in the time of technology: How storytelling is the key to empathy. *Journal of Evolution and Technology, 19*(1), 51–61.

McArdle, F., & Wright, S. (2014). First literacies: Art, creativity, play, constructive meaning-making. In G. Barton (Ed.), *Literacy in the arts: Retheorising learning and teaching* (pp. 21–137). Dordrecht: Springer.

McDonald, N., & Fisher, D. (2006). *Teaching literacy through the arts*. New York, NY: Guilford Press.

McKay, J., & Kember, D. (1997). Spoon Feeding Leads to Regurgitation: A better diet can result in more digestible learning outcomes. *Higher Education Research & Development, 16*(1), 55–67. https://doi.org/10.1080/072943 6970160105

Minarechová, M. (2012). Negative impacts of high-stakes testing. *Journal of Pedagogy*, (1), 82–100. https://doi.org/10.2478/v10159-012-0004-x

Munro, J. (2010). Enhancing students' literacy comprehension using NAPLAN data. East Melbourne: *Centre for Strategic Education Seminar Series*, Paper No. 200.

Northam, N. (2017). NAPLAN—more questions than answers. *Newsmonth, 37*(6), 1–2.

Parker, J., & Folkman, J. (2015). Building resilience in students at the intersection of special education and foster care challenges, strategies, and resources for educators. *Issues in Teacher Education, 24*(2), 43–62.

Peterson, A. (2017). *Compassion and education: Cultivating compassionate children, schools and communities*. London: Palgrave Macmillan.

Polesel, J., Dulfer, N., & Turnbull, M. (2012). *The impacts of high stakes testing on school students and their families*. Melbourne: Melbourne Graduate School of Education/Foundation for Young Australians. Retrieved from uws.edu.au

Project Compassion. (2014). *A flower in the favelas*. Retrieved from https://catholicschoolsguide.com.au/our-community/a-flower-in-the-favelas/

Raelin, J. A. (2009). The practice turn-away: Forty years of spoon-feeding in management education. *Management Learning, 40*(4), 401–410. https://doi.org/10.1177/1350507609335850

Russell-Bowie, D. (2009). Syntegration or disintegration? Models of integrating the arts across the primary school curriculum. *International Journal of Education and the Arts, 10*(28), 1–23.

Russell-Bowie, D. (2011). An Ode to Joy … or the sounds of silence? An exploration of arts education policy in Australian primary schools. *Arts Education Policy Review, 112*(4), 163–173. https://doi.org/10.1080/10632913.2011. 566099

Schaefer, T., Barta, M., Whitely, W., & Stogsdill, M. (2013). The "you owe me!" mentality: A student entitlement perception paradox. *Journal of Learning in Higher Education, 9*(1), 79–91.

Schwartzman, R. (2013). Consequences of commodifying education. *Academic Exchange Quarterly, 17*(3), 1–7.

Scott, S., Jackson, S., & Backett-Milburn, K. (1998). Swings and roundabouts: Risk anxiety and the everyday worlds of children. *Sociology, 32*(4), 689–705.

Twenge, J. M. (2013). Does online social media lead to social connection or social disconnection? *Journal of College and Character, 14*(1), 11–20. https://doi.org/10.1515/jcc-2013-0003

Walzer, M. (1984). *Spheres of justice: A defence of pluralism and equality.* Oxford: Martin Robertson.

West, C. (2012). Teaching music in an era of high-stakes testing and budget reductions. *Arts Education Policy Review, 113*(2), 75–79.

Williams, R. (2011, August 11). *Archbishop speaks in House of Lords on unrest.* Retrieved from http://aoc2013.brix.fatbeehive.com/articles.php/2152/archbishop-speaks-in-house-of-lords-on-unrest

Wright, S. (2012). *Children, meaning-making and the arts* (2nd ed.). Frenchs Forest, NSW: Pearson.

Wu, M. (2010). Inadequacies of NAPLAN results for measuring school performance. Submission to the *Inquiry into the Administration and Reporting of NAPLAN Testing*, Senate References Committee on Education, Employment & Workplace Relations, Canberra.

Yang, R. (2006). The commodification of education and its effects on developing countries: A focus on China. *Journal Für Entwicklungspolitik, 22*(4), 52–69. https://doi.org/10.20446/JEP-2414-3197-22-4-52

8

Peace, Conflict, and Empathy: Leveraging Violent Games for Global Good

Paul Darvasi

Video games have emerged from the morally suspect margins of society to become a cornerstone of the global entertainment industry. Their potency as a cultural force is such that noted media scholar Dr. Henry Jenkins believes that video games will be the defining art form of the twenty-first century (Smithsonian, 2012). In his *Manifesto for a Ludic Century*, game designer and scholar Dr. Eric Zimmerman (2013) suggests that we are at the dawn of the "ludic century", where art, design, entertainment, commerce, and education will increasingly become game-like experiences. Healthcare organizations, corporations, the military, NGOs, schools, and universities are all experimenting with video games for their propensity to train, teach, and motivate. In a twist of irony, a medium once labeled a "murder simulator" might now become an effective tool to support peace education and conflict resolution.

This chapter will review a handful of digital games set in zones of global conflicts for their potential to produce empathy and ultimately support the work of peace. Kampf and Cuhadar (2015) stress that empathy is considered "the most critical element by many scholars in the

P. Darvasi (✉)
Royal St. George's College, York University, Toronto, ON, Canada

© The Author(s) 2019
G. Barton, S. Garvis (eds.), *Compassion and Empathy in Educational Contexts*,
https://doi.org/10.1007/978-3-030-18925-9_8

conflict resolution literature" (p. 542), and a body of research draws links between digital gameplay with the production of empathy (Bachen, Hernández-Ramos, & Raphael, 2012; Belman & Flanagan, 2009; Chen, Hanna, Manohar, & Tobia, 2018; Flanagan & Nissenbaum, 2014; Greitemeyer, 2013; Kidd, 2015; Kral et al., 2018). Despite promising findings, the links between digital games and empathy continues to be tenuous, primarily because the "motivational, emotional, and social effects of gaming are … complex and hard to disentangle" (Granic, Lobel, & Engels, 2014, p. 70). Interactions between humans and digital games are complex, and nuanced emotions like empathy are a challenge to measure accurately, particularly when seeking to understand longitudinal effects. Moreover, there is a paucity of studies that specifically look at how digital games might be leveraged for the work of peace and conflict resolution. Consequently, this chapter will draw from research in diverse fields including game studies, psychology, virtual peace education, sociology, health and medicine, and trauma studies to shed some light on the topic and expose gaps for further work. Four games will be explored for their potential to cultivate and direct empathy through perspective-taking, negotiating ethical dilemmas, and promoting intercultural understanding. The final section will discuss the importance of context and reflection when implementing digital games to foster social and emotional development, concluding with a discussion on how they might produce long-term, sustainable changes to behaviors and attitudes.

In the interest of clarity, the term "digital game(s)" will be used as a catchall that includes both *video games* (games played on dedicated game consoles) and *computer games* (games played on computers), as many of the games described are available for either platform (Flanagan & Nissenbaum, 2014).

Serious Games

Digital games used for education, training, and learning broadly fall into two categories: commercial off-the-shelf (COTS) games or games that were deliberately instrumentalized for purposes other than entertainment

(Kafai & Burke, 2015; Klopfer, Osterweil, & Salen, 2009). However, the digital games ecology has grown in scope and sophistication, and now there are games that indistinguishably fuse entertainment and instruction, such as Ubisoft's *Valiant Hearts: The Great War* about World War I and iNK Stories' *1979 Revolution: Black Friday.* These can be classified as *serious games*, which are digital games that seek to entertain while addressing complex societal issues (Sanford, Starr, Merkel, & Kurki, 2015).

Serious games are generally produced by smaller, independent studios and/or universities and are designed for training and learning, or as catalysts for promoting awareness and effecting positive social change (Marchand & Hennig-Thurau, 2013). Notable examples include *Darfur Is Dying*, where players walk in the shoes of a Sudanese villager living through a humanitarian crisis; *Papers Please* confronts the ethical predicaments of a Soviet era customs officer; *This War of Mine* deals with civilians surviving in a war zone; *Czechoslovakia 38–89: Assassination* examines the lives of a handful of victims of the Nazi occupation during World War II; *Hush* tackles a Tutsi mother hiding from a Hutu patrol during the Rwandan genocide; *Fight for Freedom* puts the player in the role of an American slave, and *The Dragon, Cancer* is based on the designers' true story about losing their young son to terminal cancer.

The term "serious game" has been variably defined, but Marsh (2011) provides a definition suitable to present purposes:

> Digital games, simulations, virtual environments and mixed reality/media that provide opportunities to engage in activities through responsive narrative/story, gameplay or encounters to inform, influence, for well-being, and/or experience to convey meaning. The quality or success of serious games is characterized by the degree to which purpose has been fulfilled. Serious games are identified along a continuum from games for purpose on one end, through to experiential environments with minimal or no gaming characteristics for experience at the other end. (p. 63)

Conflict resolution education has long relied on live simulations and role-play (Hatipoglu, Müftüler-Baç, & Murphy, 2014), which is why Marsh's (2011) inclusion of simulations is especially applicable in this context.

Perspective-Taking and Empathy in Digital Games

Empathy is defined as "the ability to understand and share in another's emotional state or context" (Cohen & Strayer, 1996, p. 988) and is a necessary and vital foundation for the process of conflict resolution (Kampf & Cuhadar, 2015). Research in neuroscience has determined that empathy can "increase social understanding, lessen social conflict, limit aggression, increase compassion and caring, lessen prejudice, increase emotional competence, and motivate prosocial behavior" (Feshbach & Feshbach, 2009, in Kidd, 2015). These qualities are clearly beneficial for reducing intergroup conflict, but how can they be cultivated through digital games and computer simulations? Perhaps even more importantly, can empathy that transpires from playing a digital game lead to sustained and meaningful changes in behavior and attitude?

Perspectives and Perspective-Taking in Digital Games

Perspective-taking is the active consideration of an another's mental state, points of view, and motivation. Cuhadar and Kampf (2014) claim that perspective-taking "is one of the most important outcomes in conflict resolution and a prerequisite for developing empathy" (p. 515). Todd and Galinsky (2014) reviewed empirical research and found that perspective-taking helped negotiate social complexities, diminish biases, improve intergroup attitudes, and encourage a view of outgroups as more "self-like" and a sense of the self as more "outgroup-like". Cohen (2001) claims that by "introducing other perspectives and persuading others to identify with them, new possibilities for understanding are opened that may result in attitude change" (p. 260). The potential to positively impact attitudes with digital games is rooted not only in their aptitude to grant perspective but also in their status as instruments of persuasion. Bogost (2007) proposes *procedural rhetoric* in digital games as "the art of persuasion through rule-based representations and interactions, rather than the spoken word, writing, images, or moving pictures" (p. ix). A well-intentioned and effective game design that combines perspective-taking with procedural rhetoric has the possibility of effecting positive and beneficial changes in a player's attitudes and behaviors.

Digital games can grant players the agency to guide the actions and decisions of an in-game avatar in a responsive environment, which may deepen identification and enhance the effects of perspective-taking (Klimmt, Hefner, & Voderer, 2009). However, perspective-taking does not guarantee favorable results. For example, it has been found to be deleterious if enacted by someone who suffers from low self-esteem or identifies too strongly with their ingroup. Perspective-taking can also lead to negative outcomes in highly competitive contexts, or under the circumstances of a prolonged or intractable conflict (Todd & Galinsky, 2014). In digital games, the perspective the game affords can have profound implication for the player's perception of events.

Digital games encompass a sprawling ecology of interactive virtual worlds that range from simple 2D puzzlers to highly immersive digital environments. Depending on the game, players can control and interface with objects, characters, and environments and adopt a variety of perspectives. The first-person perspective, for one, tends to dominate the aptly named first-person shooter (FPS) genre, which includes blockbusters franchises like *Call of Duty* and *Bioshock*. Action genres like *Assassin's Creed*, MMOs (Massive Multiplayer Online) like *World of Warcraft* and 2D platformers like the classic *Donkey Kong* and *Braid* are played from a third-person perspective, where the in-game avatar is wholly visible to the player. The second-person perspective, which addresses the player directly, is rare and most typically used by interactive fiction and text-based games like *Depression Quest*, which delves into the life of a person suffering from depression and anxiety. Strategy games like *Civilization* and *Age of Empires* employ an omniscient or "God-like" point of view, much like that of a board game. Additionally, some games like *Skyrim*, an open-world sword and sorcery role-playing game, and *Minecraft*, a world building game, let players switch between first-person and third-person, while *This War of Mine* and *Mass Effect* allow for the control of multiple characters at once.

Each of these deployments of perspective will have a different impact on how a player identifies with their in-game personas and will variably shape player attitudes, affective and cognitive responses. For example, the first-person perspective creates a close identification between the player and their in-game avatar. The player does not see their own face any more than one would in real life while they are anchored in their character's visual and auditory perspective. This convention is a powerful immersion strategy, but if the game seeks to create identification with a victim or outgroup member represented by the player-controlled avatar, it may not afford the critical distance to think about one's in-game persona in a meaningful way. Newman (as cited in Smethurst & Craps, 2015) suggests that when a game is most immersive and interactive, and the feedback loop is most complete, players can lose sight of their in-game identity which, in turn, diminishes the possibility for empathy with their avatar. Likewise, Cohen (2001) suggests that "identification is likely to increase enjoyment, involvement, and intense emotional responses, but it is less likely to produce critical stances" (p. 260). An over-identification between player and avatar may "collapse" the two identities and attenuate the critical distance necessary to contemplate the "nonequivalent singularity" of the other (Simon, 2014).

When most engaged by the game, the player's affective focus tends to shift from their in-game persona to their contextual game environment (Smethurst & Craps, 2015). For example, *Homefront* can generate empathy for the plight of the victims of war but, for commercial and functional reasons, it was designed in the style of an FPS. Recognizing that the player would have "no mirror to see how the character's actions would be received socially" (Flanagan & Nissenbaum, 2014, p. 102), the designers included three companions (or visible "others"), whose emotional reactions to their difficult circumstance can elicit empathy for their suffering as collateral victims of war.

These findings underscore that, to better understand the operations of empathy and digital games, further research should address the nuances of how players respond to and are affected by the various in-game perspectives.

Cognitive and Affective Empathy in Digital Games

Empathy comprises both cognitive and affective (emotional) dimensions, and "perspective-taking can increase intergroup positivity through both forms of empathic responding" (Todd & Galinsky, 2014, p. 79). Belman and Flanagan (2009) suggest that games would profit from combining both modes to effect a lasting and productive change in the player, and Happ, Melzer, and Steffgen (2015) write that "either component on its own does not fully describe empathy, as affect and cognition are typically linked in empathy" (p. 81). Although the two modes work in conjunction with each other, the examples that follow will look at how they function independently of each other in digital games to better grasp their individual operations. Cognitive empathy will be explored with *PeaceMaker*, a government simulation game about the Palestinian/Israeli conflict, while *Hush*, a game set during the Rwandan genocide, will be used to demonstrate the production of emotional or affective empathy.

PeaceMaker: Cognitive Empathy and the Two-State Solution

Cognitive empathy requires active thought about the motivation, positionality, and circumstance of the other. It is the intellectual process of assessing the motivations, beliefs, cultural norms, and mindset of the other, and is closely tied to perspective-taking. Examples of cognitive empathy might include a teacher thinking about what causes a student to act out in class, or two diplomats who familiarize themselves with each other's motives and goals before undertaking a delicate negotiation.

In *PeaceMaker*, players assume the role of either the Israeli prime minister or the Palestinian president and endeavor to achieve a tenable two-state solution. Cognitive empathy is exercised in the game because, regardless of what side is chosen, players must think about the needs of their own stakeholders as well as the mindset and circumstances of their opponent (Belman & Flanagan, 2009). Belman and Flanagan (2009) suggest that players take the role with which they do not identify and/or support to gain a broader view of the conflict. As a virtual site that enables context-specific political decisions and negotiations, *PeaceMaker* differentiates itself from live conflict resolution simulations in that it lets players experiment with multiple perspectives in an environment where actions and decisions precipitate tangible and immediate consequences. The game also incorporates authentic newsreels and photos depicting emotionally difficult scenes that provide an affective counterweight to the intellectual management of the conflict at the political and military level.

Cuhadar and Kampf (2014), who studied *PeaceMaker* for its potential to support peace education, found that all participants who played the game demonstrated significant increases in knowledge pertaining to the Israeli-Palestinian conflict. The study found notable changes in attitude about the conflict by third-party participants (American and Turkish students) but, conversely, measured almost no effect on the attitudes of Israeli and Palestinian participants who were direct parties to the conflict. The researchers concluded that when "attitudes are linked to self-defining values and reference groups, which is often the case in intractable conflicts, they are very much resistant to change" (Cuhadar & Kampf, 2014, p. 543). This is consistent with other research on perspective-taking that found limited success with participants who identified strongly with their ingroup (Todd & Galinsky, 2014). These results, however, are contingent on a specific game, length of exposure, and other contextual factors. Had the game, for example, involved the use of realistic third-person avatars, as opposed to a largely omniscient and disembodied point of view, there may have been deeper investment in the perspective. Nevertheless, the effect on third-party participants is promising because it demonstrates that a game-based intervention can produce a measurable change in attitude. As research, technology, and design improve perhaps, in time, these benefits might eventually impact the chief stakeholders in the conflict.

Hush: Terror, Truthfulness, and Emotional Empathy

Emotional empathy is an immediate and visceral response to the feelings of others, and is subcategorized into *parallel empathy* and *reactive empathy* (Belman & Flanagan, 2009, p. 6). Parallel empathy is "roughly equivalent to the lay understanding of empathy as the vicarious experience of another's emotional state" (p. 7), and reactive empathy is an emotional response which is at variance with what the other is experiencing, such as feeling guilt for another's loss or pain. *Hush*, set during the Rwandan genocide, provides a good example of how a game can provokes both parallel and reactive empathy.

In *Hush*, a Rwandan Tutsi mother named Liliane hides in an abandoned house with her baby while armed Hutu troops patrol nearby. The object of the game is simple: sing a quiet lullaby to prevent the baby from crying and attracting the unwanted attention of the nearby soldiers. To "sing" the lullaby, players type keys that correspond to a rhythm of materializing letters, but, if they fall out of sync, the baby's cries grow louder. Too many mistimed letters cause the mother and child to be discovered and an unsettling red screen marks the end of the game and, presumably, their murder at the hands of the patrol. If the player keeps pace with the rhythm of the letters and pacifies the baby, the soldiers pass and the mother and child flee to safety.

Visually, the game is rendered in a simplistic, but disturbing, abstract style of dim lights, shadowy figures, and gloomy landscapes. The disconcerting soundtrack includes angry soldiers barking orders, unseen victims pleading and screaming, machetes slicing flesh, and startling bursts of machine gun fire. The terrifying soundscape and nightmarish art unsettle players as they try to perform the otherwise simple task of keeping synch with the lullaby. The stress, tension, and anxiety the player can feel are, to some degree, analogous to that of the mother's, thus provoking parallel empathy. The crying baby, however, elicits reactive empathy, as the player's concern for its life and safety are at variance with the cause of the child's unhappiness (cold, hunger, discomfort, etc.). The game's designers explain that "the player isn't viewing this horrific event from a distance and attempting to 'solve the problem.' They're in the middle of it, experiencing the terror of the Hutu raid" (Flanagan & Nissenbaum, 2014, p. 146). They add that "it's a tense and anxiety-producing experience, but hopefully players come away with new empathy for the victims and survivors of the Rwandan genocide" (Flanagan & Nissenbaum, 2014, p. 147).

There is little doubt that the game provokes uncomfortable emotions, but it's a far cry from the experience of a real victim. The player is not really "in the middle of it", as the designers suggest, but merely reacting to a low-stakes representation of a horrific and traumatic event. Keyboarding is not the same as being a petrified mother stumbling through a lullaby to protect the life of her child. Is five minutes of gameplay enough to create even a tenuous connection to the complex and drawn-out emotional experience it hopes to communicate?

The limits of representing reality is an important consideration when thinking about how digital games can produce prosocial emotions. Despite its limitations, the game produces a genuine and meaningful affective connection between the player and the represented victim. *Hush* personalizes trauma in a way that Hirsch and Spitzer (2009) term "narrative truth" or "truthfulness" which "can tell more about the *meaning* of an event … than about the event itself" (p. 162). A mother hiding with her child is a recurrent event in war zones and sites of armed conflict; it does not have to be historically located or specific to evoke empathy, create awareness, and spur curiosity to learn more. In the right context, *Hush* can encourage players to think, feel, and care about the Rwandan genocide, but it also universalizes the plight of victims and survivors in all zones of conflict.

This War of Mine: Ethical Dilemmas and Quiet Moments in the Warzone

This War of Mine is an antidote to mainstream digital games that glorify war and conflict as it shifts from the more common perspective of the combatant to that of the civilian. The game centers on a band of civilians who struggle to survive in a war-torn city inspired by the 1992–1996 Siege of Sarajevo during the Bosnian War. Supplies are scarce, and the survivor must scavenge by night to avoid daytime sniper fire.

The game combines both cognitive and affective empathy as players negotiate difficult ethical dilemmas to survive the wreckage of war. Whether robbing an elderly couple or denying limited supplies to other survivors, players are regularly confronted with hard choices. Toma (2015) speaks to the game's capacity to rouse empathy in an evocative and instructive way when she observes that *This War of Mine* is a "saddening and profound experience of war, famine, murder, suicide and failure, bringing the player closer to its victims, which are similar to them, thus having the potential for becoming a counter pedagogy of war" (p. 216).

Players can intellectualize the conditions of the victims and understand the difficult decisions they are forced to make (cognitive empathy), but also parallel their characters' guilt and remorse for having to make those hard choices (affective empathy). Occasionally, an in-game character will become unresponsive when they fall into a depression, which renders them temporarily unplayable. The frustration a player feels from losing control of a depressed character who might otherwise be put to productive work is an example of reactive empathy.

Smethurst and Craps (2015) write that "games work with the concept of psychological trauma in ways that are unprecedented in other media" (p. 172) because they offer alternative, and perhaps even more fruitful means of representing personal and social histories of suffering and injustice. Flanagan and Nissenbaum (2014) also see digital games as potent sites for moral deliberation because "games reach deep parts of the human psyche [and] … not only reflect and express, but also activate these beliefs and values in powerful ways" (p. 3). An online post discussing *This War of Mine* highlights digital games' unique capacity to provoke empathy, elicit emotion, and disseminate awareness:

> *This War of Mine* … shows you the cost of war—body, mind, and soul. I've read plenty of great anti-war novels, seen plenty of great anti-war films. *This War of Mine* joins *Spec Ops: The Line* in a growing, prestigious genre of anti-war games. It speaks for the most silent, unrepresented victims of war unflinchingly, sincerely. It reveals the cost of war; not with the over-the-top set pieces and faceless macho protagonists, but with quiet moments. (Spirit, 18 November 2014, as cited in Toma, 2015, p. 220)

These "quiet moments" may be a key to how digital games can produce meaningful and, perhaps, even transformational instances of empathy. Cognitive and emotional empathy do not typically occur at the heights of interactive play, but rather when "a player is not actually capable of influencing the game state: unskippable scripted or prerecorded cutscenes, for instance, or loading screens" (Smethurst & Craps, 2015, p. 273). These moments of relative inactivity open a space where players have occasion to reflect on their actions and experience.

Digital gameplay oscillates across a spectrum of active and passive engagement. When involved in highly immersive, interactive play, a player may not feel empathy in that moment, but they are steadily reminded of the consequences of their decisions. In other words, "by putting their hands on the controller and becoming part of the player/game feedback loop—players become complicit with the events portrayed therein" (Smethurst & Craps, 2015, p. 277). Toma (2015) highlights this process when reflecting on playing *This War of Mine*:

> The game oriented us … toward considering how we felt about our actions, how these actions affected us as persons, for the results of our decisions in the game and their effect on the characters may not be anticipated. The game has thus a strong moral component … by playing it we learned that we must take responsibility for our actions, regardless of what the future brings…. Difficult decisions encourage self-reflection. (p. 215)

Player choices in digital games can precipitate palpable reactions and emotionally compelling outcomes: arriving too late with the medication leads to the death of a family member; or in *Fight for Freedom* an American slave's choice to sabotage their master may lead to the beating or death of a falsely accused fellow slave. Game worlds respond to players and hold them accountable for their actions, but they are also forgiving. If a choice leads to an undesirable result, there is usually the option to reset and try again. Moreover, the digital game spaces are safe rehearsal sites as consequences tend to be low-stakes because they occur in a virtual dimension; however, the lessons can translate to the real world. Zagal (2009) found that players who negotiate moral and ethical dilemmas in games like *This War of Mine* can feel personally invested in their choices. He characterizes digital games as "perfect-test bed[s]" (p. 8) to teach and learn about ethical reasoning.

This War of Mine is inspired by the Siege of Sarajevo but set in a fictional setting and is thus largely decontextualized from lived culture and history. *1979 Revolution: Black Friday*, however, is a striking example of how a digital game can replicate the complex and ambiguous ethical dilemmas faced by individuals in a historically and culturally specific zone of conflict.

Digital Game as Documentary: Intercultural Understanding in *1979 Revolution: Black Friday*

1979 Revolution: Black Friday is an adventure interactive drama set during the Iranian Revolution. It follows a young Iranian photojournalist named Reza Shirazi as he negotiates and documents the complex political and emotional landscape of his country in turmoil. The game's cultural and historical fidelity blur the lines between digital game and documentary, which imports a unique value to the discussion of how digital games can produce empathy to benefit peace education and conflict resolution.

Unlike *PeaceMaker*'s omniscient perspective, *Black Friday* personalizes the experience and connects the player directly to the ground-level activities of the aspiring photojournalist and his family as they are torn asunder by the violent ideological conflicts of the revolution. Throughout, players contend with morally ambiguous dilemmas as they are pressed to make choices through dialogue and action. The options are never black and white and, as the game's developer Navid Khonsari describes, players must "choose randomly between two horrible decisions, which reflects the reality reported by those who lived through the revolution" (N. Khonsari, personal communication, July 8, 2016). The choices affect Reza's political alignments and interpersonal relationships, but the historical outcome remains unchanged. Choices in *Black Friday* subvert right/wrong or good/evil binaries and, instead, evoke the complex moral, ideological, and political dilemmas faced by the various stakeholders in Iran during the revolution.

Black Friday strives for historical and cultural accuracy and shares characteristics with the vérité mode in documentary film, which led its developers to classify it as a "vérité game". Iranian-born Khonsari and his team curated the game with authentic artifacts and documents from the revolution, including films, photos, and recorded speeches from the Ayatollah Khomeini. The development team accessed a wide range of relevant documents, interviewed scholars and advisors, and recorded conversations with forty Iranians who experienced the revolution first-hand, many of whose stories were woven into the game's narrative (N. Khonsari, personal communication, July 8, 2016). Real locations are referenced, such as the nefarious Evin political prison and the Cinema Rex, which was deliberately set on fire leading to the tragic deaths of the 470 people trapped inside. Finally, local culture is experienced from the perspective of an Iranian, introducing players to Persian tea protocols, the delights of street bread, and a smattering of Farsi. Additional information and media are available through unobtrusive in-game menus for those who want to learn more about Iran, Persian culture, and the revolution.

According to Harris (2009), the development of *intercultural understanding* is a pillar of the peace education process, as it "promotes respect for different cultures and helps students appreciate the diversity of the human community" (p. 81). This concept is closely tied to the idea of ethnocultural empathy, or the acceptance and appreciation of another culture in comparison to one's own (Wang et al., 2003). In *Black Friday*, these concepts are fostered by transporting players to Tehran at a critical juncture in Iranian history with the intention, as Khonsari claims, to "use this extremely powerful tool to create a better understanding of what is going on around the world and reconcile multiple perspectives" (N. Khonsari, personal communication, July 8, 2016). Gonzalez, Saner, and Eisenberg (2012) found that better information and knowledge about a conflict and/or an outgroup gained through gameplay helps mitigate the influence of political and religious affiliations on peace process strategies. It also helps to understand and reflect on the roots and complexities of conflict, and the choices faced by those affected.

Finally, *Black Friday*'s unique cultural and historical affordances might be studied to determine if the game might also be used to support the production of historical empathy (Schrier, 2015) and global empathy (Bachen et al., 2012; Zappile, Beers, & Raymond, 2016), both of which contribute to the acquisition and development of intercultural understanding.

Optimizing Outcomes Through Design, Context, and Reflection

Digital games are complex cultural artifacts. Like all media texts, they invite manifold interpretations that are influenced by contingencies such as, but not limited to, game design, technological affordances, approach to gameplay, time spent playing, and user disposition. These variables can be better controlled and directed to meet specific ends by contextualizing gameplay with ancillary material to encourage productive discussion, community building, and spaces for reflection.

Empathy is generally thought to be a desirable trait, but it should be approached carefully in both game design and implementation because, under certain circumstances, it can lead to negative outcomes. For example, an empathetic identification with an antisocial or violent character in a game can increase antisocial and aggressive behavior in the player (Happ et al., 2015). Belman and Flanagan (2009) also caution that empathy without attendant mindfulness or thought will not produce "significant shifts in … players' beliefs about themselves, the world, or themselves in relation to the world" (p. 10). Gorry (2009) speculates that empathy generated from decontextualized interactions with virtual spaces may not transfer to the real world. Empathy alone does not automatically produce an understanding of outgroups members or the social and historical forces that shape instances of injustice and suffering.

Furthermore, a game designed to elicit empathy may not be received as intended. Besides unfavorable player dispositions, Carvalho (2014) and Toma (2015) observe that a digital game can be played as "just a game" where its content can be ignored by a player who is driven to efficiently "beat the system", finish, and win. This emphasis on gameplay over game content not only impedes the production of empathy but also can run counter to learning and affective outcomes.

Managing the instructional context is an effective means to counter the effects of "gaming the game" at the expense of the content. For example, two studies carried out by Happ et al. (2015) found that priming players prior to a gameplay session with videos and readings that promote empathy led to greater prosocial behavior and empathy for the characters in the game. Jin (2011) also found that "presenting pregame narratives has been successfully shown to mitigate the deleterious effects of violent games on behavior" (as cited in Happ et al., 2015, p. 83). Therefore, gameplay might be prefaced with materials to help guide participants toward desired goals and outcomes.

An additional contextual consideration is the inclusion and creation of spaces for dialogue, collaboration, and reflection. Whether face-to-face discussions, online forums, or computer-mediated communication

(CMC), the effectiveness of collaborative learning around games in formal and informal forums has received broad support from educational games scholars (Ang, Zaphiris, & Wilson, 2010; Gee, 2003; Jenkins, Purushotma, Weigel, Clinton, & Robison, 2009; Steinkuehler & Duncan, 2008; Toma, 2015; Turkay, Hoffman, Kinzer, Chantes, & Vicari, 2014). Learning communities that contextualize games have been shown to construct, share, and exchange knowledge socially, solve problems collectively, and partake in evidence-based debates (Steinkuehler & Duncan, 2008). These interactions also build community, encourage positive social interactions (Ang et al., 2010), and, if effectively established and guided, could work in the service of a conflict resolution process.

Opportunities for reflection during gameplay can better dispose players to empathy and mindfulness (Simon, 2014; Smethurst & Craps, 2015), and individual and/or collective reflection outside the game should also be encouraged. Ang et al. (2010) advocate for "collective-reflective play", where players give thought to their in-game experiences and also "reflect on individual roles, goals, and knowledge shared in the group" (Ang et al., 2010, p. 375). Guided reflection can produce deeper thought on a subject, mindfulness, and can attend to particular aspects of the game that may further a learning agenda, produce empathy, or gain new knowledge and perspectives on both ingroups and outgroups. Reflection can also incite players to "recognize and engage with the material relations that continue to structure individual and collective identities" (Simon, 2014, p. 211) and, consequently, catalyze action as well as changes in attitude and behavior.

A key to success in using digital games used in school curricula, or for any other instructional or educational purpose, is the creation of a suitable context targeted to produce specific learning outcomes.

Changes in Behavior and Attitude in Digital Games

In many games, players are held accountable for their decisions, reinforcing the reality that actions and choices have consequences. On the other hand, empathy tends to occur at moments of diminished agency, where a player is more passive and has occasion to reflect on the consequences of their choices. As the pendulum swings between these two states, action, agency, responsibility, and empathy combine in any number of ways to produce a range of emotions, understandings, and responses. But what is the lasting effect? Can digital games alter behavior and shape new attitudes?

There is some evidence to support that games can produce significant changes in players. Zagal (2009) suggests that digital games have the capacity to affect a player's ethical mindset, while third-party participants to the Palestinian/Israeli conflict who played *PeaceMaker* were observed to experience a change in attitude (Kampf & Cuhadar, 2015). Additionally, Evan Narcinne's review of *This War of Mine* states that "It's the kind of game that could potentially change the way you watch the news, treat others or cast a vote in an election" (as cited in Toma, 2015, p. 218). Bogost's (2007) claim that games are instruments of persuasion also implies that games can influence thought and action. Digital games seem to demonstrate the possibility to produce changes in players, but are these changes in behavior and attitude sustainable in the long term? Do changes experienced immediately after gameplay persist and transfer to the real world?

Children at play assume roles, work through feelings, and experiment with a wide range of social, emotional, and behavior constructs that inform their relationship with the real world (Piaget, 1962). Similarly, the digital game space is a site for playful simulation, rehearsal, and experimentation that may transfer to real life. Presumably, this dynamic is not confined to children. Recent studies that look at whether digital games can successfully alter behavior tend to cluster in health and medicine research (e.g., Duncan, Hieftje, Culyba, & Fiellin, 2014). There is some evidence, however, that players will apply social skills and prosocial behavior learned in digital games to relations outside the gaming environment (Gentile & Gentile, 2008; Gentile et al., 2009 as cited in Granic et al., 2014). Likewise, Happ et al. (2015) found that "when playing an avatar in a video game, one can still experience empathy for an opponent, and thus act more prosocially or experience a positive change in attitude toward others" (p. 91). Furthermore, research in neuroscience supports that gameplay can physically alter the brain which, in turn, can alter an individual's mindset and behavior (Kral et al., 2018). Buckley and

Anderson (2006) found that frequent exposure to certain types of media affect internal variables (emotions, cognitions, etc.) and can lead to permanent changes in personality (as cited in Happ et al., 2015). Likewise, Bavelier et al. (2011) describe digital games as "controlled training regimens" (p. 763) and suggest that improved performance in gameplay is "paralleled by enduring physical and functional neurological remodeling" (p. 763). However, additional research is critical to better understand how to design games to target specific and sustained changes in behaviors and attitudes.

Discussion and Conclusion

Despite their violent content, the judicious use of the games discussed can provide safe spaces for contact and collaboration, encourage perspective-taking, produce empathy, help negotiate ethical and moral dilemmas, stimulate intercultural understanding, and facilitate the acquisition of historical and cultural knowledge. The hope is that these benefits will have a lasting effect on individuals and cause positive and sustainable changes in behaviors and attitudes. However, much work remains before this emergent, complex, and rapidly evolving medium can be more effectively leveraged for the ends of social good.

In the meantime, design and implementation must proceed cautiously, as digital games are powerful tools whose mismanagement can backfire and achieve unintended consequences. Essentializing complex subjects, cultural appropriations, and unproductive or misplaced emotional manipulations and "emotioneering" are some perils to be avoided. Sanford et al. (2015) sum up the situation well when they advise that "creating simplistic games that are unsophisticated and non-immersive run the risk of doing the opposite of what they intend, that is, they can trivialize vitally important world issues" (p. 102). This view is counterbalanced by Carvalho's (2014) observation that designers be weary of creating overly complicated games or risk alienating players, especially those who have limited experience playing digital games. As the field progresses, designers will be challenged to negotiate the fine lines that distinguish the complicated from the complex, and representation from misrepresentation.

A critical approach must underpin the successful use of digital games as instruments of emotional growth and social justice. As media texts and sites of literacy, digital games are subject to the same interrogative process that underpins the responsible design and consumption of all media. Who and what is selected for representation? Who and what is suppressed? Whose narrative perspective is privileged? Whose is ignored? What is the ideology and rhetoric implicit in the design? Does the treatment of the subject provoke thought, empathy, or action? If so, how? If not, does it still have value? Are there specific elements about *how* digital games transmit their message that make them more or less effective than other media or modes of representation? Who has access to game, and who does not? These questions are by no means exhaustive but mark a path by which the once maligned and now pervasive influence of digital games can be leveraged for the causes of justice, equity, civility, and peace.

References

Ang, C. S., Zaphiris, P., & Wilson, S. (2010). Computer games and sociocultural play: An activity theoretical perspective. *Games and Culture, 5*(4), 354–380.

Bachen, C. M., Hernández-Ramos, P. F., & Raphael, C. (2012). Simulating REAL LIVES: Promoting global empathy and interest in learning through simulation games. *Simulation & Gaming, 43*, 437–460. https://doi.org/10.1177/1046878111432108

Bavelier, D., Green, C. S., Han, D. H., Renshaw, P. F., Merzenich, M. M., & Gentile, D. A. (2011). Brains on video games. *Nature Reviews Neuroscience, 12*, 763–768.

Belman, J., & Flanagan, M. (2009). Designing games to foster empathy. *Cognitive Technology, 14*(2), 5–15.

Bogost, I. (2007). *Persuasive games: The expressive power of videogames*. Cambridge: MIT Press.

Buckley, K. E., & Anderson, C. A. (2006). A theoretical model of the effects and consequences of playing video games. In P. Vorderer & J. Bryant (Eds.), *Playing video games: Motives, responses, and consequences* (pp. 363–378). Mahwah, NJ: Lawrence Erlbaum Associates Publishers.

Carvalho, G. (2014). Virtual worlds can be dangerous: Using ready-made computer simulations for teaching international relations. *International Studies Perspectives, 15*(4), 538–557. https://doi.org/10.1111/insp.12053

Chen, A., Hanna, J. J., Manohar, A., & Tobia, A. (2018). Teaching empathy: The implementation of a video game into a psychiatry clerkship curriculum. *Academic Psychiatry, 42*(3), 362–365.

Cohen, J. (2001). Defining identification: A theoretical look at the identification of audiences with media characters. *Mass Communication & Society, 4*, 245–264.

Cohen, D., & Strayer, J. (1996). Empathy in conduct-disordered and comparison youth. *Developmental Psychology, 32*, 988–998.

Cuhadar, E., & Kampf, R. (2014). Learning about conflict and negotiations through computer simulations: The case of PeaceMaker. *International Studies Perspectives, 15*(4), 509–524.

Duncan, L. R., Hieftje, K. D., Culyba, S., & Fiellin, L. E. (2014). Game playbooks: Tools to guide multidisciplinary teams in developing videogame-based behavior change interventions. *Translational Behavioral Medicine, 4*(1), 108–116. https://doi.org/10.1007/s13142-013-0246-8

Flanagan, M., & Nissenbaum, H. (2014). *Values at play in digital games.* Cambridge: MIT Press.

Gee, J. P. (2003). *What video games have to teach us about learning and literacy.* New York: Palgrave Macmillan.

Gentile, D. A., & Gentile, J. R. (2008). Violent video games as exemplary teachers: A conceptual analysis. *Journal of Youth and Adolescence, 37*(2), 127–141.

Gonzalez, C., Saner, L. D., & Eisenberg, L. (2012). Learning to stand in the other's shoes: A Computer video game experience of the Israeli–Palestinian conflict. *Social Science Computer Review, 31*(2), 236–243.

Gorry, A. (2009). Empathy in the virtual world. *The Chronicle of Higher Education, 56*, B10–B12.

Granic, I., Lobel, A., & Engels, R. C. (2014). The benefits of playing video games. *American Psychologist, 69*(1), 66.

Greitemeyer, T. (2013). Playing video games cooperatively increases empathic concern. *Social Psychology, 44*(6), 408–413. https://doi.org/10.1027/1864-9335/a000154

Happ, C., Melzer, A., & Steffgen, G. (2015). Like the good or bad guy— Empathy in antisocial and prosocial games. *Psychology of Popular Media Culture, 4*(2), 80.

Harris, I. (2009). Peace education: Definition, approaches, and future directions. *Peace, Literature, and Art, 1*, 77.

Hatipoglu, E., Müftüler-Baç, M., & Murphy, T. (2014). Simulation games in teaching international relations: Insights from a multi-day, multi-stage, multi-issue simulation on Cyprus. *International Studies Perspectives, 15*(4), 394–406.

Hirsch, M., & Spitzer, L. (2009). The witness in the archive: Holocaust studies/memory studies. *Memory Studies, 2*(2), 151–170.

Jenkins, H., Purushotma, R., Weigel, M., Clinton, K., & Robison, A. J. (2009). *Confronting the challenges of participatory culture: Media education for the 21st century.* Cambridge: MIT Press.

Kafai, Y. B., & Burke, Q. (2015). Constructionist gaming: Understanding the benefits of making games for learning. *Educational Psychologist, 50*(4), 313–334.

Kampf, R., & Cuhadar, E. (2015). Do computer games enhance learning about conflicts? A cross-national inquiry into proximate and distant scenarios in Global Conflicts. *Computers in Human Behavior, 52*, 541–549.

Kidd, J. (2015). Gaming for affect: Museum online games and the embrace of empathy. *The Journal of Curatorial Studies, 4*(3), 414–432.

Klimmt, C., Hefner, D., & Voderer, P. (2009). The video game experience as "true" identification: A theory of enjoyable alterations of players' self-perception. *Communication Theory, 19*, 351–373.

Klopfer, E., Osterweil, S., & Salen, K. (2009). *Education arcade.* Cambridge, MA: MIT Press.

Kral, T. R., Stodola, D. E., Birn, R. M., Mumford, J. A., Solis, E., Flook, L., ... Davidson, R. J. (2018). Neural correlates of video game empathy training in adolescents: A randomized trial. *npj Scientific of Learning, 3*, 13.

Marchand, A., & Hennig-Thurau, T. (2013). Value creation in the video game industry: Industry economics, consumer benefits, and research opportunities. *Journal of Interactive Marketing, 27*(3), 141–157.

Marsh, T. (2011). Serious games continuum: Between games for purpose and experiential environments for purpose. *Entertainment Computing, 2*(2), 61–68.

Piaget, J. (1962). *Play, dreams and imitation* (Vol. 24). New York: Norton.

Sanford, K., Starr, L. J., Merkel, L., & Kurki, S. B. (2015). Serious games: Video games for good? *E-Learning and Digital Media, 12*(1), 90–106.

Schrier, K. (2015). EPIC: A framework for using video games in ethics education. *Journal of Moral Education, 44*(4), 393–424.

Simon, R. (2014). *A pedagogy of witnessing: Curatorial practice and the pursuit of social justice.* New York: SUNY Press.

Smethurst, T., & Craps, S. (2015). Playing with trauma: Interreactivity, empathy, and complicity in *The Walking Dead* video game. *Games and Culture, 10,* 269–290.

Smithsonian Institute. (2012). *The art of video games exhibition trailer.* Retrieved from http://americanart.si.edu/exhibitions/archive/2012/games/artists/

Steinkuehler, C., & Duncan, S. (2008). Scientific habits of mind in virtual worlds. *Journal of Science Education and Technology, 17*(6), 530–543.

Todd, A. R., & Galinsky, A. D. (2014). Perspective-taking as a strategy for improving intergroup relations: Evidence, mechanisms, and qualifications. *Social and Personality Psychology Compass, 8*(7), 374–387. https://doi.org/10.1111/spc3.12116

Toma, E. (2015). Self-reflection and morality in critical games. Who is to be blamed for war? *Journal of Comparative Research in Anthropology and Sociology, 6*(1), 209.

Turkay, S., Hoffman, D., Kinzer, C. K., Chantes, P., & Vicari, C. (2014). Toward understanding the potential of games for learning: Learning theory, game design characteristics, and situating video games in classrooms. *Computers in the Schools, 31*(1), 21.

Wang, Y.-W., Davidson, M. M., Yakushko, O. F., Savoy, H. B., Tan, J. A., & Bleier, J. K. (2003). The scale of ethnocultural empathy: Development, validation, and reliability. *Journal of Counseling Psychology, 50,* 221–234.

Zagal, J. P. (2009, August). Ethically notable videogames: Moral dilemmas and gameplay. In *DiGRA conference.*

Zappile, T. M., Beers, D. J., & Raymond, C. (2016). Promoting global empathy and engagement through real-time problem-based simulations. *International Studies Perspectives, 18*(2), 194–210.

Zimmerman, E. (2013). *Manifesto for a ludic century.* Retrieved from http://kotaku.com/manifesto-the-21st-century-will-be-defined-by-games-1275355204

9

Exploring How Quality Children's Literature Can Enhance Compassion and Empathy in the Classroom Context

Georgina Barton, Margaret Baguley, Martin Kerby, and Abbey MacDonald

Introduction

When teachers make space for children to chart parallels between their own emotional states and those of characters depicted in texts, they create opportunities for deeply transformative learning; the kind of learning where children can probe their evolving sense of self, and understand where more profound and complex emotions spring from (Garner & Parker, 2018; Katch, 2018; MacDonald & Baguley, 2012). Allowing

G. Barton (✉)
School of Education, University of Southern Queensland, Brisbane, QLD, Australia
e-mail: georgina.barton@usq.edu.au

M. Baguley • M. Kerby
University of Southern Queensland, Brisbane, QLD, Australia
e-mail: margaret.baguley@usq.edu.au; martin.kerby@usq.edu.au

A. MacDonald
University of Tasmania, Hobart, TAS, Australia
e-mail: Abbey.MacDonald@utas.edu.au

© The Author(s) 2019
G. Barton, S. Garvis (eds.), *Compassion and Empathy in Educational Contexts*,
https://doi.org/10.1007/978-3-030-18925-9_9

165

students to explore emotions through, reading, writing, making and responding provides opportunity for meaningful emotional development and cultivation of wellbeing. Opportunities for teachers to work with students to explore the genesis and implications of emotional responses in their daily lives are integral to their development of self and social awareness and management.

Empirical studies conducted over at least the past 30 years have shown emotions that are evoked by language can be powerful (Lindquist, MacCormack, & Shablack, 2015; Velten, 1968), and can impact upon judgements and decision making (Johnson & Tversky, 1983; Lerner, Li, Valdesolo, & Kassam, 2015). There has also been significant research exploring how images can depict emotion alongside language choice in texts such as picture books (Lewis, 2001; Unsworth, 2013). Despite this, Havas, Glenberg and Rinck (2007) suggest that "the interaction between emotion and language is not well understood" (p. 436). The opportunity to draw upon the plethora of individual daily experiences of students in order to explore emotional interactions within the visual and (sometimes) textual world of children's picture books through a focussed approach can assist in developing effective life-skills (ACARA, n.d.).

This chapter situates itself within a broader conversation around the challenges and opportunities for learning about emotions and associated capabilities that children and their teachers can encounter within children's literature. To do this, we utilise examples of children's literature to explore the complexities of what it might mean to be a child growing up in Australia today. In doing so, this chapter shares a process of experiential inquiry, adopting the Australian Curriculum, Assessment and Reporting Authority (ACARA) General Capability of *Personal and Social Capability* (ACARA, n.d.) as a guide to formulate strategies a teacher could use to discuss the complexities of human emotions such as compassion and empathy with their students.

With each of the authors drawing from their own encountered or observed experiences of working with children's picture books from Australian authors and illustrators we unfold how the ACARA General Capabilities of *Personal and Social Capability* (n.d.) might be adapted by teachers to inform a practical framework for teasing out complex thematic explorations pertaining to empathy and compassion. The general capabilities which also include literacy, numeracy, information and communication technology, critical and creative thinking, ethical understanding and intercultural understanding play a significant role in the *Australian Curriculum* in equipping young Australians to live and work successfully in the twenty-first century (ACARA, n.d.). We propose that strategies that can support teaching and learning opportunities in complex and changing circumstances are essential in fostering personal and social capability.

A Brief Review of the Literature

Children's Picture Books and Compassion and Empathy

The use of language, image and other modes in quality literary texts, such as children's picture books and animated films, can evoke powerful emotive visuals for readers/viewers. According to Harper (2016), "picture books can provide the framework for building empathy, tolerance, and friendships and reinforce social-emotional, problem-solving, and conflict resolution skills in young children" (p. 81). Building such skills in children is important as it can manifest feelings of wanting to help others without wishing anything in return (Almerico, 2014), that is, they learn to become compassionate and empathetic people.

Feelings such as compassion and empathy can also be enhanced through effective dialogic practice in the classroom. Harper (2016) noted that when teachers use quality pictures books as resources in the classroom, they are able to "heighten their awareness of emotions, enhance their sensitivity to other's feelings, promote empathetic behaviours toward others, and foster moral development" (p. 81). Research from UNESCO (2006, p. 4) contends that introducing learners to artistic processes, such as those in picture books, "cultivates in each individual a sense of creativity and initiative, a fertile imagination, emotional intelligence, and a moral 'compass', a capacity for critical reflection, a sense of autonomy, and freedom of thought and action". Costa (2001) suggested that engaging students in reading and thinking can support their learning about themselves and others, including what we can become. These approaches are increasingly vital in preparing twenty-first-century learners and are in direct contrast to the Western celebration of competitive individualism.

The Individual and Society

For children to understand others is important in contemporary times. Over the last several decades, theoretical researchers (Barry et al., 2013) and social commentators (Lasch, 1979; Wolfe, 1976) have argued that a liberal, affluent, secular and consumer-oriented North American culture has increasingly engendered narcissistic qualities of individualism and self-absorption (Thompson, 2015, p. 608). The self-esteem movement of the 1980s encouraged an approach to personal development in which self-esteem was considered the cure-all to a "plethora of social, academic, and mental health problems" (Barry et al., 2013, p. 146). In this approach to personal development, self-esteem and personal value "became equated not with doing good but simply with feeling good". Timms (2004, cited in Baguley & Fullarton, 2013, p. 29) highlights the impact of this more broadly by noting how "the special interests of the individual have triumphed over concern for general welfare".

Baguley (2007) found that the myth of the triumphant individual has been deeply inculcated in Western thinking with recent movement towards collaborative and cooperative approaches in a range of sectors. Thompson (2015, p. 608) argued that there is an overblown preoccupation with self-fulfilment and self-realisation by a generation who have attempted to alleviate the anxieties of an uncertain world. The importance of personal and social capabilities, such as evidenced in the *Australian Curriculum*, is seen as a foundation for both learning and citizenship as students are better able to manage their own emotions and behaviours, understand others, and seek to maintain positive relationships (ACARA, n.d.).

Curriculum Considerations

Internationally, compassion and empathy are key attributes expected to be taught in educational contexts. UNESCO (2017), for example, reports that peace across the world needs to be initiated through tolerance and acceptance towards others. In this sense, they believe that empathy is the "foundation of a better world" (UNESCO, 2017) and organised a photobook that high-lighted the power of images and text in order to "pass on the values of solidarity, empathy and altruism" to the reader (Bokova, 2017, p. 4). (http://unesdoc.unesco.org/images/0025/002591/259191m.pdf).

Similarly, in Australia, the *Australian Curriculum* features seven general capabilities of which *Personal and Social Capability* is one. This general capability understands how and why it is important for students in schools to learn about themselves and others, including their communities. ACARA (n.d.) states that:

> Personal and social capability involves students in a range of practices including recognising and regulating emotions, developing empathy for others and understanding relationships, establishing and building positive relationships, making responsible decisions, working effectively in teams, handling challenging situations constructively and developing leadership skills. (p. 1)

This general capability acknowledges that there are four key ideas that support the development of personal and social capabilities. These are self-awareness, self-management, social management and social awareness.

Self-Awareness

According to ACARA, *self-awareness* involves "students developing an awareness of their own emotional states, needs and perspectives" (n.d.). Through this process, students are able to explain and identify aspects that may impact on their own personal responses to incidents. In this way, students are able to "develop a realistic sense of their personal abilities, qualities and strengths through knowing what they are feeling in the moment, and having a realistic assessment of their own abilities and a well-grounded sense of self-knowledge and self-confidence" (n.d.). In order to this, students are expected to be able to effectively reflect on and evaluate their learnings. This concept supports the

- recognition of emotions,
- recognition of personal qualities and achievements,
- understanding of students as learners and
- development of reflective practice.

Self-Management

Self-management develops students' critical-thinking capacities further by developing meta-cognitive skills. Students are able to effectively select and use appropriate skills to manage themselves in different contexts. ACARA (n.d.) states, "Students effectively regulate, manage and monitor their own emotional responses, and persist in completing tasks and overcoming obstacles". They also develop organisational skills and identify the resources needed to achieve goals. Students need to be able to work independently but also work within teams. This involves being able to deal with failure. As such, self-management means that students can

- express emotions appropriately,
- develop self-discipline and set goals work independently and
- show initiative and become confident, resilient and adaptable. (n.d.)

Social Awareness

Social awareness is important when working with others. According to ACARA (n.d.), this aspect includes knowing when and how to help other people. Students do this by acknowledging and identifying particular emotions. This particular aspect of the curriculum capability supports students' skills in respecting others. Students "learn to participate in positive, safe and respectful relationships, defining and accepting individual and group roles and responsibilities" (p. 1). When students have high social awareness, they are able to advocate for a just world and be critical citizens who can advocate for compassionate and empathetic understanding within the community. This involves students

- appreciating diverse perspectives,
- contributing to civil society and
- understanding relationships.

Social Management

Social management is different from self-management as it is about working with others. This requires being able to communicate productively and work well in teams towards positive outcomes. The curriculum outlines that students should be able to develop the "ability to initiate and manage successful personal relationships, and participate in a range of social and communal activities" (p. 1). It involves knowing how to

- communicate effectively,
- work collaboratively,
- make decisions,
- negotiate and resolve conflict and
- develop leadership skills.

It is therefore important to consider how these attributes can be explicitly taught as well as fostered in the classroom.

Research Design

In understanding how quality children's picture books deal with issues related to compassion and empathy, we have drawn on the aforementioned *Australian Curriculum's* General Capability: Personal and Social Capability (ACARA, n.d.) and three quality Australian picture books—*The Red Tree* (2001) by Shaun Tan, *The Short and Incredibly Happy Life of Riley* (2007) by Colin Thompson and Amy Lissiat and *Alfred's War* (2018) by Rachel Bin Salleh and Samantha Fry. All authors are award winning and often address social and cultural issues and emotions as themes within their texts.

We used the four elements of self-awareness, self-management, social awareness and social management to identify aspects within the three picture books that relate to these areas. Further, we analysed both the use of language and image in the books to show how the authors expertly weave messages of compassion and empathy throughout their work. In analysing the images we used a social semiotic tool (Barton, 2018; Kress & van Leeuwen, 2006) in the first instance to identify the representational, interpersonal and compositional meanings within the images, and then we, as artists, explore the artistic-aesthetic elements of the work that address the themes identified. Elements including colour, shape, form, line, light, framing and camera angles were all explored in order to determine how the author/illustrators portrayed the themes present in each book. The next section shares the analysis of each book.

Research Findings

Book-Case 1: *The Red Tree* by Shaun Tan

The Red Tree by Shaun Tan features a small red-haired girl who is facing significant challenges in her life, as depicted through her daily activities. The story begins with the words *Sometimes the day begins with nothing to look forward to … and things go from bad to worse.* Her bedroom fills with dead brown leaves that are overwhelming, making it difficult for her to enter the outside world. We can, however, see one single red leaf framed on the wall.

Tan's use of colour and shape enhances the meaning of oppression in this image. The pile of dead brown leaves is overpowering, making it difficult for the little girl to leave her room. The blind is drawn and little light enters the room. The text and font size increases and is written in an uneven way indicating the uncertainty of entering the outside world.

The girl continues her day walking down the street. A huge menacing creature hovers over her and she hides in a bottle covered by an underwater mask—a metaphor for making it difficult to breathe. Tan displays an image of the girl with a tiny light bulb in her chest but the world remains big, unwieldy and uncaring—*a deaf machine without sense or reason.*

The girl experiences time going slowly and then returns home. As she enters the same room in which the book began daylight streams through the door. The little red leaf that appeared on each page throughout the book—a symbol of hope—has transformed into a luscious and bright red tree. It is the first time we see the girl look directly at the reader with a smile.

Throughout this text, the author beautifully illustrates the movement of the main character through a day and a "sequence of striking landscapes" (DNLR, 2016). While Tan uses a simple text to describe the happenings and feelings within the narrative, it is the images that represent the themes most deeply. The emotions of depression, despair and isolation feature through the use of colour, shape and symbolism.

The following table shows how the text may address each of the personal and social capabilities in the Australian Curriculum. Ideas for teachers' work in the classroom are also listed. These activities support the development of compassion and empathy in students (Table 9.1).

Book-Case 2: *The Short and Incredibly Happy Life of Riley* by Colin Thompson and Amy Lissiat

The text narrative in *The Short and Incredibly Happy Life of Riley* by Thompson and Lissiat focuses upon the life of Riley the rat and the situational and environmental factors that shape, align and contrast with his sense of self-satisfaction and happiness. Entwined with this text narrative are two additional characters, a man and a woman, recurrent in the images around Riley's narrative that assert provocations and perplexities regarding human nature. The interplay between the literary narrative which speaks more explicitly from and to Riley's philosophy and attitude towards life and happiness creates juxtapositions for reflection. The arrangement of Riley's textual narrative and depicted visual narrative entwines to create the story of Riley the rat, who is presented as being satisfied with a simple life, where all of his basic needs for happiness are described and met. Running parallel to the storyline describing Riley's life of contentment, we see some provocative juxtapositions drawn between Riley and the Moustached man, searching for happiness.

Table 9.1 *The Red Tree's* analysis according to personal and social capabilities and meta-semiotic meanings

	Representational—characters and setting	Interpersonal—relationship between the viewers	Compositional—layout
Self-awareness	The girl's body language shows strong emotions such as sadness, despondency, etc.	Children may recognise some of the feelings in the text. Teachers can support students in discussing different emotions and their strengths and express this via multiple modes.	The composition of the image and text creates a number of interpretative possibilities around depression and loneliness.
Self-management	Limited evidence through the text. Although the symbol of hope—the red leaf—indicates there are possibilities.	Although self-management does not feature heavily in the book, teachers can encourage students to express their emotions appropriately.	Symbol of hope is present on each page. The colour red (leaf and girl's hair) indicates hope and empowerment.
Social awareness	The girl is depicted with an unhappy demeanour until the last page.	The reader is enticed to feel compassion for the little girl and show empathy through actions. The teacher could develop activities based on how students would support the girl in her emotions.	Throughout the text "others" are illustrated as not caring or interested. The colour palette is brown and grey.
Social management	The characters in the book show no interest in supporting the girl.	Children may consider their friends who feel the same. Teachers can support children in understanding how to support and communicate effectively with others.	As above.

The text opens with a picture of a baby, sitting with a balloon pinned to its nappy, accompanied by the text *Everyone wants to live forever*. This opening page and image of the baby with a vibrant yellow, buoyant balloon creates an immediate and obvious parallel point for the cover art, where we see Riley comforting a very small (literally in scale), emaciated and downtrodden looking Moustached man; one of the central visual protagonists depicted throughout the picture book. Later versions of the text cover page (2017 reprint) incorporated the *Children's Book Council of Australia—Picture Book of the Year* medal into a balloon, which is tied to the Moustached man's wrist.

The reader can see how the Moustached man on the front page holds a much less buoyant, dull and somewhat misshapen or deflated looking balloon. From the very beginning of the story, we are positioned to consider the depicted relationship between animal and human, need and want, contentment and desire, and how gratitude and appreciation for what one has, as opposed to what one has not, is imperative to cultivating a sense of self-satisfaction and contentment.

In another vignette, we gain a sense of Riley's joy at finding the perfect stick to scratch a part of his back that he cannot quite reach: *All Riley wanted was a little stick with a pointy end to scratch the bit of his back he couldn't reach himself.*

This satisfied description (and depiction) of Riley's contentment is juxtaposed with a highly provocative image of the Moustached man, looking grey, sad and isolated from a semi-circle of men with their backs to him. The Moustached man, wearing a tiny peace symbol on his breeches, is pierced with sticks, with the text: *People, of course, should never be allowed to have sticks with pointy ends, because they stick them into each other.*

An interesting point for exploration here is why we should/should not feel pity for the Moustached man, particularly given some of the previous descriptions of the attitudes and behaviours of people as greedy, all consuming, competitive and cruel. This provocation can be explored with older children about the sweeping statements regarding people, and how we as an audience ascribe to a particular collective of humanity.

The following table shows how consideration of the General Capability—*Personal and Social Capability*—can be used to identify and unpack opportunities to examine self and social awareness and management for teachers' working with *The Short and Incredibly Happy Life of Riley* in their classroom. These discussion points and ensuing strategies and activities present a pedagogical approach to help support the development of compassion and empathy in relation to examination of the key ideas captured in this picture book (Table 9.2).

Book-Case 3: *Alfred's War* by Rachel Bin Salleh and Samantha Fry

At the centenary of the First World War, a plethora of children's picture books dealing with various aspects of the conflict were published. By 2017, such publications become a "torrent" (Lawn, 2015). (For a selection, see Bogle and Whatley (2015), Everett and McGuire (2007), Hannaford and Hannaford (2015), Hoy and Johnson (2006), Jorgensen and Harrison-Lever (2004), Kerby, Tuppurainen-Mason, and Baguley (2017), Metzenthen and Camilleri (2015), and Walters and Mullins (2008).) Each is pervaded, to a greater or lesser extent, by the "increasingly sentimentalised construct of the Australian soldier as a victim of trauma and the traditional use of Australian war literature to explore national identity" (Kerby, Baguley, Lowien, & Ayre, 2018).

Rachel Bin Salleh and Samantha Fry's *Alfred's War* (Bin Salleh & Fry, 2018) gently exposes the historical absence of Indigenous servicemen or women from the nation's history contextualised with the broader story of Indigenous Australians.[1] They do this by drawing on familiar tropes, ones that pervade the Australian imagining of conflict, thereby seeking an integration of the Indigenous experience rather than the creation of a separate mythological tradition. By seeking to engender compassion rather than outrage, to seek admission to the mythology rather than redress for decades of ostracism, *Alfred's War* fits seamlessly into the Australian literature of war.

---

[1] Though officially barred from service, approximately 1200 indigenous Australians enlisted during the First World War by hiding their Aboriginality, taking advantage of regional disparities in process, or by taking advantage of the decision to allow enlistment to those with one white parent or who had assimilated sufficiently. Contemporary press reports of Indigenous service were used as a means of shaming white men into enlisting. The reference to Albert mourning for his lost mates reflects the fact that an Indigenous soldier tended to meet with racism at the entry and exit points of his military service rather than in the field.

Table 9.2 *The Life of Riley's* analysis according to personal and social capabilities and meta-semiotic meanings

	Representational—characters and setting	Interpersonal—relationship between the viewers	Compositional—layout
Self-awareness	• Riley—aware of his needs in relation to his sense of happiness; • Moustached man—Always appears to be in search of ways to satisfy his needs and achieve happiness; • Blonde woman—appears always in relation to Moustached man, and similarly in search of love • The need to be loved appears to be inextricably linked to sense of self and happiness.	• Children may recognise how some of the rich descriptions emphasise excess and greed, love and lust, desire and need. • Use of famous/recognisable imagery (i.e. Van Gogh, Raphael, Da Vinci, Munch) in relation to fame/desirability self-worth/value.	• Story opens with minimal, but powerful/evocative, text, centre position for emphasis. • Text at times is overwhelming and saturating, alluding to rhetoric of superficial love/lust, need to consume/acquire as many things as possible (consumerism) • Text falls off the linear/slips to droop on page adding further emphasis emotive quality/weight of words.
Self-management	• Teachers can use rich textual descriptions and accompanying imagery to facilitate conversations around the differences and how these can support the reflective self.	• Scope for discussion around role of pets in relation to emotional health and wellbeing. • Provocation for discussion—the difference between an animal and a pet (Riley vs Moustached man's dog).	• Interesting to explore the role of the Moustached man's little dog, who appears to be with him at most times where the man is grappling with his sense of self-worth. The dog is always looking expectantly at the man, tail wagging (suggested through use of line).

(continued)

Table 9.2 (continued)

	Representational—characters and setting	Interpersonal—relationship between the viewers	Compositional—layout
Social awareness	• Riley consistently presents us with a sense of satisfaction, contentment and happiness—depicted through facial expression and bodily gesture. • Moustached man depicts a range of emotions through the above, most of which are doubtful, depressed, insecure, perhaps misplaced contentment.	• Through Riley, we are positioned to reflect upon how being satisfied with less and simplicity supports self-happiness and satisfaction. • Through Moustached man and Blonde woman, we are positioned to reflect upon the complexities of human nature, where consumerism, greed, fear and lust disrupt and distort our capacity to be satisfied with simplicity and less.	• Colours and shade/tone are used pointedly and powerfully to allude to emotive weight—warm colours for exertion, cool colours for sadness, darkness for loneliness.
Social management	• The three key characters unfold across the story separate to each other, yet speaking powerfully to complex human emotions, and how to inhibit/enable happiness • Being appreciative/expressing appreciation.	• The provocative nature of imagery in relation to text alludes to powerful potential outcomes/implications of greed, fear, lust and acceptance. • Topics such as war, betrayal, deception, loss, searching and settling create rich opportunities for reflection/discussion/debate • Scope to reflectively examine own views/perceptions/parameters of/for happiness.	• Visual information can be examined in relation to key characters, and how material things create a particular dynamic between characters and text narrative—transferable from the text to our own lives.

Bin Salleh calls on familiar tropes in her portrayal of the main character Albert, *always with his hat on, his billy tied to his swag and holes in the soles of his shoes,* as he walks *from town to town looking for work.* It is a powerful image not because it disrupts our national mythology but because it extends it to include an otherwise marginalised character. Albert is not a threatening "other". He is appealing, unthreatening and his later suffering stirs our compassion because we see ourselves in his journey, and perhaps our complicity.

There is no send off for Albert, who merely writes to his family that he *has signed up for adventure and travel.* This is perhaps the most significant sentence in the book for it is an overt effort to separate Alfred from the actual prosecution of the war, for that would emphasise his agency at the expense of his victimhood. As Bin Salleh and Fry may have sensed, any attempt to communicate Indigenous trauma within the parameters of Australian military history is inevitably problematic. Though understandable, any attempt to link the Indigenous struggle against European settlement and military service after 1901 is, in Padraic Gibson's (2014) view, "fundamentally mistaken. There is a real danger of the proud tradition of Aboriginal resistance to British invasion being used to bolster the militaristic, nationalist ideology being carefully cultivated through the ANZAC centenary" (p. 2).

Trauma rather than glory becomes the central motif in this text. Albert also does not return unscathed, but his "gammy leg" is merely a visible scar, for his greatest wounds are psychological: *Every so often, Alfred could hear the never-ending gunfire in his head and the whispers of young men praying. On those days, he curled into a ball and slept in the shadows.*

The illustrator portrays this through the use of swirling images around Alfred's head as he sleeps which contain horses and men he knew juxtaposed against grey clouds of smoke and memory. There is a sense that perhaps he feels closest to his friends sleeping on the ground and under the stars. Albert's struggles occur before and after the war, not during, and this is an important distinction. For there is no mention of an enemy nor even where the battles that so traumatised him were fought. It is the ostracism of Alfred in peacetime Australia that is offered as the "real" trauma. When suffering from flashbacks, he enters the world of shadows. When attending Anzac Day services, Albert continues to dwell in those shadows, *until he heard the lament of the bugle, and then he quietly joined the people gathered in the morning light.*

Bin Salleh in fact has a far more reverential take on Anzac Day than a reader might initially have expected. She does not question the commemoration or its place in the national psyche, and in fact is quite restrained in her views and conservative in her literary choices. A reader might assume that Albert's plight was a matter of oversight rather than reflecting deeply entrenched views about race. For though "Alfred had fought in the Great War … his bravery was not a part of the nation's remembering. He was one of the forgotten soldiers". Even the historical postscript is un-emotive in its reference to the lack of recognition afforded Aboriginal and Torres Strait Islander servicemen. The concluding observation that "it would take years" before they were "acknowledged and valued" communicates a reassuring message that Albert's story is very much a matter for the historical record rather than a contemporary issue (Table 9.3).

Discussion and Strategies for Classroom Practice

It is evident that each of these books can be used as powerful resources to teach children about issues related to compassion and empathy. Each author beautifully and effectively portrays their characters in ways that evoke the reader's concepts of emotion and relationships albeit in different contexts, times and spaces.

Tan's work highlights the need for social awareness of mental health issues such as depression and feelings of isolation. Through the use of complexly illustrated pages that feature a symbol of hope, a red leaf, Tan effectively portrays the character's sensation of oppression and hopelessness. The reader is drawn into these sensitivities and it is apparent that one becomes sympathetic to the red-headed girl's plight. The final depiction of a lush, bright and hopeful Red Tree provides a slight sense of optimism, despite the possibility that the girl may continue to face her challenges.

In *The Short and Incredibly Happy Life of Riley*, Thompson and Lissiat represent basic happiness. Without striving to outdo other people and to appreciate what we have, the book highlights the secret to happiness.

Table 9.3 *Alfred's War's* analysis according to personal and social capabilities and meta-semiotic meanings

	Representational—characters and setting	Interpersonal—relationship between the viewers	Compositional—layout
Self-awareness	With no citizenship rights in his own country, Alfred is neither honoured as a returned soldier. The images depict Alfred pursing a lonely life, often in natural settings such as the bush, until each Anzac Day when he quietly joins the Dawn Service.	Children may recognise the injustice of Alfred's situation. They may also recognise some of the emotions Alfred experiences such as the excitement of going to war, the friendships he made during this time. A photograph depicts respect: 'Me and my mates, Great War 1917'.	The book begins with a double page spread of Alfred fishing depicted in pencil and soft washes of watercolour. Very minimal text is used which is often centred. Nature is a predominant theme throughout with mainly a blue/green palette used. Alfred is isolated until the final sepia photograph—depicting him as equal.
Self-management	Alfred overcomes a range of obstacles to maintain his independence. He is plagued by the horrifying memories of war which become worse at night when he is sleeping alone.	Teachers can encourage students to consider why it is difficult for Alfred to express his emotions. They can also consider loss and discuss any family histories that may include servicemen and women. Students could also discuss the cover image.	The book begins with Alfred alone and ends with him in a photograph with his mates. He is proud and happy with a sense of comradeship. The images throughout have a dream-like quality of remembrance.

(continued)

Table 9.3 (continued)

	Representational—characters and setting	Interpersonal—relationship between the viewers	Compositional—layout
Social awareness	Alfred is depicted alone throughout most of the book. He is aware there are places Aboriginal people are not allowed to be in, and in group situations, he appears on the periphery.	The reader is positioned as an observer of Alfred a World War I ex-serviceman as he wanders the country, remembering his fallen comrades and trying to ignore the pain of his war-time injuries. Teachers can make students aware of the Australian government's failure to recognise Indigenous servicemen and women when they returned from active service. They can also assist students in understanding the importance of Acknowledgement of Country.	Alfred's face is not fully visible until several pages into the text, perhaps suggesting his erasure from this aspect of history. Two pages of historical facts at the end of the book about Aboriginal and Torres Strait Islander veterans provide important information to assist students in understanding this important aspect of Australian history.
Social management	Alfred is portrayed as respectful and humble throughout the book; however, he is not treated equally on his return and is described as a "forgotten soldier".	The imagery is gentle and inviting. The text is minimal and complements the character of Alfred. Loneliness is a pervasive theme throughout the book as is duty and respect.	The image of Alfred with his swag and billy is similar to the typical Australian bushman. The same type of swag he used as a soldier appears with him as an older man as a unifying device.

Riley is always happy because he does not compare himself to other people. He is content with what life has provided him and the cycle of life which he embarks on in a much shorter timeframe than that of most humans provides an important message that the reader is able to relate to.

Alfred's War by Bin Salleh and Fry explores the concept of trauma experienced by returned Indigenous servicemen and women, including not being recognised upon their return. This is displayed powerfully through the use of colour, framing, angle and language. The softly rendered illustrations complement the character of Alfred who moves softly through the landscape with minimal interaction. His positioning as a non-citizen on his return from the war is juxtaposed with the way he was accepted as an equal in the army as detailed in the notes at the end of the book. Albert displays qualities of courage, service, dignity and respect even though he returns wounded and without the recognition of the service he gave to his country.

Each of our selected picture books has displayed how curriculum intentions, such as those in the *Australian Curriculum*'s Personal and Social Capabilities, can be present within the language and images in the texts. With appropriate knowledge and skills, teachers can use the texts as powerful stimuli to support the growth of children's and young people's compassion and empathy. The following section shares some strategies teachers can use to effectively use these picture books.

Strategies for Use of Quality Picture Books to Develop Compassion and Empathy

Know the Resources

It is important that teachers spend some time selecting appropriate picture books to use with their students. Not all books will be able to support learning around compassion and empathy so time needs to be well spent selecting a book and also developing learning activities around elements of that book (as we have shown in our book case studies). Teachers can clearly link teaching and learning about compassion and empathy to curriculum and educational policy.

Know the Students

Each classroom is different and students may have had deep-seated experiences related to negative emotions such as those displayed in our texts (e.g. depression, trauma, feelings of isolation, inequality, social disadvantage). Teachers should carefully work with students in supporting their own personal and social development. Using quality picture books can assist in multiple ways including supporting students who need it, creating safe classrooms for all students and enhancing students' own capabilities individually, socially and culturally.

Carefully Create Learning Activities

Using quality picture books to support social and personal proficiencies requires careful thought. Cam (2012) suggests teachers firstly identify an ethical issue for teaching and learning purposes. This could include one of the following: personal and social awareness or management. Next teachers should set an agenda for the students. This can be done in creative ways such as providing an arts-based learning experience initially and then discussing this experience using appropriate meta-language based on the capabilities. The teacher can then suggest other ideas and opinions, inviting students to reason why particular situations are explored in the books. Further, students can evaluate the use of language and image in the texts and reach reliable conclusions, solutions or resolutions (Cam, 2012, p. 72).

Continue Professional Learning

Schools and classrooms are constantly changing so it is critical that teachers keep up to date with skills related to teaching the concepts of compassion and empathy on one hand and how these may be illustrated in a range of teaching resources such as picture books, as well as compassionate and empathetic understanding of students towards others on the other hand. Much research in the field of language and literacy, for example, posits the importance of students viewing texts, whether print only or multimodal, critically so as to uncover sociopolitical and sociocultural underpinnings (Kalantzis, Cope, Chan, & Dalley-Trim, 2016).

Conclusion

Children's picture books offer an ideal opportunity to engage students in learning about emotions and how to regulate them. The three books discussed in this chapter encourage students to individually interact with both images and text to explore and share the emotions of the characters. Compassion and empathy which are the focus of this chapter occur when students can identify with another person and the challenges they are understanding. Moving the perspective away from themselves to consider the impact of particular situations on other people, such as evidenced in *Alfred's War*, can promote the development of compassion and empathy through understanding.

The three book case studies provide examples for teachers to encourage students' personal and social capabilities of self-awareness, self-management, social awareness and social management by exploring how the characters and settings, the interpersonal relationships between the characters and the reader and the design elements and principles have been used by the author and illustrator to further enhance meaning. The multi-modality of children's picture books also offers an engaging way for students to explore complex emotions by moving between text and image which can also have multiple interpretations depending on a student's gender, cultural background and visual and textual reading ability. Students are being increasingly exposed to violence and intolerance through increased access to technology. Therefore, enhancing the qualities of compassion and empathy in the classroom through devices such as children's picture books is an important opportunity to provide them with the skills and abilities to respond in ways that are critical for their future.

References

ACARA. (n.d.). *Personal and social capability.* Australian Curriculum. Retrieved from https://www.australiancurriculum.edu.au/f-10-curriculum/general-capabilities/personal-and-social-capability/

Almerico, G. M. (2014). Building character through literacy with children's literature. *Research in Higher Education Journal, 26*, 1–13.

Baguley, M. (2007). *Partnership or Perish? A study of artistic collaborations.* Unpublished Doctoral dissertation, University of Tasmania, Tasmania.

Baguley, M., & Fullarton, L. (2013). The education of artistic vision: A collaboration between the community and the Academy. *International Journal of Pedagogies and Learning, 8*(1), 27–38.

Barry, M. M., Clarke, A. M., Jenkins, R., & Patel, V. (2013). A systematic review of the effectiveness of mental health promotion interventions for young people in low and middle income countries. *BMC Public Health, 13*(1), 835.

Barton, G. M. (2018). *Music learning and teaching in socio-culturally diverse contexts: Implications for classroom practice.* London: Palgrave Macmillan.

Bin Salleh, R., & Fry, S. (2018). *Alfred's war.* Broome: Magabala Books.

Bogle, E. & Whatley, B. (2015). And the band played waltzing Matilda. Crows Nest, NSW: Allen & Unwin.

Bokova, I. (2017). *The power of empathy* [Photobook]. Retrieved from http://unesdoc.unesco.org/images/0025/002591/259191m.pdf

Cam, P. (2012). *Teaching ethics in schools: A new approach to moral education.* Australia: Australian Council Educational Research (ACER).

Costa, A. L. (2001). *Teaching for, of, and about thinking. Developing minds: A resource book for teaching thinking* (pp. 354–358). Victoria, Australia: Hawker Brownlow Education.

David Newmonic Language Resources (DNLR). (2016). *The Red Tree. An analysis of Shaun Tan's luminous work of art.* Retrieved from http://www.speech-language-resources.com/the-red-tree.html

Everett, V., & McGuire, B. (2007). *The house that was built in a day: Anzac Cottage.* Crawley, WA: University of Western Australia Press.

Garner, P. W., & Parker, T. S. (2018). Young children's picture-books as a forum for the socialization of emotion. *Journal of Early Childhood Research, 16*(3), 201–304. https://doi.org/10.1177/1476718X18775760

Gibson, P. (2014). Imperialism, Anzac nationalism and the Aboriginal experience of warfare. *Cosmopolitan Civil Societies Journal, 6*(3), 63–82. https://doi.org/10.5130/ccs.v6i3.4190

Hannaford, R., & Hannaford, R. (2015). *My Gallipoli.* Adelaide: Working Title Press.

Harper, L. J. (2016). Using picture books to promote social-emotional literacy. *Young Children, 71*(3), 80–86.

Havas, D. A., Glenberg, A. M., & Rinck, M. (2007). Emotion simulation during language comprehension. *Psychonomic Bulletin & Review, 14*(3), 436–441.

Hoy, C., & Johnson, B. (2006). *My grandad marches on Anzac day*. South Melbourne: Lothian Books.

Johnson, E. J., & Tversky, A. (1983). Affect, generalization, and the perception of risk. *Journal of Personality and Social Psychology, 45*(1), 20.

Jorgensen, N., & Harrison-Lever, B. (2004). *In Flanders field*. Fremantle: Sandcastle Books.

Kalantzis, M., Cope, B., Chan, E., & Dalley-Trim, L. (2016). *Literacies* (2nd ed.). London: Cambridge University Press.

Katch, J. (2018). Seeing me in you: Teaching empathy and learning courage through picture books. *Schools: Studies in Education, 15*(2), 216–227.

Kerby, M., Baguley, M., Lowien, N., & Ayre, K. (2018). Australian not by blood, but by character: The Digger and the Refugee in Australian Picture Books. In M. Kerby, M. Baguley, & J. McDonald (Eds.), *Palgrave handbook of cultural and artistic responses to war* (Vol. 1). London: Palgrave Macmillan.

Kerby, M., Tuppurainen-Mason, E., & Baguley, M. (2017). *Voices from the Trenches*. Ellipsis Media: Toowoomba.

Kress, G. R., & Van Leeuwen, T. (2006). *Reading images: The grammar of visual design* (2nd ed.). London: Psychology Press.

Lasch, C. (1979). *The culture of narcissism*. Warner Books.

Lawn, J. (2015). *Gallipoli books for children open an enlightening window on the reality of war*. Retrieved from http://www.watoday.com.au/entertaining-kids/parenting-and-childrens-books/gallipoli-books-for-children-open-an-enlightening-window-on-the-reality-of-war-20150420-1mmcfl.html

Lerner, J. S., Li, Y., Valdesolo, P., & Kassam, K. S. (2015). Emotion and decision making. *Annual Review of Psychology, 66*(1), 799–823. https://doi.org/10.1146/annurev-psych-010213-115043

Lewis, D. (2001). *Reading contemporary picturebooks: Picturing text*. London: Routledge Falmer.

Lindquist, K. A., MacCormack, J. K., & Shablack, H. (2015). The role of language in emotion: predictions from psychological constructionism. *Frontiers in Psychology, 6*, 444. https://doi.org/10.3389/fpsyg.2015.00444

MacDonald, A., & Baguley, M. (2012). How three Tasmanian teachers use and respond to emotion in the secondary English classroom. In *Proceedings of the AARE conference 2011: Researching across boundaries* (pp. 1–15). Hobart: Australian Association for Research in Education.

Metzenthen, D., & Camilleri, M. (2015). *One minute's silence*. Sydney: Allen & Unwin.

Thompson, M. B. (2015). Authenticity in education: From narcissism and freedom to the messy interplay of self-exploration and acceptable tension. *Studies in Philosophy and Education, 34*(6), 603–618.

Timms, P. (2004). *What's wrong with contemporary art?* Sydney, NSW: University of New South Wales Press.

UNESCO. (2006). *Road Map for Arts Education.* The World Conference on Arts Education: building Creative Capacities for the 21st Century, Lisbon, 6–9 March. Retrieved from http://www.unesco.org/new/en/culture/themes/creativity/arts-education/official-texts/road-map/

UNESCO. (2017). *The power of empathy.* Retrieved from https://en.unesco.org/events/power-empathy

Unsworth, L. (2013). Re-configuring image-language relations and interpretive possibilities in picture books as animated movies: A site for developing multimodal literacy pedagogy. *Journal of English Language, 64*, 15–48. https://doi.org/10.5007/2175-8026.2013n64p15

Velten, E., Jr. (1968). A laboratory task for induction of mood states. *Behaviour Research and Therapy, 6*(4), 473–482.

Walters, C., & Mullins, P. (2008). *Only a donkey.* Melbourne: Puffin Books.

Wolfe, T. (1976). *Mauve gloves and madmen, clutter and vine.* New York: Farrar, Straus and Giroux.

Part IV

Compassion and Empathy for Teachers

10

Moderating the Adverse Consequences of Compassion and Empathy for Teachers in Modernity: Dimensions of Stress, Burnout and Resilience of Teachers in Social Development Schools in Hong Kong

Lai Kuen Brenda Lo and Richard G. Bagnall

Background to the Research

School teaching in modern societies—in which a high value is placed on instrumental learning and competitive individualism—has long been recognised as a vocation that is particularly demanding of its practitioners (Guarino, Santibañez, & Daley, 2006). In such a cultural context, societies in general, and schooling regulators and employing authorities in particular, increasingly are evaluating teaching success in terms of the extent to which it enhances students' future prospects (Education Bureau, 2016). Working in such a cultural context, in itself, leads to elevated levels of stress and burnout in teachers (Cheng, 2009a). However, the traditional qualities of teachers as compassionate and empathetic carers of

L. K. B. Lo (✉) • R. G. Bagnall
Griffith University, Brisbane, QLD, Australia
e-mail: r.bagnall@griffith.edu.au

© The Author(s) 2019
G. Barton, S. Garvis (eds.), *Compassion and Empathy in Educational Contexts*,
https://doi.org/10.1007/978-3-030-18925-9_10

their students may also be seen as exacerbating the stress of working within the contemporary cultural context, since the stress (and burnout) from teaching to meet the performance-based expectations and targets feeds on their compassion, empathy and care—in its heightening of their efforts to succeed (Center & Callaway, 1999). In that degenerative chain of events, the stress arising from teachers' efforts to meet the performance expectations and targets of their contemporary cultural work context are seen as being exacerbated by the compassion, empathy and care that they have for their students. Increased stress may lead to burnout and hence to reduced performance, further exacerbating teachers' sense of failure, leading, then, to their dropping out of teaching in many cases (Chang, 2009).

That degenerative pattern may be argued, though, to be disrupted by ameliorating the levels of stress and hence reducing the likelihood of burnout and dropout (Chan, Chen, & Chong, 2010). Such disruption may take the form of teacher *resilience* to the stressors of their situation (Day & Gu, 2014). The notion of resilience has been developed to explain the capacity of individuals to resist the depredations of adversity and to preserve their sense of well-being in face of adversity (Hong, 2012). Research to date has focused particularly on the dimensions of resilience, on factors that contribute to it or are associated with it, and on ways in which it may be enhanced. It has been taken to be a complex construct of two major types: individual and organisational resilience (Day & Gu, 2014). Individual resilience embraces attributes of individuals that have been found to be associated with (and which are presumed to contribute to) resilience, including initiative, independence, insight, empathy, interpersonal relationships, humour, creativity and morality (Siebert, 2006). Organisational resilience involves attributes of the organisational work context that are seen as contributing to the capacity of individuals to be resilient, including a supportive and caring organisational culture that encourages openness among peers, active learning from experience and strong interpersonal relationships (Grove, 1997). Resilience has been taken (and confirmed) to be an attribute of individuals and organisations that may be enhanced through learning, education and organisational change (Mansfield, Beltman, Price, & McConney, 2012).

There is thus introduced the idea that teacher resilience to stressors may not only disrupt the degenerative pattern of association between stress, burnout and dropout but also be something that could be *learned* by teachers as part of their initial teacher training and continuing professional development (Day, 2013). The dimensions of teacher resilience to stress, however, have been essentially unrecorded and un-researched (Day & Gu, 2014).

It may also be argued that the degenerative changes and the disruptive or corrective effects of resilience to stress may be particularly marked in teaching situations involving emotionally and behaviourally challenged (EBC) students, which not only attract teachers with high levels of compassion, empathy and care for their students but also where the achievement of contextually generated student learning goals and expectations is particularly challenging (Hong Kong Mood Disorders Centre, 2004). Teachers in such situations have been reported as experiencing especially high levels of stress and burnout (Billingsley, 2004).

That relationship suggested the study reported here, into the experience of stress, burnout and resilience among the teachers of EBC students in Hong Kong special schools—termed 'social development schools' (SDSs) in Hong Kong.

The Research Context

Since the official transfer of sovereignty over Hong Kong from Britain to China in 1997, there has been constant educational reform in the 'Hong Kong Special Administrative Region' (HKSAR). The HKSAR government has sought to reform education within a lifelong learning framework focusing on individual development in a globalising cultural context (Bagnall & Wong, 2014). The remarkable and rapid educational and curricular reforms (Tse, 2005) have inevitably placed teachers in the position of experiencing considerable controversy, offence, misfortune and blame (Democratic Alliance for the Betterment of Hong Kong, 2006). These reforms, in themselves, have added greatly to the demands on teachers, which have been further exacerbated by the traditional cultural pressure in Hong Kong for everyone to work hard and for long hours, regardless of their productivity (Cheng, 2009a). Within that context, EBC students have tended to be regarded as a problem, to be handled, ultimately, through the SDSs and for whom there has been little public support for or expectation of their further development and contribution to society (Pang, 2012). Teachers in SDSs thus tended to be seen publicly as minders of problem children (Chong & Ng, 2011), but they have commonly seen their role and contribution to society as that of lifting their pupils from lives of failure and self-deprecation into lives of educational success and self-confidence (Pang, 2012).

The education and curriculum reforms have also led to changes in the workplace atmosphere (Cheng, 2009b). 'Value-adding' and 'redundancy' have become fashionable terms in education and have often been used by authorities (Cheng, 2009a). There has been a common belief among teachers that they are under constant pressure, not only to deal with student misbehaviour but also to 'value-add' to themselves, working hard, not only at school but also after school, by attending as many professional development courses as possible, 14 hours a day, 6 days a week (Hong Kong Professional Teachers' Union, 2008). With such a climate of change and uncertainty, teachers have been experiencing increasing levels of stress (Chan et al., 2010). New methods of student performance assessment and the quality assurance practices have also been seen as contributing to teacher stress (Committee on Teachers' Work, 2006).

The 'Language Proficiency Assessment' (LPA) and the mandatory requirements of continual professional development (CPD) have also contributed to teacher stress (Hong Kong Professional Teachers' Union, 2005). While facing heavy workloads in school, teachers have had to spare energy and time for their CPD and the benchmarking examinations of the LPA. Teachers have also faced heavy workloads in lesson preparation and assessment planning for the new curriculum and the additional paperwork associated with the reforms. The rising suicide rates of both teachers and students in the past ten years—although unexplained—have also created alarm in the education sector (Committee on Teachers' Work, 2006).

The reforms have also contributed to an intensification of the climate of competition among subsidised schools, and between private schools and direct subsidised schools (Tse, 2005). Market forces have come to operate in the education system, with the comparative presentation of school public examination results, annual reports and quality assurance inspections, external school reviews, benchmarking exercises, increased parental rights (including parents on school boards) and changing contract terms of teachers' employment, all of which have been seen as contributing to high levels of teacher stress.

The education reforms have included policies of educational inclusion in special education: emphasising equality of educational experience, with students being placed in mainstream schools and classes, regardless of any differences in academic performance and special educational needs (SENs) (Forlin & Lian, 2008). Special schools for students with special educational needs and EBCs have been made redundant. Teachers in the seven special schools who survived as SDSs have faced the continuing threat of school closure and redundancy, which has contributed further to their stress (Hong Kong Professional Teachers' Union, 2005)

There has also been a progressive decline of new student numbers, with demographic changes in Hong Kong (Hong Kong Professional Teachers' Union, 2003). The falling birth rate has led to primary year-one student numbers dropping from 60,214 (2003) to 49,914 (2013), and secondary year-one student numbers from 81,555 (2003) to 51,649 (2013) (Education Bureau, 2013). This drop in the number of newly enrolled students has been reflected in cuts to the number of classes in schools, the closure of schools and teacher redundancies (Hong Kong Professional Teachers' Union, 2013). The trend of school closure and teacher redundancy has been projected to continue at least until 2020, contributing to a widespread feeling of job insecurity among teachers in Hong Kong.

The stressors on teachers in those SDSs were thus further heightened (Hong Kong Professional Teachers' Union, 2003) making them an a priori paradigmatic case of the impact of stress on teachers, teachers' resilience to the stressors, and the relationship between their stress and burnout. Although there have been a range and number of international studies of teacher stress, burnout and resilience, there has been only limited research focusing specifically on SDS teachers in Hong Kong. The research, accordingly, sought to focus on population of 146 EBC teachers in the seven Hong Kong SDSs.

The Research Methodology

The research called for a mixed-methods research approach (Creswell, 2003). The need to confirm the previously indicated relationships between teacher stress, burnout and resilience in the relatively extreme case of SDS teachers of EBC students in Hong Kong was addressed through a structured survey research approach (Larkin, Watts, & Clifton, 2006). The levels of stress, burnout and resilience experienced by the participating teachers and the numerical relationships between those three categories of experience were therein structured by traditional inter-pretations and measures to ensure their meaningful comparability with research findings to date. The primary research aim, though, was to explore the dimensions of resilience of the more resilient SDS teachers, which called for an interpretative research approach (Reid, Flowers, & Larkin, 2005). The field work to collect data was undertaken during the early stages of policy implementation: over the 2007–08 and 2008–09 school years.

The survey research data were collected through a written, self-administered questionnaire of the total SDS teacher population. The questionnaire focused on five validated scales totalling 94-item state-ments to examine the conditions of and correlations between stress, burnout and resilience in the SDS teachers. A four-point Likert scale was used for all 94-item statements. The respondent demographic items sought information on their gender, age, teaching experience and level, special education training, and self-rated stress, burnout and resilience levels. There followed an invitation to those who perceived themselves to be resilient teachers to volunteer for an interview.

Respondent stress levels were measured by the 'Source of Teacher Stress' (STS) scale, a 28-item scale focusing on student misbehaviour, lack of professional recognition, poor school ethos, and workload and time pressure (Chan, 2006). Teacher burnout was measured by the Modified Maslach Burnout Inventory-Educator Survey (MBI-ES) (Lau, Yuen, & Chan, 2005), based on the original MBI-ES scale developed by Maslach and Jackson (1981). It consists of 22-item statements loading onto a three-factor subscale structure: emotional exhaustion, personal accomplishment and depersonalisation. Teacher resilience was measured in terms of both individual and organisational aspects, using 44 items from three validated scales: the 'teacher sense of efficacy' scale (Rutter, 1990), the 'resilience scale' (Siebert, 2006) and the 'collective teacher self-efficacy' scale (Schwarzer & Schmitz, 1999).

Of the 146 questionnaires sent out, 118 were returned, 12 of which were discarded as incomplete. The remaining 106 returns (73% of the total population) were used for the data analysis. Analysis involved initial data cleaning and the calculation of Cronbach's alpha coefficients (Nunnally, 1978) to determine the internal consistency of the data sets. Descriptive statistics were generated to describe the demographic characteristics of participants. Mean scores for each respondent on the ten subscales of teacher stress (four subscales), burnout (three subscales) and resilience (three subscales) were computed to observe the stress, burnout and resilience levels of each individual respondent. Total and mean scores and standard deviations were calculated on each of the ten subscales. Pearson product moment correlation coefficients were calculated to ascertain the correlations between the stress, burnout and resilience factors.

The interpretative exploration of the dimensions of resilience of the more resilient SDS teachers involved in-depth conversational individual interviews (Miles & Huberman, 1994) to explore each participant's understanding of their situation in the light of their past experiences. Interview participants were selected from those who volunteered at the time of their completing the questionnaire and who also scored above the average of all respondents on each of the three resilience subscales in the questionnaire. Fifteen of the questionnaire respondents volunteered to be interviewed, of whom 11 were found to have met the resilience criterion and were selected for interviewing. Standard procedures for such interviews (Denzin & Lincoln, 2005) were used. Similar questions and probes were used for all respondents by drawing on an interview protocol, but the order in which the questions were posed was open, according to how each individual interview progressed. The duration of each interview was between 45 and 60 minutes. Key points were noted during and after the interviews. The interviews were conducted in Cantonese and were audio-recorded and transcribed verbatim. A summary of key points from each transcript was sent to the interviewee for validation. The Chinese transcripts were then translated into English for analysis. Data analysis followed the procedures of interpretative phenomenological analysis (IPA) drawn together by Smith and colleagues (Smith, Flowers, & Larkin, 2009).

The Research Findings

The Respondent Population

The respondents were quite evenly distributed by gender and age, suggesting a demographically balanced population. Years of teaching experience represented the solid depth of experience in the population. The teaching levels of respondents showed a concentration in secondary schooling, reflecting the distribution across classes in the seven schools. Ninety-four (89%) had received some type of special education training, at some level, in working with students with special educational needs (SEN). Only a small proportion (11%) had not received any SEN-related training.

The mean scores on the four stressor scales suggested moderate levels of EBC teacher stress. The MBI-ES burnout scale data indicated that all three burnout subscale scores fell within the factor score ranges representing a moderate level of burnout. The resilience data on the teacher self-efficacy scale indicated a moderate-to-high level of self-efficacy. The data on the collective teacher self-efficacy scale gave mean scores over the midpoint on all items, suggesting a moderate-to-high level on this scale also.

The concepts of teacher burnout and resilience both emerged as reasonably coherent and hence unitary. The concept of stress, though, suggested that it had two different dimensions in the study: one encompassing the student misbehaviour and workload and time pressure subscales, the other the poor school ethos and lack of professional recognition subscales.

The Relationship Between Stress, Burnout and Resilience

The analyses indicated that the stress factors of student misbehaviour, lack of professional recognition, poor school ethos, and workload and time pressure correlated positively with total teacher burnout, and the factors of emotional exhaustion and depersonalisation. Teachers who felt high levels of stress thus tended to experience high levels of burnout, emotional exhaustion and depersonalisation, and low levels of personal accomplishment.

Teacher sense of efficacy correlated negatively with student misbehaviour and lack of professional recognition. Collective teacher self-efficacy was negatively associated with lack of professional recognition, emotional exhaustion and depersonalisation. High levels of teacher sense of efficacy, individual resilience and collective teacher self-efficacy were associated with high levels of personal accomplishment, suggesting a significant negative association between the mean burnout scores and the mean resilience scores.

Stress, burnout and resilience factors were thus significantly interrelated, and their correlations were in the hypothesised directions. That validation of the relationships among stress, burnout and resilience thus confirmed the validity of the SDS teacher population as appropriate for the primary research aim: that of exploring the dimensions of SDS teacher resilience.

The Dimensions of Resilience

The factors that the more resilient teachers saw as enhancing their resilience and the strategies they used to enhance that resilience are reported here as dimensions of resilience, in the two categories recognised in the study: (1) individual dimensions and (2) organisational dimensions. The identified dimensions of resilience in both of those categories are presented here in the order of their relative importance as revealed by higher frequency of occurrence and re-occurrence in respondents' interview narratives. The illustrative narrative extracts, presented here in plain italicised text, have been translated from Cantonese to English to retain the *meaning* of their utterance, rather than to preserve their linguistic structure. They are attributed in each case to their author, using his or her research pseudonym and are used to evidence and ground the general form of each dimension.

(1) Individual Dimensions of Teacher Resilience

The eight emergent individual dimensions of teacher resilience were (1) being positive, (2) being committed, (3) being a lifelong learner, (4) being responsive, (5) being reflective, (6) being purposeful, (7) being detached and (8) having a higher calling.

Being positive was identified by all 11 interviewees as most important to their resilience. It involved having a positive attitude, being optimistic and converting any situation that was emotionally toxic into something emotionally nutritious:

> It was the attitude of seeing the 'glass half-full' instead of 'half-empty'. (Peter)

> Resilience has to do with sticking around wholeheartedly and being a positive force to influence others. (Cathy)

> Being resilient? A lot of it is about attitude. Keeping it positive. (Monica)

Being committed was also identified by all 11 participants. They saw themselves as being motivated by love, as having a commitment to education and as choosing to teach in such disadvantaged schools because of an 'inner calling':

> I think these kids need someone who can help them and who knows what is going on; they need a teacher like me. ... I respect them for what they are doing. (Ah Man)

> I am not just here for a job, for money, I am actually working to contribute; not only to change, but to build those EBC students' values and skills and knowledge. (Wing)

Being a lifelong learner was identified by eight interviewees. They saw themselves as having the initiative to further their study and the willingness to enhance their teaching effectiveness through attending continuing professional development programmes. They expressed their willingness to take short-term in-service training programmes in special and inclusive education for their continuing professional development, seeing the programmes as:

> Nutrition that could enhance our teaching effectiveness, and opportunities to meet teachers from other schools to share, to listen, and to tell. (Monica)

Six respondents were undertaking or planning to pursue a higher degree pertinent to teaching of EBC students. They talked of having a positive lifelong learning mindset to continually push themselves to learn.

Being responsive was identified by eight interviewees. It involved being flexible in response to situational demands, being creative in addressing challenging situations, and using a problem-solving approach:

> *I think, as a teacher, it probably has to be with an open mind, being flexible and open to new ideas ... and continuing to be innovative.* (Alice)

> *I know how to balance and be flexible. I will step forward to deal with a problem proactively, and then step back to rest and re-energise myself relaxingly.* (Cathy)

Being reflective was identified by seven participants. It involved being able to learn from experience through reflection on their teaching practice. They saw their reflection as being not just about how they thought but also about how they constructed their experience, looking at it from different perspectives, making independent judgements, and taking responsibility for their actions:

> *I learn from experience and know how to help prevent the same mistake from recurring. I think it important that I am reflective. ... The big thing in being resilient is looking back and learning how to examine your mistakes.* (Alvin)

> *I do a lot of reflecting by self-questioning. ... I never think about any negative points. I only think of 'what I can', 'how I can', 'what they can' and 'how they can'.* (Clayton)

Being purposeful was identified by seven of the interviewees. They saw it as their having goals in their work life, having a sense of direction, holding beliefs that gave life purpose, aims and objectives, and deriving from their work a sense of success. Teachers who understood their job's wider purpose— such as the vision and mission of education—saw themselves as being happier and more engaged. When they saw how their roles fitted into the school's goals, they recognised their teaching effectiveness as being enhanced:

[In the SDS,] work has meaning in some way. No matter what you do, you and your job are existing for some reason. When you know that reason ... or when you understand how your efforts make the world better, you have found your purpose. (Cathy)

For wellness of students and, in particular, their positive future, the concept of making a meaningful difference was one that resonated strongly with me for my staying in the field. (Ah Lee)

Being detached was identified by six participants. It involved externalising events, depersonalising situations, detaching oneself from them, maintaining a work-life balance and having a sense of humour. When a difficult event occurred, they would assess what was happening and make judgements from different viewpoints. They would shy away from seeing the event as purely their own fault, feeling guilty about it or taking it too personally. They would seek not to let it overwhelm them, facilitated for some by a sense of humour about the situation:

My mentor taught me how to depersonalise without being aloof and inhumane. I care, but I do not take it personally. I can distance myself from the problem and step back and tell myself 'that's his choice, it has nothing to do with me'. I need not take things personally. (Alice)

I take care of myself, pay attention to my own feelings and engage in sports activities. ... That helps to keep my mind and body well-informed to deal with situations requiring a state of resilience. Meditation helps me to build connections and restore hope too. (Duck)

Having a higher calling, whether it was a belief in a higher power (God) or a more general sense of spirituality, was identified by five interviewees as a dimension of their resilience:

I am practising Buddhism. ... I believe humans are born equal. My students have become lost and they need help to transform. My mission is to create value [in life]. I enjoy teaching here as I can fulfil my mission. (Kelvin)

I have support from my church. I am a Christian. ... I have always had faith that I am going to be taken care of and I always look for opportunities to serve and to help. I will never give up my mission to be the effective SDS teacher of EBC students that God leads me to be. (Alvin)

(2) Organisational Dimensions of Teacher Resilience

The four emergent dimensions of organisational resilience were (1) a positive school climate, (2) positive and supportive relationships, (3) trust and recognition, and (4) team membership.

A positive school climate was identified by all 11 interviewees. It may be seen as the primary organisational dimension of resilience, to which each the following three dimensions contributed. It was articulated by each participant as a positively supportive and encouraging work context or climate in the school:

Under positive school climates, we were able to build our resilience by sharing the joy of our students' improvement and advancing our professional lives. (Alice)

When we have a work environment that is inspiring and supportive, it is easier for us to stay connected to the deeper meaning of our work. (Ah Lee)

Positive and supportive relationships was identified as the most important component of a positive school climate, all 11 reporting it:

Good relationships in the school are important for my development of resilience. To accept help and support from others who strengthen me. (Peter)

Interviewees commonly used terms like *trust, togetherness, support, respect, mutuality, understanding* and *caring* to describe their positive and supportive relationships in school.

The relationships were with their work supervisors and school administration:

My school is terrific. We have a sense of togetherness. … When supervisors want to suggest some new things, they will consult you and ask you if you are OK, always in a non-threatening and not a boss-like manner. (Monica)

But also with their fellow teachers:

We are supportive, mutually supportive. … We have mutually agreed that if anyone needs a break or support, we will 'trade off' students. We are collaborative. We are together, and we are never alone. (Wing)

And with students:

I'm pretty good at building up relationships with my students. I make an effort to remember their names. … After school, I chat with them to understand their needs. We … care for and trust each other. (Kelvin)

But also with the parents of students:

We are grateful to have parents' contributions as we always work together for the good of our kids. (Cathy)

And the broader school community:

The activities were good for community relationship-building. Our students joined community service activities regularly to help the needy. We were all happy and fulfilled. (Ah Lee)

Strong mentorship in the school was also an important component of this dimension:

My mentor was really awesome. She could understand my difficulties. She realised that this year was my first time teaching and I had not been assigned to teach my elective subject [music]. When I planned to have the music interest class and the mini concert, she 100 per cent supported me. (Alice)

Trust and recognition amongst students, teachers, parents and administrators was identified by six of the participants:

Trust, support, and recognition of my work were the fuel in motivating me to carry on. (Wing)

The students are very different now. I have respect from them. Actually, we are mutually respectful. Students' behaviour has improved: no more fighting and no more anger; they all behave. (Duck)

Team membership was identified by four of the interviewees. Working in a team they saw as reinforcing their strength and helping them to feel supported:

When handling problem students, we work in a team. We work together to share the best approach to handling the same case. There's always a team spirit to it. (Alice)

Teamwork is very important. You can vent and release your frustration to team-mates and accept their understanding and advice; they can also support you if you are having trouble. (Monica)

Contributions of the Study to Existing Knowledge

These findings are broadly in agreement with those of other studies internationally. The findings from the survey component part of the study, though, may be seen as raising the level of certainty about the interrelationships between stress, burnout and resilience, confirming the hypothesised patterns between and among them. The study is also unique in its detailed articulation of the different dimensions of individual SDS teachers' lived experiences of resilience, and it adds greatly to previous knowledge of those dimensions, both in terms of the details of each dimension and in terms of the particular dimensions identified. It stands, as well, as the only study in the Hong Kong SDS context that has systematically examined the interrelationships between stress, burnout and resilience in SDS teachers. In the SDS context, the study has evidenced the importance of the identified eight individual and four organisational dimensions of teacher resilience. It may also be seen as an exemplar of how different research approaches and instruments may be combined effectively into a unitary study.

A number of previous studies (e.g. Chong & Au, 2008; Chong & Ng, 2011; Ho, Leung, & Fung, 2003; Pang, 2012) in Hong Kong have suggested that student misbehaviour was the major factor that led to teacher stress. In contrast, this study indicated that workload and time pressure were more important.

The combined impact of the resilience dimensions identified in this study may also be seen as providing a credible explanation of the unexpectedly moderate stress and burnout levels of the SDS teachers, in contrast to the findings of previous local studies, which have created a general belief that all teachers alike suffered similarly high levels of stress and burnout (Chan et al., 2010; Chang, 2009).

While the impact of the resilience dimensions points to the likelihood of stress significantly contributing to burnout, it also raises the potential role of managing stress by focusing attention on the important stressors identified in this study through building resilience: a point that is particularly important in moderating the negative impact of teachers' commonly high levels of compassion, empathy and care for their students, which can exacerbate their levels and burnout.

While the study has involved the SDS teachers in Hong Kong, the findings stand, at the very least, to be used in other educational jurisdictions and contexts to sensitise the management of stress and the reduction of burnout through the building of resilience, both individual and organisational. Through that understanding, the way is opened-up for educational policy and practice to support teachers in building their resilience.

Implications of the Study for Educational Policy and Practice

While acknowledging the exploratory and interpretative nature of this study, its findings may be seen as suggesting a number of implications for educational policy and practice in relation to teacher preparation and practice in Hong Kong. However, like the findings themselves, those implications may be seen also as raising considerations for special education in other jurisdictions with similar structures, cultures and traditions. They are as follows.

(1)   *Teachers should understand and develop their resilience*

The findings of the study indicate the importance of resilience as a moderator of stress and possible burnout in the SDS teaching context. Since an important part of that moderating effect involved teachers' awareness of the resilience dimensions, it is evident that teachers should be aware of the dimensions that could enhance their resilience. They could then use the dimensions as strategies.

(2)   *School leadership and management should focus on building teacher resilience*

The findings of the study indicate that resilience can be learned and reinforced through an encouraging and supportive school culture, suggesting the importance of school leadership and management focusing attention on creating and sustaining school cultures that build, support, sustain and reward teacher resilience.

(3)   *Teacher education should embrace resilience-enhancing content*

Similarly, initial teacher education and ongoing professional development should focus on building knowledge and strategies of resilience in teacher trainees and professionals.

(4)   *Educational policy should encourage the adequate resourcing of teaching*

The study found that workload and time pressure were the most important stressors for SDS teachers. That finding points to the importance of making adequate resources available to moderate teachers' workload, reduce the pressure on their time, and hence to build their resilience.

Conclusions

This study of the stress, burnout and resilience in SDS teachers in Hong Kong confirmed the hypothesised correlations between stress, burnout and resilience. They confirmed that SDS teacher stress was positively correlated with teacher burnout and that SDS teacher resilience was negatively correlated with their stress and burnout. The model of teacher stress leading to teacher burnout, moderated by teacher resilience, may thus be seen as being congruent with the findings. The study confirms also the hypothesised exacerbation of teacher stress by their compassion, empathy and care for their students in the contemporary cultural context. The building of teacher resilience to stress thus emerges as a constructive approach to moderating or alleviating that negative impact of teacher compassion, empathy and care.

From the in-depth conversational interviews with more resilient SDS teachers, a number of dimensions that might be managed to reduce burnout by building resilience and alleviating stress were identified: both individual and organisational dimensions. Identified individual dimensions of resilience were (1) being positive, (2) being committed, (3) being a lifelong learner, (4) being responsive, (5) being reflective, (6) being purposeful, (7) being detached and (8) having a higher calling. Organisational dimensions of resilience identified were (1) a positive school climate, (2) positive and supportive relationships, (3) trust and recognition, and (4) team membership.

It is suggested that the findings of the study might be used to contribute to the building of teacher resilience through (1) facilitating teacher understanding and strategies of resilience, (2) ensuring that educational leadership and management focus on building teacher resilience, (3) including appropriate resilience-enhancing content in initial teacher education and professional development programmes, and (4) ensuring that educational policy encourages the adequate resourcing of teaching.

However, in considering the findings and recommendations from the study, it must be recognised that the study of the dimensions of resilience was exploratory and limited in its scope. The findings and recommendations, accordingly, should be seen as suggestive interpretations, rather than affirmative assertions of reality.

References

Bagnall, R. G., & Wong, K. L. (2014). Applied learning policy in Hong Kong as a contribution to lifelong learning. *International Journal of Continuing Education and Lifelong Learning, 7*(1), 93–118.

Billingsley, B. S. (2004). Special education teacher retention and attrition: A critical analysis of the research literature. *Journal of Special Education, 38*, 39–55.

Center, D., & Callaway, J. (1999). Self-reported job stress and personality in teachers of students with emotional and behavioural disorders. *Behavioural Disorders, 25*, 41–51.

Chan, R. M. (2006). *A research study on Hong Kong teachers' stress: A preliminary analysis*. Hong Kong: Hong Kong primary education research association and education convergence (in Chinese).

Chan, A., Chen, K., & Chong, E. (2010). *Work stress of teachers from primary and secondary schools in Hong Kong* (Proceedings of the International Multi Conference of Engineers and Computer Scientists 2010) (Vol. III). Hong Kong: IMECS.

Chang, M. (2009). An appraisal perspective of teacher burnout: Examining the emotional work of teachers. *Educational Psychology Review, 21*, 193–218.

Cheng, Y. C. (2009a). Teacher management and educational reforms: Paradigm shifts. *Prospects, 39*(1), 69–89.

Cheng, Y. C. (2009b). Hong Kong educational reforms in the last decade: Reform syndrome and new developments. *International Journal of Educational Management, 23*, 65–86.

Chong, S., & Au, M. L. (2008). What works for teachers of students with emotional and behavioural difficulties in Hong Kong's special schools? *The International Journal on School Disaffection, 6*(1), 25–34.

Chong, S., & Ng, K. (2011). Perception of what works for teachers of students with EBD in mainstream and special schools in Hong Kong. *Emotional and Behavioural Difficulties, 16*, 173–188.

Committee on Teachers' Work. (2006). *CTW final report*. Retrieved August 13, 2007, from http://www.legco.gov.hk/yr06-07/english/panels/ed/papers/ed0212cb2-1041-6-e.pdf

Creswell, J. W. (2003). *Research design: Qualitative, quantitative, and mixed methods approaches* (2nd ed.). Thousand Oaks, CA: Sage.

Day, C. (2013). *Passionate teachers, passionate learners: Why technical skills are a necessary but insufficient measure of quality*. London: Routledge.

Day, C., & Gu, Q. (2014). *Resilient teachers, resilient schools: Building and sustaining quality in testing times*. London: Routledge.

Democratic Alliance for the Betterment of Hong Kong. (2006). *Press release: A survey on alleviating teacher workload and stress*. Retrieved July 16, 2011, from http://www.dab.org.hk/UserFiles/Image/News%20centre/News/doc/2006/20060110poll.pdf (in Chinese).

Denzin, N. K., & Lincoln, Y. (2005). *The sage handbook of qualitative research*. Thousand Oaks, CA: Sage.

Education Bureau. (2013). *Information sheet: Education, figures and statistics.* Retrieved January 27, 2014, from http://www.edb.gov.hk

Education Bureau. (2016). *Performance indicators and school self-evaluation tools* [online]. Retrieved September 30, 2016, from https://www.edb.gov.hk/attachment/en/sch-admin/sch-quality-assurance/performance-indicators/PI-2016_Eng.pdf

Forlin, C., & Lian, M. G. J. (Eds.). (2008). *Reform, inclusion and teacher education: Towards a new era of special education in the Asia-Pacific Region.* London: Routledge.

Grove, K. S. (1997). *Architecture for a resilience organisation: Survive, grow and prosper in a downsized environment.* Unpublished dissertation, The Union Institute, Cincinnati, OH.

Guarino, C. M., Santibañez, L., & Daley, G. A. (2006). Teacher recruitment and retention: A review of the recent empirical literature. *Review of Educational Research, 76*(2), 173–208.

Ho, C., Leung, J., & Fung, H. (2003). Teacher expectation of higher disciplinary problems and stress among Hong Kong secondary school teachers. *Educational Research Journal, HKIER, 18*(1), 41–55.

Hong, J. (2012). Why do some beginning teachers leave the school, and others stay? Understanding teacher resilience through psychological lenses. *Teachers and Teaching: Theory and Practice, 18*(4), 417–440.

Hong Kong Mood Disorders Centre. (2004). *Teacher stress and mood disorders survey* (text in Chinese). Retrieved March 13, 2011, from http://www.hmdc.med.cuhk.edu.hk/report/report19.html

Hong Kong Professional Teachers' Union. (2003). *Survey study on occupational stress of Hong Kong teachers* (text in Chinese). Retrieved January 30, 2011, from http://www.hkptu.org.hk

Hong Kong Professional Teachers' Union. (2005). Quality education impossible with teacher's higher burnout rate (text in Chinese). *PTU News, 498,* 127. Retrieved January 30, 2011, from http://www.hkptu.org.hk

Hong Kong Professional Teachers' Union. (2008). *Survey on Hong Kong teachers' occupational stress and mental health* (text in Chinese). Hong Kong: Commission to Hong Kong Institute of Asia-Pacific Studies. Retrieved January 30, 2011, from http://www.hkptu.org.hk

Hong Kong Professional Teachers' Union. (2013). *Measures for stabilising secondary schools and enhancing quality education* (text in Chinese). Hong Kong: Action Group of Secondary Schools of HKPTU. Retrieved May 25, 2014, from http://www.hkptu.org.hk

Larkin, M., Watts, S., & Clifton, E. (2006). Giving voice and making sense in interpretative phenomenological analysis. *Qualitative Research in Psychology, 3*(2), 102–120.

Lau, P., Yuen, M., & Chan, R. (2005). Do demographic characteristics make a difference in teacher burnout in Hong Kong secondary schools? *Social Indicators Research, 71*, 491–516.

Mansfield, C. F., Beltman, S., Price, A., & McConney, A. (2012). "Don't sweat the small stuff": Understanding teacher resilience at the chalkface. *Teaching and Teacher Education, 28*(3), 357–367.

Maslach, C., & Jackson, S. (1981). The measurement of experienced burnout. *Journal of Occupational Behaviour, 2*, 99–113.

Miles, M. B., & Huberman, A. M. (1994). *Qualitative data analysis*. Thousand Oaks, CA: Sage.

Nunnally, J. L. (1978). *Psychometric theory* (2nd ed.). New York, NY: McGraw-Hill.

Pang, I. W. (2012). Teacher stress in working with challenging students in Hong Kong. *Educational Research for Policy and Practice, 11*(2), 119–139.

Reid, K., Flowers, P., & Larkin, M. (2005). Exploring lived experience: An introduction to interpretative phenomenological analysis. *The Psychologist, 18*(1), 20–23.

Rutter, M. (1990). Psychosocial resilience and protective mechanisms. In J. Rolf, A. S. Mastern, D. Cicchetti, K. H. Nuechterlein, & S. Weintraub (Eds.), *Risk and protective factors in the development of psychopathology* (pp. 181–214). Cambridge: Cambridge University Press.

Schwarzer, R., & Schmitz, G. (1999). Collective self-efficacy of teachers: A longitudinal study in ten German states. *Zeitschrift für Sozialpsychologie, 30*(4), 262–274.

Siebert, A. (2006). *The survivor personality: Why some people are stronger, smarter, and more skilful at handling life's difficulties*. Oakland, CA: Berrett-Koehler Publishers.

Smith, J. A., Flowers, P., & Larkin, M. (2009). *Interpretative phenomenological analysis: Theory, method and research*. London: Sage.

Tse, K. C. (2005). Quality education in Hong Kong: The anomalies of managerialism and marketisation. In L. S. Ho & P. Morris (Eds.), *Education reform and the quest for excellence* (pp. 99–124). Hong Kong: Hong Kong University Press.

11

Early Childhood Education: From Maternal Care to Social Compassion

Geoff Taggart

Introduction

Early childhood education and care (ECEC) is based on a rich tradition of research in child development which recognizes that young children learn holistically, involving mind, body and emotions (e.g. Neaum, 2010). In contrast to traditional school learning, young children's learning is necessarily creative and spontaneous. Relationship is central and, as Murray (1998, 149) observes, since 'toddlers do not have the cognitive ability to grasp the employment relationship of which they are a part', we can only assume that they think practitioners come to work with them every day because they love them. Where provision is in tune with child development, working with young children therefore requires a high degree of responsiveness, empathy, alertness and flexibility. Attitudes of care, attentiveness and receptivity are as central to learning as the skill in providing an appropriate cognitive challenge or connecting learning to the child's own experience. In ECEC, care involves intensive experiences of both 'caring

G. Taggart (✉)
Institute of Education, University of Reading, Reading, UK
e-mail: g.taggart@reading.ac.uk

© The Author(s) 2019
G. Barton, S. Garvis (eds.), *Compassion and Empathy in Educational Contexts*,
https://doi.org/10.1007/978-3-030-18925-9_11

for' and 'caring about' (Noddings, 1984), the former concept involving direct physical contact and the latter involving emotional concern (even worry) about the cared-for. In using both forms, the work of practitioners and teachers ranges from simple intimate physical care to the exercising of empathy, receptiveness, responsiveness and benevolent concern.

However, expertise in provision of this care often seems to be purely adventitious rather than a result of deliberate training or qualification. Certainly, a number of practitioner-focused texts outline the various 'roles of the adult' (e.g. Rose & Rogers, 2012), but such portrayals tend to be normative and idealized. Perhaps as a result, researchers such as Davis and Dunn (2018, 919) recognize that 'there seems to be difficulty in conceptualizing emotional qualities of relationships and what they mean as part of professional, intentional practice'.

I intend to argue that the principal reason for this difficulty lies in the way in which qualities of care and compassion, particularly for the old, sick and very young, continue to be associated with inherited ideals of feminine identity, rather than being seen as generic human capacities. The particular skills and attitudes of compassion come to be lost within the ill-defined parameters of 'women's work', even concealing the fact of care as a form of labour involving skills and knowledge. Women continue to carry out the bulk of 'caring for' functions, in both Western democracies and the developing South (e.g. Graham, 1983; Fisher, 1990; Ungerson, 1983) and men in such roles are seen as oddities, or at least biologically disadvantaged. It would therefore seem that, if the skills and qualities associated with care are to be accorded explicit professional status, they need to be disentangled from their patriarchal history. De-gendering compassion is the first step in professionalizing ECEC and in identifying compassion as an attribute which can be encouraged and cultivated through education and training rather than being relied on as a feminine virtue.

Love, Care and Professional Status

As feminist commentators have noted (e.g. Lloyd, 1984), Western expectations of a caring identity for women, aligning them principally with their child-rearing role, arose in Renaissance cultures in which women were increasingly seen as immune to reason and excluded from public discourse. For example, Ruddick (1989, 31) comments that 'an idealized figure of the Good Mother casts a long shadow on many actual women's lives'. This Good Mother is compassionate and self-sacrificial, instinctive and non-rational. As Chodorow (1978) famously argues, she is an invention of the historical revolution in manufacturing in which a familial division of labour was necessitated by the demise of cottage industries and the recruitment of men into factories.

ECEC can be seen as a kind of pseudo-mothering activity where this archetypal maternal identity can flourish. For example, although practitioners are neither employees nor friends of the families they serve, they establish deep emotional ties with them and maintain diverse kinds of physical contact with the children, including 'touching, hugging, holding, cuddling, rocking, carrying, wiping and restraining' (Murray, 1998, 156). The sector tends to attract young women who, in the absence of other forms of capital, need to call upon their perceived 'feminine capital' (Huppatz, 2009) for employment in the low paid caring work for which such capital apparently suits them as potential mother/carers. As various researchers have shown (e.g. Colley, 2006; Vincent & Braun, 2010; Osgood, 2012; Skeggs, 1997), early years training programmes, typically undertaken in community or further education colleges, shape the caring dispositions associated with 'respectable' femininity, recalling nineteenth-century training schools for urban girls (Read, 2017). ECEC, particularly in the case of child-minding, often blurs the boundaries between home and work, between instinctive care and contractual employment, so that one's private and public identity overlaps. In England, practitioners often move into this work as a result of needing to find childcare for their own children. Osgood (2004, 19) notes that they therefore tend to draw upon their experience as caring mothers when discussing good practice, using value-laden terms such as 'empathy', 'support', 'collaboration' and 'care'. Certainly, many see it as a natural disposition (Cousins, 2017).

In a short-lived attempt to raise the professionalism of ECEC, the New Labour government introduced graduate competency standards for 'Early Years Professional' status in 2006 (now Early Years Teacher status). However, the now-defunct Children's Workforce Development Council removed from the standards all emotive terms which could evoke 'amateur' motherliness:

'love', 'care' and 'compassion' went unmentioned. The assumption was that such things are ipso facto unprofessional and incompatible with professionalism. However, as I have argued (Taggart, 2011), the consequences of such misplaced aims at professionalism are that love and care necessarily continue to be valued in practice but exist as unacknowledged forms of 'emotional labour' (Hochschild, 1986). In other words, practitioners split themselves between an 'official' persona, focused on educational outcomes and 'school readiness', and a more informal persona rooted in love and care (Cousins, 2017; Davis & Degotardi, 2015; Osgood, 2012). Davis and Dunn (2018), for example, contrast the language of practitioners with the language of the curriculum frameworks followed, demonstrating that the relational aspects of the work are largely rendered invisible. Practitioners are encouraged by official policy to talk about care and 'positive relationships' and 'love' may be conspicuously absent in conversation (Rouse & Hadley, 2018). Where this discourse is investigated and owned by practitioners themselves, it is used more confidently. For example, Recchia, Shin and Snaider (2018, 155) made an interesting finding amongst practitioners: 'rather than conceiving of love as conflicting with professionalism, loving their students turned out to be a core element of their emerging professional identities'. In order to capture and articulate the affective dimension of ECEC work, a concept of 'professional love' has been advanced (Page, 2011) as a focal point for this discourse. In defining this, Page (2018) proposes that professional love ideally arises as an outcome of the three-way relationship between parent, practitioner and child (a 'triangle of love' model) and that it can be fostered deliberately by practitioners as they cultivate dispositions of self-awareness and emotional resilience. It occurs when practitioners are able to 'decentre' from their own pre-occupations and immerse themselves in encounters with children and parents, growing in authenticity and a capacity for emotional intimacy.

I would contend that this discourse of love in an ECEC context, whilst offering a valuable voice of dissent amongst the clamour for 'school readiness', may not be the best way to professionalize the skills of receptivity, care and patience which practitioners demonstrate. There are three main reasons why a discourse of compassion may be more successful in articulating and promoting it. The first is ambivalence about the appropriateness of 'love' in a professional context. In Western societies, love is typically expressed in particular, dyadic relationships within a domestic context. Page (2011) found that not all practitioners were comfortable using the term 'love' in their work and this is probably culturally determined. Although the forms of love are diverse and numerous, such as *philia* (belonging) or *agape* (self-sacrifice), many affluent Western cultures are dominated by *eros*, a form that is private rather than social and instinctive rather than rational. It also prevents members of the public from seeing male practitioners in ECEC settings as anything other than deeply suspect. Therefore, whilst it is cheering that Hungarian parents applaud the 'child-loving' attitudes of practitioners (Campbell-Barr, Georgeson, & Varga, 2015), promoting ECEC as 'professional love' more globally may simply entrench the view of it as a form of irrational, pseudo-domestic 'women's work' whose loving character necessarily disqualifies men from participating. By contrast, compassion is a gender-neutral virtue and, in the pantheon of ideals, there is a Gandhi or Dalai Lama for every Mother Teresa.

The second reason why compassion presents itself as appropriate in this context is that it resolves a tension within the theoretical underpinnings provided for professional love. Page (2018) identifies attachment theory (Ainsworth, Blehar, Waters, & Wall, 1978; Bowlby, 1958) as a key inspiration for this construct. As a biologist studying cases of maternal separation and deprivation, Bowlby proposed that young mammals have a care-seeking instinct which ensures their survival and that, when met with sensitive care-giving, allows them to build accurate 'internal working models' of themselves and the world. Love is patently central to this relationship. At the same time, Page also acknowledges the criticisms which have been levelled against attachment theory as imposing a particularly dyadic and Western model of ideal child-rearing which is strongly focused on the mother. In this sense, carers are constructed by attachment theory as substitutes in this one-to-one relationship, even though a broader pattern of relating may be more beneficial to the child. In considering infant mental health, for example, McHale (2007) argues that intervention strategies need to take into account caregivers beyond the immediate family. As regards practice in ECEC, Degotardi and Pearson (2009) point out that emphasis upon attachment relationships can inhibit a child's capacity to play and explore the environment more widely. From a philosophical perspective, Barnes (2015) urges us to see ethic of care as multidimensional rather than only two way. In sociological terms, Aslanian (2015) notes that the popularity of attachment theory can largely be explained simply because of its usefulness in challenging the dominance of behaviourism in twentieth-century thinking about health and social care. These arguments suggest an ambivalence surrounding the use of attachment theory in ECEC work because its affective/psychological basis does not acknowledge the social/political context in which it operates. As I will argue, compassion brings both of these elements together.

The third advantage of compassion is that it suggests a means by which the constitutive skills and dispositions can be developed in practice. Page (2018, 129) admits that the triangle of love model is a 'utopian abstraction [which] is rarely if ever fully achieved in practice' and it is intended as a normative ideal type. Although Page portrays very clearly what professional love looks like in the sense of 'best practice', it is not clear what steps a novice could take to cultivate this attribute if it were lacking: this might be because the notion of 'love' is itself so broad and far-ranging. Therefore, in the rest of this chapter, I argue that the concept and practice of compassion provides both a social and psychological framework for ECEC which includes and celebrates the relational qualities previously characterized as 'women's work', providing clues about how they can be 'taught' as well as 'caught'.

From Maternal Care to Social Compassion

A form of professionalism needs to be established which can acknowledge, cultivate and celebrate the relational context of work of ECEC without recourse to gender essentialism, and the concept of compassion can provide a suitable platform for it. As indicated, one of the advantages of compassion over the more general term of 'love' is that it has an explicit social and active dimension as well as a personal, affective dimension. This is shown in that human activities which would be described as compassionate are usually those which seek to alleviate suffering, vulnerability or inequality in a public sphere whilst also calling upon distinct emotions for their motivation. As Hugman (2005, 51) remarks, 'compassion is the emotion that bridges the public and the private'. Writers as diverse as Nussbaum (2001) and Haidt (2012) have articulated the connection between compassion and socio-political consciousness since compassion is only extended towards those whom we consider *deserve* it, whether they are stressed business leaders or homeless people, thus revealing our own affiliations. Koopman-Holm and Tsai (2017) bring together a wealth of studies demonstrating the way compassion is shaped by class and culture. For example, in a study of 23 nations, participants from less affluent countries were more likely to help others than those from wealthier ones (Levine, Norenzayan, & Philbrick, 2001). It also seems to be the case that, within the same society, poorer people are mostly more compassionate than the richer ones (Piff & Moskowitz, 2017) and that compassionate attitudes are most strongly associated with a liberal and progressive political perspective (Haidt, 2012). Compassionate attitudes also seem to vary over time in accordance with dominant political attitudes and, bearing in mind the dominance of Reaganite, neoliberal thinking over the last 30 years, it may not be surprising that measures of compassion in the United States seem to indicate a sustained decline (Zarins & Konrath, 2017).

This socio-political dimension of compassion seems to reflect very well the social justice commitments embedded in many early childhood projects, ranging from the early experiments in nursery schooling by the radical McMillan sisters in London to the more recent Head Start/Sure Start community programmes. To take one English example, Pen Green Children's Centre arose as a community response to the declining steel industry in an east midlands town, offering parenting advice and basic skills tuition as well as childcare: it quickly became a pioneering example of compassionate practice (Whalley, 2017). In these programmes, the promotion of play, flourishing and self-expression are integral to the compassionate approach, and this reflects the continuing influence of the humanistic Freudian Left (e.g. Brown, 1959; Fromm, 1959; Marcuse, 1965) whose alternatives to bureaucratic capitalism centred on a celebration of play, creativity and collaboration which are central to the building of community and solidarity. For the childcare worker, it would seem, compassion may describe both their psychological orientation and their political vision.

From the perspective of moral psychology, a widely held definition of compassion is that it is a sense of caring concern that arises when we are confronted with the suffering of another and feel motivated to relieve it (Jinpa, 2015). It can be understood in diverse ways, both as a short-term motivation to help in response to immediate events and as a longer-term personality trait/disposition which can be identified through self-report measures such as the Multidimensional Compassion Scale (Goldin & Jazaeiri, 2017). One of the most relevant points about compassion in relation to ECEC is being shown by evolutionary biology, that the 'hard-wiring' of human beings to act in a compassionate way in a general sense has been strongly selected for and refined over tens of thousands of years because of the specific benefits it provides in terms of *child-rearing* (e.g. Batson, 2011; Carter, Bartal, & Porges, 2017; Porges, 1998; Goetz, Keltner, & Simon-Thomas, 2010). It should be pointed out here that, in hunter-gatherer groups, the neurobiological skills of patience and responsiveness would be expected from all adults in a kind of informal daycare since alloparenting (shared parenting) would be the norm (Boyette, 2015). Being able to anticipate needs of the vulnerable and postpone one's own gratification became essential, bearing in mind that human babies are born more prematurely than any other mammal, requiring a degree of care unparalleled elsewhere in nature if they are to reach maturity. It is these same 'neural circuits' that prompt us to nurture and care which also allow us to suppress self-interest when encountering unmet needs among people more widely. In other words, 'there seems to be a common neural network for caring, feelings of social connection and altruism' (Klimecki & Singer, 2017, 111). It is not surprising, therefore, that the empathic competences which are especially important to compassion, identified by Gilbert and Mascaro (2017), would be recognizable by most early childhood teachers. These include the ability to see the other as more than a means of satisfying one's own needs, having enough 'distress tolerance' to engage with the vulnerability of others, treating them with a closeness similar to family and being able to select an appropriate response to expressed need, such as feeding, soothing or picking up.

This evolutionary perspective has the effect of widening the scope of compassion beyond *suffering* and its stereotypical association with nurses attending to the diseased and dying. Compassion is at once both more ordinary and fundamental. Whitebrook (2002) argues that the notion of suffering should be replaced by that of 'vulnerability' and, bearing in mind our common vulnerability in early life, sickness and old age, this conception of compassion emphasizes its universal relevance. This argument is clearly significant for ECEC since, by emphasizing the role of compassion in addressing *need* or *vulnerability* in general rather than suffering specifically, it is extended to include the work of early childhood practitioners. This extension is not so unnatural if one remembers the etymological roots of 'compassion' itself which, in Semitic languages, are close to that of the word for 'womb' (Armstrong, 2011): the emphasis is on holding and containment of the vulnerable.

Our understanding of the relationship between child-rearing and compassion has been enhanced by advances in the ability to detect and measure oxytocin, a neuropeptide which plays a central role in the capacity for and expression of social traits and emotion (e.g. Rockliff et al., 2011). It conditions both parents' bonding with children and is released during activities such as feeding, soft vocalization and affectionate touch. Research with non-human mammals suggests that oxytocin fosters prosocial, compassionate activities both with partners and with outlier groups, modifying the stress reaction that normally occurs (Feldman, 2012). Carter et al. (2017, 177) argue that it effectively allows one to witness vulnerability in others without being overcome oneself. It would therefore seem as though the *child-rearing* dispositions of parents and alloparents (listening, anticipating, responding, mirroring, etc.) and the *compassionate* dispositions we express as social adults share the same underlying neurobiological mechanisms, indicating that, in child-rearing situations managed by non-kin relations, *compassionate pedagogy* may describe the practice most appropriately (Taggart, 2016).

One of the advances demonstrated by the relatively new field of 'compassion science' (Seppala et al., 2017) is that an individual's capacity for compassion is not fixed but, like most dispositions, can be encouraged and expanded through deliberate attention. Through organizations such as the Center for the Greater Good at the University of Berkeley, the Center for Compassion and Altruism Research and Education at Stanford University and the Center for Investigating Healthy Minds at the University of Wisconsin, there is increasing evidence that our capacity for care, empathy and compassion is like a muscle which can grow stronger through practice and 'that we can indeed train the brain to become more compassionate' (Davidson, 2012, 118). This muscle may be underdeveloped as a result of our own early experience, but it does not mean that it is lost or incapable of growth. In fact, the very belief that it can grow is likely to be a self-fulfilling prophecy. Understanding of this neurological plasticity underpins the various programmes of compassion training which have emerged over recent years, their empirical benefits measured in many cases through functional magnetic resonance imaging (Klimecki & Singer, 2017). They show that, although altruistic emotions such as compassion can be short-circuited by the fear associated with self-preservation, deliberate cultivation of compassionate attitudes can modulate lower brainstem function, making the compassionate response stronger and more resilient (Carter et al., 2017). Common features of programmes include mindfulness practice, reflective writing, group discussion and provision of an organizing ethical framework (Skwara, King, & Saron, 2017). Although a pattern of eight weekly sessions is common, Weng et al. (2013) and Klimecki, Leiberg, Lamm, and Singer (2013) reported that participants showed a willingness to engage in more demanding altruistic behaviour in much shorter periods of time. In their review of the literature on compassion training, Skwara et al. (2017) identify several common benefits across a range of interventions such as greater social sensitivity and responsiveness, increased ability to identify feeling states, higher levels of tolerance to distress/vulnerability and reduced personal stress.

Of particular relevance here are the programmes which are specifically oriented to those working with children such as teachers and parents since the skills involved are similar to those used by practitioners in ECEC. Welford and Langmead (2015) describe their 'Care to Achieve' programme which focuses on teaching staff as well as pupils. Participants learn to understand their own 'affect regulation system' via a model described by Gilbert (2009). This system describes three different modes of feeling and acting, each controlled by a different chemical messenger. Two of these modes are well-known, the fight and flight mode regulated by cortisol and the excited mode which dopamine maintains, for example, when we get a 'like' on social media or pass a test. However, Gilbert points out that the third mode occurs more rarely and this is characterized by the feelings associated with belonging, safety, warmth and intimacy, all associated with the production of oxytocin and a kind, compassionate disposition. Engaged in the kinds of activities listed above, teachers learn to identify the constituent elements of the 'compassionate mind' and reflect upon how it would respond to various teaching scenarios. With kindergarten teachers included in their sample, Lavelle, Flook and Ghahremani (2017) outline their Sustainable Compassion Training (SCT) which draws out the relational dimension of care by helping educators and students recognize that one needs to learn to *receive* care in order to be empowered to extend this same caring attitude towards others. Involving similar activities, there are three stages to the process, receiving care, deep self-care and extending care, echoing Noddings' key principle of care ethics (1984) that the practice of kindness depends and draws upon one's own experience of being cared for and receiving kindness. Run in 30 schools in the United States, the aim was to help teachers nurture their caring capacities for the benefit of their own health and wellbeing and to help them embody and model these skills in the classroom. Overall, research shows that school-based programmes such as these are most successful when implemented across school and focus strongly on the teachers. Compassion training for educators leads to improvements across a range of measures such as reduced stress and improved attention, and these are linked with quality of interactions with children (Jennings, Frank, Snowberg, Coccia, & Greenberg, 2013; Jennings & Greenberg, 2009).

Compassion programmes focused on parenting have developed out of mindfulness trainings (e.g. Duncan & Bardacke, 2010; Reynolds, 2013) which aim to help parents to reflect upon their automatic, habitual ways of responding to challenging behaviour which have the effect of intensifying or prolonging conflict. We can assume that parents do not decide at the outset to yell at children or mistreat them but, it is proposed, this happens because of an overactive or automated threat system. So parents are invited to understand how their brain functions and how this impacts on relationships. Swain and Ho (2017) argue that the sensitivity needed to cultivate an attachment bond and the reflective self-understanding needed to communicate successfully are skills involved in compassionate parenting. They also speculate that, because 'parenting a child involves regular, heated challenges for the parents' compassion' (Swain & Ho, 2017, 67), the relationship becomes a 'crucible for compassion' for all parties involved. With this in mind, Kirby (2017) has sought to build on existing evidence-based parenting programmes such as Triple P (Sanders, 2012) and the Incredible Years (Webster-Stratton, 1998) to develop a specific programme aimed at cultivating compassionate parenting. Typically, the older programmes are focused on teaching techniques to address behavioural problems, rather than training participants about how a 'compassionate mind' can be cultivated and strengthened. The compassionate parenting programme fosters a range of social competences such as empathy, distress tolerance and awareness of parenting style, framed by Gilbert's model of emotion processing described above. Soothing and pacifying the engrained fear response is key since it seems that 'when parents feel threatened and uncertain, they are more likely to engage defensively, potentially responding impulsively' (Kirby, 2017, 96). Advocates of this approach are keen to point out that it 'simply does not mean 'being nice' to your children' (Kirby, 2017) since a genuinely helpful stance often challenges the child (i.e. insisting on completion of homework) rather than indulging them. These challenges induce feelings of self-doubt and guilt in parents, indicating why carers need to direct compassion to themselves as well as to the vulnerable other.

Conclusion

Such programmes demonstrate that, in a psychological sense, compassion is a developmental quality and elsewhere (Taggart, 2015, 2019). I have demonstrated the implications of this for the professional development of early childhood teachers. Taken together, the political and psychological dimensions of compassion described above can help us to understand the practices in ECEC of child advocacy and relational pedagogy (Papatheodorou & Moyles, 2008) more fully and deeply. For centuries, much ECEC practice has been based on the inherited assumption that it is women's work because of an innate capacity to nurture, a view which has prevented it from being seen as a profession. Although top-down forms of professionalization aim at increasing status by minimizing the nurture role or reshaping it in instrumental terms, a manifesto for a compassionate profession may validate love and care whilst also advocating for greater social justice and equality.

References

Ainsworth, M. D., Blehar, M. C., Waters, E., & Wall, S. N. (1978). *Patterns of attachment: A psychological study of the strange situation*. London: Routledge.

Armstrong, K. (2011). *Twelve steps to a compassionate life*. London: Bodley Head.

Aslanian, T. (2015). Getting behind discourses of love, care and maternalism in early childhood education. *Contemporary Issues in Early Childhood, 16*(2), 153–165.

Barnes, M. (2015). Beyond the dyad: Exploring the multidimensionality of care. In M. Barnes (Ed.), *Ethics of care: Critical advances in international perspective*. Bristol: Policy Press.

Batson, C. D. (2011). *Altruism in humans*. Oxford: OUP.

Bowlby, J. (1958). The nature of the child's tie to his mother. *International Journal of Psycho-Analysis, 39*, 350–373.

Boyette, A. H. (2015). The long view: Evolutionary theories of early childhood education and care. In T. David (Ed.), *Routledge international handbook of philosophies and theories of early childhood education and care*. London: Routledge.

Brown, N. O. (1959). *Life against death: The psychoanalytic meaning of history*. Middletown, CT: Wesleyan University Press.

Campbell-Barr, V., Georgeson, J., & Varga, A. N. (2015). Developing professional early childhood educators in England and Hungary: Where has all the love gone? *European Education, 47*, 311–330.

Carter, C. S., Bartal, I. B., & Porges, E. C. (2017). The roots of compassion: An evolutionary and neurobiological perspective. In E. Seppala, E. Simon-Thomas, S. L. Brown, M. C. Worline, C. D. Cameron, & J. R. Doty (Eds.), *The Oxford handbook of compassion science* (pp. 173–188). Oxford: Oxford University Press.

Chodorow, N. (1978). *The reproduction of mothering: Psychoanalysis and the sociology of Gender*. Berkeley, CA: University of California Press.

Colley, H. (2006). Learning to labour with feeling: Class, gender and emotion in Childcare, Education and Training. *Contemporary Issues in Early Childhood, 7*(1), 15–29.

Cousins, S. (2017). Practitioners' constructions of love in early childhood education and care. *International Journal of Early Years Education, 25*(1), 16–29. https://doi.org/10.1080/09669760.2016.1263939

Davidson, R. J. (2012). Toward a biology of positive affect and compassion. In R. J. Davidson & A. Harrington (Eds.), *Visions of compassion: Western scientists and Tibetan Buddhists examine human nature* (pp. 107–130). Oxford: Blackwell.

Davis, B., & Degotardi, S. (2015). Who cares? Infant educators' responses to professional discourses of care. *Early Child Development and Care, 185*(11–12), 1733–1747. https://doi.org/10.1080/03004430.2015.1028385

Davis, B., & Dunn, R. (2018). Making the personal visible: Emotion in the nursery. *Early Childhood Development and Care, 188*(7), 905–923.

Degotardi, S., & Pearson, E. (2009). Relationship theory in the nursery: Attachment and beyond. *Contemporary Issues in Early Childhood, 10*(2), 144–155.

Duncan, L., & Bardacke, N. (2010). Mindfulness-based childbirth and parenting education: Promoting family mindfulness during the perinatal period. *Journal of Child and Family Studies, 19*(2), 190–202.

Feldman, R. (2012). Oxytocin and social affiliation in humans. *Hormones and Behaviour, 61*(3), 380–391.

Fisher, B. (1990). Alice in the human services: A feminist analysis of women in the caring professions. In E. K. Abel & M. K. Nelson (Eds.), *Circles of care: Work and identity in women's lives*. Albany, NY: SUNY Press.

Fromm, E. (1959). *The sane society*. London: Routledge.

Gilbert, P. (2009). *The compassionate mind*. London: Constable.

Gilbert, P., & Mascaro, J. (2017). Compassion fears, blocks and resistances: An evolutionary investigation. In E. Seppala, E. Simon-Thomas, S. L. Brown, M. C. Worline, C. D. Cameron, & J. R. Doty (Eds.), *The Oxford handbook of compassion science* (pp. 399–420). Oxford: Oxford University Press.

Goetz, J. L., Keltner, D., & Simon-Thomas, E. (2010). Compassion: An evolutionary analysis and empirical review. *Psychological Bulletin, 136*(3), 351–374.

Goldin, P. R., & Jazaeiri, H. (2017). The Compassion Cultivation Training (CCT) program. In E. Seppala, E. Simon-Thomas, S. L. Brown, M. C. Worline, C. D. Cameron, & J. R. Doty (Eds.), *The Oxford handbook of compassion science* (pp. 237–246). Oxford: Oxford University Press.

Graham, H. (1983). Caring: a labour of love. In J. Finch & D. Groves (Eds.), *A labour of love: Women, work and caring.* London: Routledge.

Haidt, J. (2012). *The righteous mind: Why good people are divided by politics and religion.* London: Penguin.

Hochschild, A. (1986). *The managed heart: Commercialisation of human feeling.* Berkeley: University of California Press.

Hugman, R. (2005). *New approaches in ethics for the caring professions.* London: Palgrave.

Huppatz, K. (2009). Reworking Bourdieu's capital: Feminine and female capitals in the field of paid caring work. *Sociology, 43*(1), 45–66.

Jennings, P. A., Frank, J. L., Snowberg, K. E., Coccia, M. A., & Greenberg, M. T. (2013). Improving classroom learning environments by Cultivating Awareness and Resilience in Education (CARE): Results of a randomized controlled trial. *School Psychology Quarterly, 28*(4), 374.

Jennings, P. A., & Greenberg, M. T. (2009). The prosocial classroom: Teacher social and emotional competence in relation to student and classroom outcomes. *Review of Educational Research, 79*(1), 491–525.

Jinpa, T. (2015). *A fearless heart: How the courage to be compassionate can transform our lives.* New York, NY: Penguin.

Kirby, J. (2017). Compassion-focussed parenting. In E. Seppala, E. Simon-Thomas, S. L. Brown, M. C. Worline, C. D. Cameron, & J. R. Doty (Eds.), *The Oxford handbook of compassion science* (pp. 91–108). Oxford: Oxford University Press.

Klimecki, O., Leiberg, S., Lamm, C., & Singer, T. (2013). Functional neural plasticity and associated changes in positive affect after compassion training. *Cerebral Cortex, 23*(7), 1552–1561.

Klimecki, O., & Singer, T. (2017). The compassionate brain. In E. Seppala, E. Simon-Thomas, S. L. Brown, M. C. Worline, C. D. Cameron, & J. R. Doty (Eds.), *The Oxford handbook of compassion science* (pp. 109–120). Oxford: Oxford University Press.

Koopman-Holm, B., & Tsai, J. L. (2017). The cultural shaping of compassion. In E. Seppala, E. Simon-Thomas, S. L. Brown, M. C. Worline, C. D. Cameron, & J. R. Doty (Eds.), *The Oxford handbook of compassion science* (pp. 273–286). Oxford: Oxford University Press.

Lavelle, B. D., Flook, L., & Ghahremani, D. G. (2017). A call for compassion and care in education: Toward a more comprehensive prosocial framework for the field. In E. Seppala, E. Simon-Thomas, S. L. Brown, M. C. Worline, C. D. Cameron, & J. R. Doty (Eds.), *The Oxford handbook of compassion science* (pp. 475–486). Oxford: Oxford University Press.

Levine, R., Norenzayan, A., & Philbrick, K. (2001). Cross-cultural differences in helping strangers. *Journal of Cross-Cultural Psychology, 32*(5), 543–560.

Lloyd, G. (1984). *The man of reason: 'Male' and 'female' in western philosophy.* London: Routledge.

Marcuse, H. (1965). *One dimensional man.* London: Routledge.

McHale, J. P. (2007). When infants grow up in multiperson relationship systems. *Infant Mental Health Journal, 28*(4), 370–392.

Murray, S. B. (1998). Child care work: Intimacy in the shadows of family life. *Qualitative Sociology, 21*(2), 149–168.

Neaum, S. (2010). *Child development for early childhood studies.* Exeter: Learning Matters.

Noddings, N. (1984). *Caring: A feminine approach to ethics and moral education.* Berkeley: University of California Press.

Nussbaum, M. (2001). *Upheavals of thought: The intelligence of emotions.* Cambridge: CUP.

Osgood, J. (2004). Time to get down to business? *Journal of Early Childhood Research, 2*(1), 5–24.

Osgood, J. (2012). *Narratives from the nursery: Negotiating professional identities in early childhood.* London: Routledge.

Page, J. (2011). Do mothers want professional carers to love their babies? *Journal of Early Childhood Research, 9*(3), 310–323.

Page, J. (2018). Characterising the principles of professional love in early childhood care and education. *International Journal of Early Years Education, 26*(2), 125–141.

Papatheodorou, T., & Moyles, J. R. (2008). *Learning together in the early years: Exploring relational pedagogy.* London: Routledge.

Piff, P. K., & Moskowitz, J. P. (2017). The class-compassion gap: How socioeconomic factors influence compassion. In E. Seppala, E. Simon-Thomas, S. L. Brown, M. C. Worline, C. D. Cameron, & J. R. Doty (Eds.), *The Oxford handbook of compassion science* (pp. 317–330). Oxford: Oxford University Press.

Porges, S. W. (1998). Love: An emergent property of the mammalian autonomic nervous system. *Psychoneuroendocrinology, 23*(8), 837–861.

Read, J. (2017). Maternalist discourse in nursery nurse training at Wellgarth Nursery Training School from 1911 to 1939: Current dilemmas of class and status in historical context. *Gender and Education, 31*(2), 171–188. https://doi.org/10.1080/09540253.2017.1302076

Recchia, S. L., Shin, M., & Snaider, C. (2018). Where is the love? Developing loving relationships as an essential component of professional infant care. *International Journal of Early Years Education, 26*(2), 142–158.

Reynolds, D. (2013). Mindful parenting: A group approach to enhancing reflective capacity in parents and infants. *Journal of Child Psychotherapy, 29*(3), 357–374.

Rockliff, H., Karl, A., McEwan, K., Gilbert, J., Matos, M., & Gilbert, P. (2011). Effects of intranasal oxytocin on 'compassion focused imagery'. *Emotion, 11*(6), 1388–1396.

Rose, J., & Rogers, S. (2012). *The role of the adult in early years settings.* Maidenhead: OU Press.

Rouse, E., & Hadley, F. (2018). Where did love and care get lost? Educators and parents' perceptions of early childhood practice. *International Journal of Early Years Education, 26*(2), 159–172.

Ruddick, S. (1989). *Maternal thinking: Towards a politics of peace.* New York, NY: Beacon Press.

Sanders, M. R. (2012). Development, evaluation and multinational dissemination of the Triple P Positive Parenting Program. *Annual Review of Clinical Psychology, 8*, 1–35.

Seppala, E., Simon-Thomas, E., Brown, S. L., Worline, M. C., Cameron, C. D., & Doty, J. R. (Eds.). (2017). *The Oxford handbook of compassion science.* Oxford: Oxford University Press.

Skeggs, B. (1997). *Formations of class and gender.* London: Sage.

Skwara, A. C., King, B. G., & Saron, C. D. (2017). Studies of training compassion: What have we learnt; What remains unknown? In E. Seppala, E. Simon-Thomas, S. L. Brown, M. C. Worline, C. D. Cameron, & J. R. Doty (Eds.), *The Oxford handbook of compassion science* (pp. 219–236). Oxford: Oxford University Press.

Swain, J. E., & Ho, S. S. (2017). Parental brain: The crucible of compassion. In E. Seppala, E. Simon-Thomas, S. L. Brown, M. C. Worline, C. D. Cameron, & J. R. Doty (Eds.), *The Oxford handbook of compassion science* (pp. 65–78). Oxford: Oxford University Press.

Taggart, G. (2011). Don't we care?: The ethics and emotional labour of early years professionalism. *Early Years, 31*(1), 85–95.

Taggart, G. (2015). Sustaining care: Cultivating mindful practice in early years professional development. *Early Years: An International Journal of Research and Development, 35*(4), 381–393.

Taggart, G. (2016). Compassionate pedagogy: Ethics of care in early childhood professionalism. *European Early Childhood Education Research Journal, 24*(2), 173–185.

Taggart, G. (2019). Cultivating ethical dispositions in early childhood practice for an ethic of care: A contemplative approach. In R. Langford (Ed.), *Theorising feminist ethics of care in early childhood practice: Possibilities and dangers*. London: Bloomsbury.

Ungerson, C. (1983). Why do women care? In J. Finch & D. Groves (Eds.), *A labour of love: Women, work and caring*. London: Routledge.

Vincent, C., & Braun, A. (2010). 'And hairdressers are quite seedy ...': The moral worth of childcare training. *Contemporary Issues in Early Childhood, 11*(2), 204–214.

Webster-Stratton, C. (1998). Preventing conduct problems in Head Start children: Strengthening parenting competencies. *Journal of Consulting and Clinical Psychology, 66*, 715–730.

Welford, M., & Langmead, K. (2015). Compassion-based initiatives in educational settings. *Educational and Child Psychology, 32*(1), 71–80.

Weng, H., Fox, A. S., Shackman, A. J., Stodola, D. E., Caldwell, J. Z. K., Olson, M. C., ... Davidson, R. J. (2013). Compassion training alters altruism and neural responses to suffering. *Psychological Science, 24*(7), 1171–1180. https://doi.org/10.1177/0956797612469537

Whalley, M. (2017). New forms of provision, new ways of working – the Pen Green Centre. In Whalley, M. and the Pen Green Centre Team (Eds.), *Involving parents in their children's learning* (3rd ed.). London: Sage.

Whitebrook, M. (2002). Compassion as a political virtue. *Political Studies, 50*, 529–544.

Zarins, S., & Konrath, S. (2017). Changes over time in compassion-related variables in the United States. In E. Seppala, E. Simon-Thomas, S. L. Brown, M. C. Worline, C. D. Cameron, & J. R. Doty (Eds.), *The Oxford handbook of compassion science* (pp. 331–352). Oxford: Oxford University Press.

12

Understanding Ethics of Care

Liisa Uusimaki and Susanne Garvis

Introduction

This chapter explores compassion and ethics of care. The main challenge Swedish teachers at all levels encounter includes exceptionally high level of stress especially in supporting growing number of students with mental health challenges. Approximately 10% of Swedish children under 18 suffer from some form of mental health disorder (Socialstyrelsen, 2016). Many classroom teachers in Sweden do not have the necessary skills to care for students with mental health disorders, and it is one reason why many teachers experience stress and are leaving the profession. The realities of stress and high burnout rates among classroom teaching staff, the

L. Uusimaki (✉)
Gothenburg University, Gothenburg, Sweden
e-mail: liisa.uusimaki@gu.se

S. Garvis
Department of Education, University of Gothenburg and Stockholm University, Göteborg and Stockholm, Sweden
e-mail: susanne.garvis@gu.se

© The Author(s) 2019
G. Barton, S. Garvis (eds.), *Compassion and Empathy in Educational Contexts*,
https://doi.org/10.1007/978-3-030-18925-9_12

continuous of government reforms lack of support together with a lack of student health and welfare support staff in Sweden is indicative of a school system under stress. As an alternative response to support teachers during a sense of helplessness, professional learning courses on compassion and ethics of care can be a way to alleviate and support self-care while supporting students in their wellbeing.

The Context of Sweden

Sweden is worldwide often held up with high regard to democracy and equality. In many happiness and lifestyle rankings, Sweden, together with the other Nordic countries, is often found in the top of the indexes. Part of this has been the development of societal conditions created by laws that have been in operation for a number of years. The laws have shaped a democratic welfare society and created a culture of inclusion, especially within schooling and education. Entrenched in Swedish law, for example, is the idea of an inclusive and welcoming school for all. In the law, there is a commitment to the provision of a free comprehensive education in Sweden where 'all children, young people and adults should be given the opportunity to test and develop their ability and their skills to their full potential, irrespective of age, gender or disability' (Ministry of Education & Research, 2016). The vision is that all children, young people and adults have equal access and are treated equally in schools; the purpose of education is the building blocks for the Swedish society. As such, the laws provide a foundation on how schools should operate and how teachers should work and on the rights of children, young people and their families within schools.

While the ideas promote democratic principles, neo-liberalism and public management of schools provide a different story. While education is available for all, market forces from the free market of schools directly influence the teaching profession. There are several challenges schools face that in particular has had a negative impact on Swedish teachers and the entire profession suggesting not all is well in the Swedish education sector. Firstly, there is an acute lack of qualified classroom teachers (bachelor qualified in education), and this has seen many schools compete for qualified teachers. Schools that cannot find qualified classroom teachers resort to employing unqualified teachers to fill gaps leading to concerns about student learning. The lack of qualified teachers are mostly felt in the segregated areas with large refugee and migrant populations. The acute lack of qualified classroom teachers in Sweden has resulted in an urgent need to recruit 77,000 university qualified preschool teachers within the next five years due to population growth according to the Swedish National Agency for Education (Skolverket, 2018). This is mainly because the preschool year that came into effect in autumn 2018 became compulsory for all children in Sweden.

Secondly, there is growth of mental health disorders among students under 18, with increasing rates of anxiety and depression. Sweden similar to many other countries has noted an increase in number of students identified with mental health disorders. Approximately 10% of Swedish children under 18 suffer from some form of mental health disorder (Socialstyrelsen, 2016) with the majority of students mental health disorders identified first in schools. The increase is said to be caused by the 2015 influx of refugees, arriving in Sweden. Forty-two per cent of the 35,300 unaccompanied children met the criteria for a psychiatric diagnosis within a few months after arrival, particularly PTSD. Understandably this has caused high levels of stress among Swedish classroom teachers with many teachers choosing to leave the profession altogether and change careers. Especially, since classroom teachers do not have the specialist and necessary skills to care for students with mental health disorders.

Swedish undergraduate teacher education programmes do not offer courses in mental health disorders (Uusimaki, Garvis, & Sharma, 2018). The reason is that there is an assumption that teacher educators bring extensive experiences working with students with a variety of special needs and infuse their experiences into the different subjects they teach. However, student teachers interested in the special needs or mental health disorder can choose courses in their area of interest in addition to the compulsory subjects in the teaching degree. To work with students with special needs is generally associated to the role of the special needs teacher or a special pedagogue that requires three years of classroom teaching experience before eligibility to apply for postgraduate study. The difference between the special needs teacher and the special pedagogue is that the former works face to face with students while the special pedagogue support the leadership of a group of schools and communities organising student support where needed (Uusimaki et al., 2018).

Sadly, the respect for Swedish teachers and teaching as a profession has been declining in Sweden with half of Swedish teachers having stated that they have regretted their decision to have chosen to become teachers. OECD (2017) reports that a mere 5% of Swedish teachers believe teaching is a highly valued profession in the Swedish society in contrast to 95% of Finnish teachers. In Finland, the teaching profession enjoy status in par with doctors and lawyers. Per Kornhall explains that the low status of teachers can be traced back to the dismantling of the Swedish school system during the 1990s, a time referred to when the *Swedish school system lost its soul.*

Based on extreme public management policies, schools, once the responsibility of the Swedish government, became the responsibility of municipalities. The introduction of tax-funded private schools and a voucher system with a promise to provide parents and students real choice of schools is what has resulted in Sweden having the most marketised school system in the world. Perhaps most damaging to the teaching profession was the end to teacher salary progressions with the school principal affording powers to decide teacher salary. This has unfortunately led to teachers' swapping schools each year to ensure themselves a guaranteed salary increase, and that has had led to negative student learning outcomes. In short, consequences of the deregulation of the Swedish educational system have been a disaster for Sweden, its teachers, students and their families.

Finally, within the Swedish context, there is a concern relating to the lack of quality professional development opportunities because of budgetary constraints and a general shortage of qualified educators to deliver professional learning programmes. The lack of quality professional development programmes especially in the area of student mental health has led many teachers leaving the profession. The other reason, as already mentioned, relates to the poor salary and salary progression for experienced teachers. To improve the attractiveness of the teaching profession, there is a promise by the current Swedish government to increase financial incentives for teachers and a promise to continue to support teachers' professional development. Whether this will be enough to reignite and develop confidence among teachers remains to be seen. The realities of burnout rates among experienced teaching staff, low salaries and particularly the acute lack of qualified classroom teachers and expert student health and welfare support staff in Swedish schools are indicative of a school system under stress.

Combined, the problems in the current schooling sector create a melting pot for teachers who are trying to survive in a complex system, with too many competing agendas created from public management policies. While Sweden and Swedish educational policies and laws are to enrich democracy *of all*, the actual lived practice of teachers differs significantly. As such, we suggest a paradigm shift starting in rethinking professional development courses with a focus on teacher self-care introducing compassion and an ethically caring perspective. This may provide teachers with a sense of agency and empowerment while supporting students' learning and wellbeing.

Altruism

A way forward to support teachers to stay in the profession is to recognise the power of altruism which means *caring for others' wellbeing*, and that is often one reason why many choose to become a teacher in the first place (Uusimaki, 2010). Acknowledging, respecting and valuing altruism can support renewing teachers' sense of purpose and motivation while building societal respect for the complex work involved in teaching. Swedish teachers, like teachers worldwide, often choose teaching for altruistic reasons (Uusimaki, 2010). This means they *care* for children's and young people's learning and wellbeing. These teachers believe in the importance of fostering positive relations with not only their students but also with students' caregivers and families. Importantly, altruistic teachers are compassionate teachers who believe in social justice and the decency of human beings. Similar to teachers in other countries, Swedish classroom teachers believe schooling is a human right and schools are safe places where all children and students are welcome and have the right to succeed in their learning. These teachers believe that their role involves supporting students in their development not only emotionally and academically but also physically. In Sweden and in other Scandinavian countries inclusive, positive and caring attitude is a given and can be attributed to the values, strong cultural traditions, and above all confidence in the national policies relating to democracy, social justice and equality (Uusimaki et al., 2018). These are teachers needed in our schools and we need to encourage and empower these teachers to remain in the teaching profession. Their trust in democracy, ethics, fairness and inclusion that they infuse in their teaching practice and relationships with students are vital to the future of Sweden and in fact all nations. Unfortunately, these are also teachers more vulnerable (because of their selflessness) to manipulation by unscrupulous principals and unfair educational policies.

As authors and educators, we suggest it is important for all educational stakeholders in Sweden to reconsider the purpose of the direction of education and especially the future of the teaching profession. This means to think about how to raise the status of the teaching profession. One way may begin with perhaps rethinking the purpose of schooling, teacher salary and career progression, and ways on how professional development courses can effectively support current classroom teachers in their complex work.

The Swedish idea of study circles is a method used successfully relating to professional development of both school leaders and teachers. There is a need for teachers and school leaders to come together to discuss and reflect on current challenges, for instance, the current challenges facing refugee children, students and their families adjusting to the Swedish schooling system. The hope for outcome of all professional development course is always to improve relationships between all parties. Empowering professional development courses are those implemented with care and that in particular has a focus on renewing teacher confidence and a belief in the teaching profession being a worthwhile endeavour. Collaborative and reflective 'study circles' allow teachers opportunities to be able to step back and enjoy for a short time, experience a sense of belonging and be empowered to recognise their collective as well as personal agency.

Ethics of Care and Compassion

Rebuilding a positive, resilient and high-quality teaching force is to consider the concepts of ethics of care and compassion as necessary components in teacher education programmes and professional development courses. The ethical caring work of the teacher aligned to altruism has been and is still today ignored in educational policy. Yet it can be a powerful and decisive motivating factor in building both wellbeing and confidence among teachers. Understanding ethical caring as 'relational' provides a stronger focus on interactions and relationships. Noddings (1984) suggest it could be embedded as a form of 'care ethics', where the carer exhibits 'engrossment' in the phenomenological encounter with the 'cared-for' while experiencing 'motivational displacement' which temporarily marginalises the carers' own concerns. Such attention also allows teachers to focus on moral emotions of care and to make sense of the ethical dilemmas and be motivated in prompting and sustaining concerns. As such, care ethics allows a model of consciousness-raising that provides a space for critical and affective ways where questions focus on the socio-political reality, where the heart and head can engage together (Taggart, 2016). Such a model also provides a strong sense of motivation for teachers in the profession as their work becomes more rewarding but also respected. Bai (2014, p. 4) describes this process as 'compassionate practice' where compassion 'involves all our faculties and facilities comprising mind-body-heart-spirit part of the ontological package called human being'. Thus, ethics of care is relational and allows teachers to reflect on the nature of teaching and learning that is both inclusive and compassionate.

According to research in neuroscience, compassion is important for human beings and that we are 'hard-wired' to respond to compassion in beneficial ways. Related to the hormone oxytocin that become stimulated by the giver of the compassionate behaviour, improving the taker's stress and benefiting immune and cardiovascular systems (Gilbert, 2011). Further, upon examining mammal development, there is an unparalleled care for offspring until maturity that is not seen in other species. From such medical research, we can suggest that compassion in teaching is important for helping reduce the stress of students and helping them develop healthy lifestyles. The importance of responding to a child's or a students' needs fulfils requirements for positive development. Fox (1999) describes the link between compassion and social justice:

> Compassion being so closely allied with justice-making, requires a critical consciousness, one that resists all kinds of 'keptnesses' … It implies a going out in search of authentic problems and workable solutions, born of deeper and deeper questions. (Fox, 1999, p. 24)

Compassion we believe is at the core of social justice and closely links to teachers' altruism. Compassion allows teachers to enhance the capabilities of 'oppressed groups and also at the heart of psychological understandings about the origins of the capacity to care' (Taggart, 2016, p. 173). There is an association between compassionate teachers' own experiences of secure attachment and the development of secure attachment with children who have experienced traumatic experiences (Tosone, Bettmann, Minami, & Jasperson, 2010).

> The ability to help others is a consequence of having witnessed and benefited from good caregiving on the part of one's own attachment figures, which promotes the sense of security as a resource and provides models of good caregiving. (Gillath, Shaver, & Mikulincer, 2005, p. 9)

Compassionate pedagogy allows teachers to draw upon new paradigms to explore new ways of working, especially within the field of teacher education. For example, Taggart (2016, p. 181) notes that 'when a graduate from a programme in compassionate pedagogy acknowledges her own nervousness in meeting a new parent … she does not need pity, only understanding'. The teachers around her are also able to support her and listen to her feelings, showing and modelling an ethics of care.

Teachers' modelling compassionate and caring behaviour provides opportunities for all children and young adults to mirror compassion in their interactions with each other. Compassionate and caring schooling is an antidote towards bullying, racism and other unacceptable social behaviours currently exacerbated with the wide access and misuse of various forms of digitalisation. The reality of digitalisation is that it is causing unnecessary harm to students especially relating to mental health and hence needs to be fully explored in order to provide ways to counteract the harm. Understanding compassionate and ethical caring are antidotes to feeling overwhelmed, experiencing anxiety, stress and burnout. Compassionate and ethical caring behaviours provide not only a deep awareness of the individual's experience but also affective responses. Compassionate care is about respect, honesty, tolerance, humility and sacrifice and it effectively supports children and students' sense of wellbeing that allows for positive learning and participation in the wider community. This is in line with Noddings (2010) and the reproduction of compassionate care in schooling is a form of an incubator for adult moral life.

The serious concerns in relation to young people experiencing mental health disorders not only in Sweden but in the world are the greatest cause of disability according to World Health Organisation (2017). The questions are what is currently being done and what can be done to prevent and to support these young people during their schooling especially with teachers themselves experiencing stress and burnout. We have provided suggestions that one way forward is providing more learning for teachers around ethics of care and compassion. This approach provides possibilities for teachers to find ways to support themselves, as well as young people in their classrooms. A focus on professional learning also provides new ways to understand the problem of mental health disorders in the world and develop real-world solutions.

Professional Learning Courses

To support ethical care and compassion among student teachers and teachers working in schools, there are different models that may be considered. We believe that professional learning can start with workshops in teacher education programmes, as well as professional learning workshops for working teachers.

One starting point for professional learning is allowing teachers space and time for reflection on their own values and beliefs of working as teachers. Swick and Brown (1999, p. 116) suggest the following questions when working with teacher education students about becoming teachers are also valuable when working with classroom teachers in the field:

- What values and beliefs am I carrying into my relationships with children, students, parents and my colleagues?
- Who am I becoming as person who will spend significant time with people who will be our future?

These are questions designed to trigger reflections about individual assumptions and emotions towards experiences of care. Reflective questions also provide opportunities for teachers and student teachers to validate their journey towards becoming caring and compassionate individuals. Compassion is viewed as a behaviour that can be learnt, or as put by Gilbert (2011, p. 432):

> Compassionate skills are things that we can practice and work on by deliberately making choices. We can learn to pay compassionate attention, to think compassionately, to engage in compassionate behaviour and practise compassionate feelings.

We suggest that the questions could be used not only in teacher education, but with all teaching staff in a school. Ethics and ethical training in schools involve compassion and ethics of care, where teachers must engage the emotions (Taggart, 2016). They could be implemented in staff meetings, school meetings and general professional learning opportunities to try and understand the purpose of teaching and begin to focus on compassion and ethics of care. The questions provide a platform for a shared understanding of altruistic beliefs and provide a sharing of perspective to develop a common set of values around relationships.

Ongoing Professional Development

The purpose of all professional development courses is to provide teachers' support and empowerment in meeting the ongoing educational needs and changes of society. The challenges of digitalisation in particular have meant new ways of understanding and approaching learning. Digitalisation has also meant a multitude of new challenges for both students and teachers that will continue to require ongoing learning. Perhaps the most important reason for all professional development is about relationship building to encourage collaboration to break the isolation still experienced by many teachers. Well-developed workshops that move beyond superficial professional learning are those that inspire, empower and engage all participants to continue learning. Particularly empowering professional development courses are those encouraging consciousness-raising that is a participator process where teachers are encouraged to share openly their feelings and experiences. Consciousness-raising contributes to powerful learning experiences and empowerment of teacher selves (Uusimaki, 2013).

There are several principles involved in the development of consciousness-raising and relational workshops that develop continuous learning (Uusimaki, 2013):

- Nonthreatening and inclusive learning environment
- Respect for the individual teacher as a knower
- Facilitation of a constructivist perspective of knowing and learning
- Provision of learning activities that relate to the teacher's personal and professional experiences, for example, case studies drawn from real-life teaching experiences, brainstorming activities
- Provision of opportunities to openly collaborate in discussion to promote (re)construction of personal epistemological beliefs.

Responses from the different activities presented in consciousness-raising courses are not to provide right or wrong answers or absolute truths; rather they provide a springboard for further discussion among participants and or for individual reflection. These discussions allow a sense of belonging, whether sharing personal values, beliefs or experiences. The sharing of intimate knowledge also develops a sense of care between teachers as they begin to discuss key points of time that have meant something to them in their teaching careers and played an important catalyst for an action to occur out of the experience.

Swedish Study Circles

One particular approach used commonly in Sweden is 'study circles'. 'Study circles' originated in the USA and was established in Lund, Sweden, in 1902 by Oscar Olsson known as the *father of the study circle* (Bjerkaker, 2014), where it spread to other Nordic countries. The popularity of 'study circles' is that it is a democratic and emancipatory method with the aim to promote societal change. Learning is at the core of study circles especially collaborative learning, and means learning is dependent on the interaction between learners. Study circles have generally between 6 and 12 participants. The work or issues of interest/concerns are determined by the participants themselves and with each responsible to participate in the knowledge building and sharing. Study circles have shown to be highly effective as a method for teacher professional development courses, university research partnerships, organisations, unions, political parties, communities and so on.

There are several principles underpinning study circle; see Table 12.1.

The principles related to *study circles* promote learning and similar to consciousness-raising can bring about change to behaviour. The principles of study circles guidelines based on democracy where open discussions and hearing all voices encourage a sense of community. In the Swedish context, we suggest that more schools and teacher education programmes implement study circles with a focus on compassion and ethics of care. We believe that this allows for a first step of inclusive professional learning and development of a learning culture based on caring relationship building. The concept of study circles may also be relevant for other countries interested in developing democratic professional learning methods to support teachers in understanding ethics of care and compassion.

Table 12.1 Study circle principles (modified from Bjerkaker, 2014)

Principle	Action
Equality and democracy among circle members	All members acting at one time as both teachers and students, reliance on dialogue and conversation rather than on lectures, outside experts or formal presentations
Liberation of members' inherent capabilities and innate resources	Empowerment to act, to influence and be influenced by social reality
Cooperation and companionship	Members working together towards agreed goals, finding 'common ground' in relationships and ideas
Study and liberty, and member self-determination	Free choice of formats and direction, based on needs and wishes and on the objectives of the sponsoring association
Continuity and planning	Providing time for conversations—all member voices are heard to overcome 'one-sidedness', withdrawal of individuals' and undue pushing of one's point of view, along with emphasis on creating interest in further study This also means planning by the members themselves, who have the ability to change plans as the need arises
Active member participation	Cooperation, joint responsibility and conversation, 'the members' active contribution is the cornerstone of democracy.... People learn best when they are active'
Use of printed study materials	Brochures, journal articles, newspaper articles, scientific texts and so on used as supplement circle conversations

Conclusion

The chapter has argued that the implementation of compassion and ethics of care in professional development courses is necessary in response to teacher stress and burnout and promotion of self-care. Without adequate training and support, it is difficult for teachers to care for others if they do not have the knowledge of self-care. We thus advocate for focused professional courses in the Swedish context on compassion and an ethics of care among stressed and burnout practicing classroom teachers.

To counteract the low status of the Swedish teacher calls for an urgent need for a paradigm shift that recognise and respect the complex work of teachers. This needs to begin with raising the status of the teaching profession through the acknowledgement of teachers' reasons for choosing teaching as a career and not be subject to feelings of choosing a lower profession because of low societal comments. Secondly, real financial incentives for all qualified teachers together with real opportunities for career progression and professional learning opportunities. Teachers should be supported and encouraged in their important work caring for their students' learning and wellbeing, as well as given adequate space to reflect on their own health and wellbeing. Part of this is providing time and space for ongoing professional development where they have opportunities to continue to reflect on their own ethics of care and sense of compassion. Ethics of care and compassion we believe are important characteristics for teachers in contemporary times and must be fostered from the beginning of teacher education and continue throughout their teaching career.

It is important to reflect on the systematic level when thinking about the schooling system in Sweden, especially from the level of policy that has led to many of the associated problems for teachers and students. For example, quick-fix solutions do not work; they never do, whether this relate to addressing the shortage of qualified teaching staff by allowing unqualified staff to work as teachers in Swedish schools or classroom teachers overworked and clearly stressed battling to meet the educational needs of refugee and immigrant students. The consequences are causing harm both to student learning and wellbeing including their teacher.

Unqualified teaching staff contribute further to the workload of qualified teachers that in turn only exacerbate the already high levels of stress. The problem in Sweden therefore has nothing to do with teachers' commitment to the teaching profession or caring for their students' learning and wellbeing, rather the problem relates to public management ideals and reforms that have led to individually negotiated and low teacher salaries. These together with a reliance on the goodwill and altruistic nature of teachers have led Swedish a vast number of quality teachers to exit the profession.

As authors, we strongly believe in aligning compassion and an ethics of care in official policy in recognition and acknowledgement of teacher's altruistic reasons for choosing teaching as a career (Uusimaki, 2010). Such a policy can be a start of a new way to restore both the status and confidence of the teaching profession not only among would-be teachers and teachers in the profession but also among members of the Swedish society. Most importantly, such a policy will be a way of restoring faith among children, students and their families in schooling. So let us start the education revolution by refocusing on compassion and ethics of care as centre stage.

References

Bai, H. (2014). Editorial introduction to special themed issue: Working compassion. *Paideusis: The Journal of the Canadian Philosophy of Education Society, 21*(2), 2–4.

Bjerkaker, S. (2014). Changing communities. The study circle – for learning and democracy. *Procedia – Social and Behavioral Sciences, 142*, 260–267.

Fox, M. (1999). *A spirituality named compassion*. San Francisco: Bear and Co.

Gilbert, P. (2011). Historical spiritual and evolutionary approaches to suffering, compassion, caring and the caring professions. In P. Gilbert (Ed.), *Spirituality and mental health* (pp. 1–20). Brighton: Pavilion.

Gillath, O., Shaver, P. R., & Mikulincer, M. (2005). An attachment-theoretical approach to compassion and altruism. In P. Gilbert (Ed.), *Compassion: It's nature and use in psychotherapy* (pp. 121–147). London: Routledge.

Ministry of Education & Research. (2016). *Towards an outstanding knowledge nation with equal education and world class research*. Swedish Government, Reference No. Article: U16.005.

Noddings, N. (1984). *Caring: A feminine approach to ethics and moral education.* Berkeley: University of California Press.

Noddings, N. (2010). *The maternal factor: Two paths to morality.* Berkeley: University of California Press.

OECD. (2017). *Education policy outlook: Sweden. European Commission.* Retrieved from http://www.oecd.org/education/Education-Policy-Outlook-Country-Profile-Sweden.pdf

Skolverket. (2018). *Stort Behov av Fler Lärare.* Skolverket. Retrieved from https://www.skolverket.se/om-oss/press/pressmeddelanden/pressmeddelanden/2017-12-18-stort-behov-av-fler-larare

Socialstyrelsen. (2016). *Utvecklingen av Psykisk Ohälsa bland Barn och Unga Vuxna.* Socialstyrelsen. Stockholm.

Swick, K. J., & Brown, M. H. (1999). The caring ethic in early childhood teacher education. *Journal of Instructional Psychology, 26*(2), 1116–1120.

Taggart, G. (2016). Compassionate pedagogy: The ethics of care in early childhood professionalism. *European Early Childhood Education Research Journal, 24*(2), 173–185.

Tosone, C., Bettmann, J. E., Minami, T., & Jasperson, R. A. (2010). New York City social workers after 9/11: Their attachment, resiliency, and compassion fatigue. *International Journal of Emergency Mental Health, 12*(2), 103–116.

Uusimaki, L. S. (2010). *Pre-service teacher education and the development of middle school teacher identity: An exploratory study.* Queensland University of Technology (QUT), Brisbane, QLD, Australia.

Uusimaki, L. (2013). Empowering pre-service teacher supervisors' perspectives: A relational-cultural approach towards mentoring. *Australian Journal of Teacher Education, 38*(7), 44–58.

Uusimaki, L. Garvis, S. & Sharma, U. (2018, December). Swedish early childhood pre-service teachers' intensions, attitudes and concerns for engagement in inclusive classrooms. *Journal of International Special Needs Education, 21*(2). Retrieved from http://jisne.org/toc/spne/0/0

World Health Organization. (2017). *Depression and other common mental disorders: Global health estimates.* Retrieved from https://apps.who.int/iris/bitstream/handle/10665/254610/WHO-MSD-MER-2017.2-eng.pdf;jsessionid=3FB61D790DBA302F4896E6BC4FA86EC5?sequence=1

Part V

Compassion and Empathy in Different Educational Contexts

13

Empathy and the Landscape of Conflict

Margaret Baguley and Martin Kerby

Introduction

In early August 2018, the Toowoomba Regional Art Gallery (TRAG) in Queensland opened a group exhibition titled *Landscape and Memory: Frank Hurley and a Nation Imagined*. The artworks created by the eight invited artists responded to official war photographer Frank Hurley's iconic images taken on the Western Front and in the Middle East in 1917 and 1918. The approach adopted by the artists was framed by the work of Samuel Hynes who argued that though the First World War was without doubt the major political and military event of the age, it was also a "great imaginative event", one which "altered the ways in which men and women thought not only about war but about the world, and about culture and its expressions" (Hynes, 1990, p. xi). This imagining is a version of the war "that confirms a set of attitudes, an idea of what the war was and what it meant" (Hynes, 1990, p. xi). Such an historical imagining is

M. Baguley (✉) • M. Kerby
University of Southern Queensland, Brisbane, QLD, Australia
e-mail: margaret.baguley@usq.edu.au; martin.kerby@usq.edu.au

© The Author(s) 2019
G. Barton, S. Garvis (eds.), *Compassion and Empathy in Educational Contexts*,
https://doi.org/10.1007/978-3-030-18925-9_13

not, however, synonymous with falsehood; instead, it refers to the layers of cultural meaning that over time encase an historical event (Badsey, 2009).

The exhibition had its genesis in a series of research and artistic initiatives led by Martin Kerby, one of the curators of *Landscape and Memory: Frank Hurley and a Nation Imagined*, and Margaret Baguley, one of the eight artists. These included two children's picture books (Kerby, Tuppurainen-Mason, Baguley, & Lynch, 2017; O'Reilly, Eldridge, Tuppurainen-Mason, & Kerby, 2015), research into Australian Children's Picture books and the First World War (Kerby, Baguley, & MacDonald, 2019; Kerby, Baguley, MacDonald, & Lynch, 2017), a Sound and Light Show, military dioramas and a series of tapestries (St Joseph's Nudgee College, 2015), an International Handbook on cultural and artistic responses to war (Kerby, Baguley, & McDonald, 2018) and a State Library of Queensland Fellowship for Kerby (2018/19). Across each of these projects, it became increasingly clear that the way artists and writers present war is shaped not so much by first-hand experience or deep historical knowledge but by other cultural artefacts. In Samuel Hynes' words, the artworks offer an imagining that is created and subsequently viewed through the prism of decades, sometimes centuries of cultural meaning. Even in the case of some of the children's picture books, when authors and artists proclaimed their pacifism, they almost universally retained a clear fidelity to the major tropes regarding the presentation of Australia and Australians at war. Central to these tropes is the experience of trauma and the desire to inculcate in viewers a sense of empathy and compassion.

The Exhibition

In a re-imagining of the battlefields of the First World War as envisaged for the *Landscape and Memory: Frank Hurley and a Nation Imagined* exhibition, Hurley's photographs were a natural starting point. His images of the lunar landscape of the Western Front and later in the Middle East have made a significant contribution to the national imagining of the conflict. These "immortal pictures" have long ago ceased to be merely a record of events and instead have "flow[n] into history" (Bickel, 1980, pp. 8–9). In some respects, they have *become* history. This is particularly true of the images of the Third Battle of Ypres in late 1917 which have almost come to exert a greater cultural influence than the event itself. For despite the fact that the Australian Imperial Force (AIF) suffered 38,000 casualties in the space of six weeks, it occupies a strangely ambiguous place in the collective memory:

> [The] battles of 1917—Bullecourt, Messines, Menin Road, Polygon Wood, perhaps even Passchendaele—elude popular cultural imagination. Ghastly though they were, they lacked the form, drama and sense of place that shape a strong heroic narrative. They presented no scaling of cliffs, no climatic moment like the charge at the Nek. They gave centre stage not to courageous individuals—though there were plenty of these—but to artillery, poison gas, air power, and all the other lethal technology of mass industrial warfare. (Beaumont, 2013, p. 391)

Even Charles Bean, the official historian and founder of the Australian War Memorial (AWM), consigned Ypres to the "periphery of that prevailing narrative of the war, the Anzac legend" (Haultain-Gall, 2016, p. 137). Bookended by Gallipoli (1915) and Pozières (1916) and the victory at Villers-Bretonneux (1918), 1917 remains "the year in between" (Gammage, 1983, p. xxv). Yet Hurley's images *are* the Western Front for many Australians. As Wilfred Owen's poetry did for the United Kingdom, Hurley's work speaks to Australians of the pity of war.

Yet this does not mean that our national mythology has remained static, for as Stephens (2012) observes, it is in fact even now being rewritten. Globalisation, multiculturalism, a newly resurgent nationalism, the ongoing debates about national identity and a population that has, in the main, no first-hand experience of war have combined to create a fertile environment for a re-imagining of the Anzac legacy. Though the experience of war is increasingly imagined as both an individual and a national trauma, it nevertheless remains a powerful expression of identity:

> During the 1920s and 1930s, a 'cult of the fallen' sat at the heart of Australia's national culture of commemoration of the First World War.1 War memorials faithfully honoured the 'glorious dead' and Anzac Day remembrance services paid tribute to the men who died overseas having

'given birth to the nation'. Such traditions emerged to assist bereaved families to grieve in the absence of a body and to preserve memories of the 60,000 battlefield dead and their 'supreme sacrifice'. (Larsson, 2009, p. 79)

In the 1960s and 1970s, just as it appeared that the Anzac story was in a "state of terminal decline, anachronistic, patriarchal, militaristic and irrelevant" (Beaumont, 2011, p. 7) and ready it would seem, to "wither away" (Inglis, 1998, p. 9), it experienced a startling reinvigoration. The imagining of a "kinder, gentler Anzac" that emerged during this period transformed the Anzac mythology from one "grounded in beliefs about racial identity and martial capacity to a legend that speaks in the modern idiom of trauma, suffering and empathy" (Holbrook, 2016, p. 19). It was not, however, a process that occurred, and continues to occur, in a vacuum, for it is part of broader societal shifts in the way Australian history is imagined:

Australians live now in a culture saturated with traumatic memories and understandings of victimhood that incite profound sympathy and give voice to those who have suffered. Think only of the stolen generations and the forgotten Australians. Their stories have changed the way Australians view history, which is more often than not seen as a wound or scar that leaves a trace on a nation's soul. (Twomey, 2015, para. 17)

There have, nevertheless, been various other factors identified as driving the "astonishing revival" of Anzac Day (Kelly, 2011) and of the growing popularity of "pilgrimages" to Gallipoli: an increasing interest in family and community history (Holbrook, 2014; Scates, 2006); its appeal as a civic religion (Inglis, 1998) or as an expression of displaced Christianity (Billings, 2015); its status as "a sacred parable we dare not question" (McKenna, 2007); an expression of the commerce and politics of nationalism (McKenna & Ward, 2007); the impact of a grand narrative that emphasises the role of Australian military engagements and the Anzac spirit in shaping the nation (Lake, 2010); proof of a "hunger for meaning", a "craving for ritual" and a "search for transcendence" (Scates, 2006, p. xx). The paradox in its recuperative character is inescapable, for this "muscular resurgence" has come just as "Australia became less British, more multicultural, less militaristic, [and] more open to feminine influence" (Kelly, 2011, para. 5). Yet for a narrative such as this is to survive, and in this case thrive, it must, as Twomey (2013, para. 7) reminds us, "speak to deeply held concerns and obsessions of the culture. Trauma is one of them". Central to this is the place of compassion and empathy, for it is something we can all experience. It allows war to engender an emotional reaction in those who have not experienced it first-hand. As McKenna and Ward (2007) observe, however, it is often ahistorical. It also raises the question of language, one that each of the artists needed to confront and overcome. For though each was convinced of the horror of war and sought to varying degrees to generate a sense of empathy in their viewers, their work threatened to be overwhelmed by the same clichés they sought to subvert:

> The coinage has been worn so thin that its value seems only marginally greater than 'Glory', 'Sacrifice' or 'Pro Patria', which 'horror' condemns as counterfeit. The phrase 'horror of war' has become so automatic a conviction that it conveys none of the horror it is meant to express. (Dyer, 1995, p. 27)

Although the exact causes driving the reinvigoration of Anzac are open to debate, both the Anzac story and its legacy command widespread allegiance (Donoghue & Tranter, 2015). Successive Australian governments from both the Left and the Right have been far from parsimonious in their funding of commemorative activities for the centenary of the First World War (Kerby, Baguley, & Tuppurainen-Mason, 2016). Over the course of four years, the public and private sectors have committed upwards of $600 million dollars, 5 times the amount spent by the government of the United Kingdom, 17 times higher than New Zealand, and 92 times that of the German commitment. It was, as Joan Beaumont (2013) observed, nothing short of a memory orgy. Though Christina Twomey (2013) suggested quite rightly that empathy generated by the appeal of trauma is an uncertain basis for national unity, her observation that by 2015 "we might all be suffering from compassion fatigue" (para. 21) has proved unduly pessimistic. That said, as Anna Clark (2017) posits, in spite of the Anzac legacy's significance in the nation's collective memory, it "has generated a commemorative space more complex and uncertain than public and official demonstrations of Anzac pride suggest" (p. 25).

Curator Martin Kerby was well aware of the evolution in the Anzac mythology, coming as he does from a history rather than arts background:

> I am politically conservative and have a longstanding affection for grand historical paintings, though I will admit to a certain weakness for British modernists like Paul Nash and CRW Nevinson. I was conscious therefore that my world view was almost inevitably going to be at odds with the artists' political and artistic predilections. I could be confident from the outset, however, that the artists were extremely unlikely to offer a celebratory or jingoistic take on Hurley's work, whatever the unspoken pressure exerted by the broader commemorative drive. Each artwork, from the most abstract to the most realistic, instead communicates something about trauma, and then by extension, inculcates a sense of empathy and compassion in the viewer.

Janet McDonald, the co-curator, is from an arts background, and though well able to draw on historical context, her expertise provided a clear theoretical framework that complemented Kerby's approach where possible and broadened it where necessary:

> The empathy that can be drawn from the contemplation of artworks can be transformative to the individual, particularly if they arouse the Aristotelian concepts of "pity and fear". Pity that we understand the feeling of pain in others, and fear that the same can and may happen to the reader at any given moment. The realisation of compassion and intellectual considerations of art are powerful empathetic tools that can be utilised by artists in the making of their work that gives voice to the suffering of others.

In particular, McDonald is cognisant both of the exhibition's capacity to interrogate and at times subvert widely held beliefs. In doing so, the viewer is asked to re-empathise with the familiar tropes of the First World War. More broadly, she also observes that:

the power of the artworks to invoke, evoke, provoke reactions and memories that transform the recollections of a war that no one alive today actually experienced [in 1914] is at the heart of the intersubjective connection that art can provide.

As the images of the artworks show, the artists did not seek to replicate Hurley's work. Instead, each worked from a photographic image as a starting point, layered as it is with historical memory, and created intensely personal interpretations shaped by and for a contemporary audience (Kerby & McDonald, 2018). In doing so, they acknowledge that the power of art is not constrained by the form of objects:

> [It] also comes in giving space to the formless possibility of what might be: to stop and pause and allow consideration of other outcomes from those that might have originally been intended, and to risk that this new path might be useless. (Siegesmund, 2013, p. 306)

Each of the artists disassembled and deconstructed Hurley's images in their search for other outcomes and in doing so reasserted art education's origins as a field of re-imaginings (Baldacchino, 2012). By creating spaces where silenced individuals might be heard, the artists, and by extension their audience, "develop an empathetic capacity to attend to their stillness" (Siegesmund, 2013, p. 306). In attending to the stillness, the artists did not need to subvert the broad trends in the Australian re-imagining of the conflict, but instead at times they subconsciously mimicked it.

The Artwork

Michael Armstrong, himself a veteran of the wars in Afghanistan and Iraq, does not consider himself a war artist. But in exploring trauma, and by extension compassion and empathy, he is engaging with the very issues that now pervade war commemoration. He submerges the drawn figures of Australian soldiers in beeswax, rendering them as silhouetted forms, stripped of their individual identity by mass industrialised warfare (Fig. 13.1). In creating these images, Armstrong has become both the viewer and the viewed:

Fig. 13.1

> What we see is not so much a landscape, but a self-portrait. By distorting and concealing the soldiers' individual forms, Armstrong also compels the viewer to see in their struggle, the struggle of all soldiers in all wars … As a veteran, Armstrong knows that each soldier will eventually wage their own war, one that will know no peace. (Kerby & McDonald, 2018)

Armstrong's exploration of this "troglodyte world" (Fussell, 1977, p. 36) prevents the viewer engaging with it as a patriotic endeavour let alone an historical record. It is instead a profoundly human exploration of suffering. One is able to metaphorically join the soldiers on their advance—or retreat?—to empathise with their stoic acceptance that they are actors on a stage with limited agency, seeking survival amidst a "new kind of infinity: more of the same in every direction, an infinity of waste" (Dyer, 1995, p. 119).

Anne Smith's *Lest We Forget* (Fig. 13.2) is also a deeply compassionate take on the experience of veterans, both those who survived and those who did not. Like Erich Maria Remarque's dedication in his clas-

Fig. 13.2

sic *All Quiet on the Western Front*, her artwork is neither "an accusation nor a confession, and least of all an adventure, for death is not an adventure to those who stand face to face with it". It is instead two veterans, one of the Second World War and the other Vietnam, interposed on an image of a First World War cemetery. Having faced death, the veterans scan the cemetery for the names of lost comrades, or perhaps their own:

> They mourn for a world now lost, but it is melancholy, rather than grief that Smith explores. For though the landscape has been touched by war, it is not overshadowed by it. The sun continues to shine on this sunburnt country, as the presence of Ian's grandson Cody, protectively placed between the two veterans, makes clear. (Kerby & McDonald, 2018)

Like many of the artists, indeed perhaps all of them, Smith who is an ex-service woman with the Women's Royal Australian Air Force is both subject to the broader emphasis on trauma, compassion and empathy and a fervent contributor to it. She recalled that after the first photoshoot with Ian and George her husband (also an ex-serviceman) quoted the poem "Ode of the Fallen Soldier" acknowledging that it was "an extremely emotional and bonding experience" (Lamb, 2018, para. 10).

Smith was overwhelmed by the sadness of the Hurley work which documented a visit to a cemetery in 1917 by soldiers presumably paying their respects to fallen comrades:

I had this strong sense that the fallen soldiers indicated in Frank Hurley's image were not forgotten and whilst laid to rest far away in Belgium, in a foreign environment, they would remain forever an integral part of the Australian landscape. The enduring impact of conflict is that no community in Australia is left untouched by the impact of the sacrifice made by their youth going to war. Images such as Frank Hurley's engender a sense of empathy which ensures the sacrifice and suffering of all those who have served and those that were left behind will never be forgotten. 'Lest we forget'.

The story of the two veterans featured in Smith's artwork, Mr George Gnezdilff and Ian Lade, "captured the hearts of media all over Australia" (Loftus & Lamb, 2018, p. 4) when they travelled from Proserpine to Toowoomba by car, a round trip of 24 hours, to attend the exhibition opening in person. In their exhibition speeches, they both mentioned how important it was for them to attend and represent their fellow servicemen who did not return home.

Garry Dolan also explores compassion and empathy, and though his artwork is tied to a specific site, in this case, the Australian National Memorial at Villers-Bretonneux, the major memorial to Australians killed on the Western Front, it is nevertheless able to transcend the particularities of place (Fig. 13.3). As trauma and suffering are universal experiences, the capacity of an artwork such as this to engender a sense of compassion and empathy among viewers is unhindered by context. Its power is certainly shaped by the pervasiveness of the Anzac mythology, but anyone who has experienced loss can engage with the artwork at a visceral level untied to the obvious historical context. Yet Dolan softens the blow:

He brings order to the chaos, perhaps even the triumph of man over nature. For here, Nature is brought under control. The land has healed and youth has returned, flowers are in bloom, and the sun is soft and nurturing. There is a promise of regeneration in *Villers-Bretonneux* and in his triptych *Bullecourt* [Figs. 13.4, 13.5, and 13.6], perhaps even resurrection. (Kerby & McDonald, 2018)

Fig. 13.3

Fig. 13.4

Fig. 13.5

Fig. 13.6

In *The Weight of the World* (Fig. 13.7), David Usher explores similar ideas but in an abstract form. His abstract landscape, which was deliberately large in order to focus on the extremes of death and suffering, seeks a balance between the man-made desolation and the sanguinity of survival and new life. While Usher acknowledges the "destructive nature of mankind's belligerent treatment of each other and the environment, this work explores themes of healing the scars of the earth and the phenomenal resilience of nature and its capacity to adapt and renew" (personal correspondence). Like the other artworks, Usher both draws on and subverts the widely held belief that the Australian people share a special relationship with the land.

Abbey MacDonald's triptych *Act 1: Recast the victims and villains, Act 2: Replay the scene* and *Act 3: Rebuild the stage* (Figs. 13.8, 13.9, and 13.10) are born of the same empathy and compassion that it seeks to

Fig. 13.7

Fig. 13.8

engender. The artist is unapologetic in acknowledging that her own background shaped her response in a far more profound manner than Hurley's photographs:

> I draw from the repertoire of my fortunate position of distance, pulling together disparate yet familiar threads that span my experience as learner, teacher, child and mother in relation to war. I dip back to my time as an art school undergrad, all at once locked in and fortuitously locked out of a dialogue with Otto Dix's *Wounded Soldier* (1924) … and this seeps into my own embodied renderings.

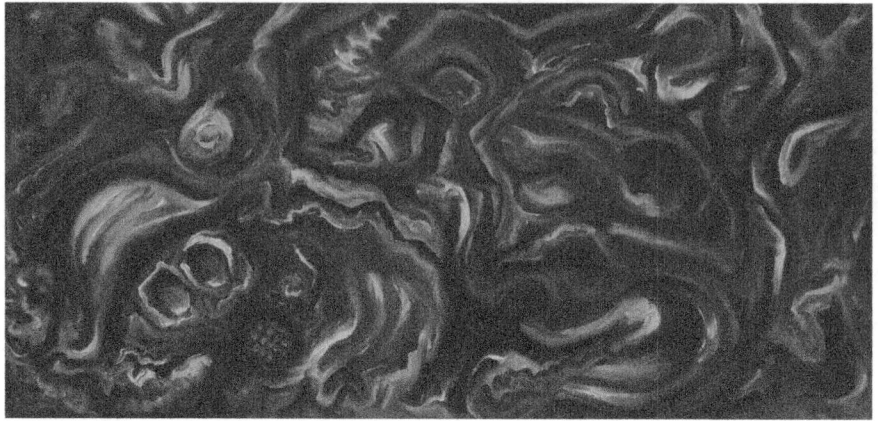

Fig. 13.9

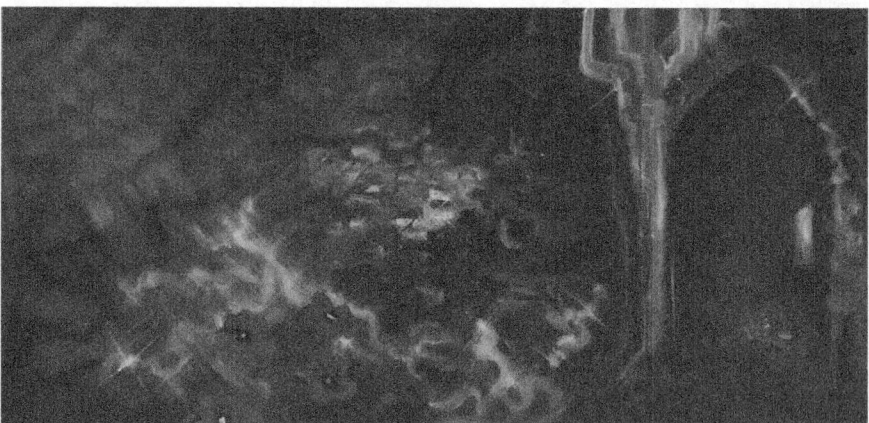

Fig. 13.10

MacDonald's artwork is, as she also acknowledges, shaped by the contemporary refugee crisis and the media's "visual saturations of tiny bodies washing up on the shores of beaches in North Africa". She personalises her response, unashamedly so, by "wondering what I myself would do as a mother facing an impossible choice". The very universality of loss and trauma ensures that viewers can respond almost in spite of context. Compassion and empathy do not need to be informed, for "there is no truth, only representations of it" (personal correspondence).

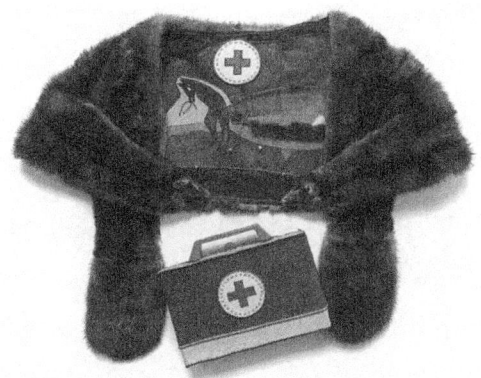

Fig. 13.11

The belief that history is a construct is also explored by Beata Batorowicz in *(A)mending WWI History* (Fig. 13.11). The artwork serves as both a residue of history while at the same time serving as a reminder of the very constructed nature of history itself, or in the words of Samuel Hynes, a re-imagining. The reference to first aid kits engenders a sense of compassion and empathy in the viewer by reminding them that the cost of the war was and is to be found not merely in the fact that "the whole circuit of the Earth is girdled with the graves of our dead" (King George VI, *The Times*, 15 May 1922). Added to "this massed multitude of silent witnesses to the desolation of war" which so moved the King on a pilgrimage to the battlefields in 1922 were the millions wounded and scared by the experience of war. In a time when post-traumatic stress disorder (PTSD) is increasingly recognised, Batorowicz encourages the viewer to decontextualise her artwork, remove it from the mud of Flanders in 1917, and seek contemporary connections and understandings.

Neville Heywood's *Ypres Sector: Belgium 25 Oct 1917* (Fig. 13.12) balances an awareness of trauma as a central motif in Australian artistic and cultural responses to war with a conventionally patriotic sensibility. He sees the Australian soldier not just the victim of a world "in turmoil, unreal, nightmarish, traumatizing and despoiled by conflict" but of the shortcomings of his own society. He argues that "frequently the tragedies of war as they affected Australian soldiers were directly linked with poor decisions, poor leadership and insufficient preparation". Indeed, he is

Fig. 13.12

named in memory of an uncle who died on March 15, 1943, along with 13 others at Moora in Western Australia during infantry training. Yet Heywood still sees value in that sacrifice despite acknowledging the waste:

> I find that the mark of returned soldiers is they do not glorify war, but value life and family and mates and the hope that it will never happen again. But it always does—and will wherever there are 'bully' countries that take nations down that path. Freedom's price is to resist that aggression at all costs.

As with a good deal of Australian war commemoration, Heywood's work is an overt honouring of sacrifice pervaded by a spirituality that is not necessarily a conscious artistic choice:

> In my art I was trying also to honour those who underwent war's horrors in service of home and country. In doing this, my paintings are an attempt to bring a spiritual dimension to the struggle and chaos of war … Hurley's generation gave sixty thousand lives in service of their country—sixty

Fig. 13.13

thousand sacrificed for a freedom that mattered and matters just as profoundly today. Sky earth and flowers bear testimony to the generations that followed.

In contrast to the peripheral importance of context displayed by the other artworks, Margaret Baguley's *It Came Upon a Midday Clear—The Battle of Jerusalem 1917* (Fig. 13.13) is firmly grounded in historical understanding. Yet even that is deceptive, despite the title placing the artwork firmly in the penultimate year of the First World War:

> She transcends that singular moment by acknowledging Jerusalem as a site of almost ceaseless warfare. Major battles are noted on each of the nine 3D printed tiles which when considered individually emphasise the contested ownership of the city and its religious and political significance for three of the world's great monotheistic religions. When considered in total, however, the tiles emphasise the profound power of each group's imagining of Jerusalem. (Kerby & McDonald, 2018)

Conclusion

The German sculptor Käthe Kollwitz (1867–1945) completed a double sculpture in 1931 revealing two figures (herself and her husband) kneeling in grief from the loss of their son in the opening months of the First

World War. Entitled *The Grieving Parents*, the statues were later placed in the Vladslo military cemetery where their son Peter is buried. Yet the narrow designation of sculptor does not do her justice, for she was "a visual poet of the human body", who as a sculptor, as a lithographer, as a woodcut designer and as a draughtswoman produced "visceral art, the art of suffering etched on human bodies" (Winter, 2017). Yet it was more than her private grief and guilt that pervades her work:

> She recognized that she was expressing something greater than her own feelings and that her art could only function if it served an entire society. Grief and loss are universal feelings that bind us, and sharing them with others leads to consolation and social transformation. (Seed, 2017, para. 2)

As Jay Winter (2017) observes, and as the curator Martin Kerby can attest, the cemetery at Vladslo is so often so wet with rain and mist that the figure Kollwitz sculpted of herself appears to shed tears. There is an element of accusation at play, both personal and general. Having given permission for her son to enlist, Kollwitz's complicity is acknowledged in a work that remains "a unique expression of the guilt of the elder generation, who had nothing to offer the young other than mass death and mutilation" (Winter, 2017, p. 257). Kollwitz's work was later labelled by the Nazis as degenerate, which was hardly surprising given their censorious view of the kind of empathy that Kollwitz's work promotes. For even now, it retains the power to stir deep feelings of loss which can "lead to collective introspection … to resistance against authoritarian politicians and those who advocate war and other forms of sacrifice and suffering" (Seed, 2017, para. 2).

The First World War is a particularly pertinent example of a time and place in history that begets much rememoration through artistic practice. The empathy produced by Kollwitz is an example of the kind of intersubjective connection that creative and cultural practices can emote/provoke in both the artists who make them and their audiences. The imaginative "projecting [of] oneself into the object of contemplation" can be profound, though it is "not always reducible to language" (Reynolds & Reason, 2012, pp. 19, 320). The Anzac mythology, "with its boy soldiers and its emaciated prisoners of war, is a story that resonates with the tenor of our times" (Twomey 2013, para. 18); hence an exhibition by contemporary artists, only two of whom possess a deep knowledge of Australia's wartime heritage, was well able to balance a respect for an inherently conservative mythology with a desire to create art that was little short of an act of empathetic understanding.

References

Baldacchino, J. (2012). *Art's Way Out: Exit pedagogy and the cultural condition.* Rotterdam: Sense.

Badsey, S. (2009). *The British Army in battle and its image 1914–1918.* London: Continuum.

Beaumont, J. (2013). *Broken nation: Australians in the Great War.* Sydney, NSW: Allen & Unwin.

Beaumont, J. (2011). The Second War in every respect: Australian memory and the Second World War. *Journal of Military and Strategic Studies, 14*(1), 1–14.

Bickel, L. (1980). *In search of Frank Hurley.* Melbourne, VIC: Macmillan.

Billings, B. (2015). Is Anzac Day an incidence of 'Displaced Christianity? *Pacifica, 28*(3), 229–242.

Clark, A. (2017). The place of Anzac in Australian historical consciousness. *Australian Historical Studies, 48,* 19–34.

Dyer, G. (1995). *The missing of the Somme.* London: Penguin.

Fussell, P. (1977). *The Great War and modern memory.* London: Oxford University Press.

Gammage, B. (1983). Introduction. In C. E. W. Bean (Ed.), *The official history of Australia in the War of 1914–1918: Volume IV: The Australian imperial force in France in 1917.* Brisbane, QLD: University of Queensland Press.

Haultain-Gall, M. (2016). Bean, the third battle of Ypres and the Australian narrative of the First World War. *Australian Historical Studies, 47*(1), 135–151. https://doi.org/10.1080/1031461X.2015.1124897

Holbrook, C. (2014). The role of nationalism in Australian war literature of the 1930s. *First World War Studies, 5*(2), 213–231.

Holbrook, C. (2016). Are we brainwashing our children? The place of Anzac in Australian history. *Ágora, 51*(4), 16–22.

Hynes, S. (1990). *A war imagined: The First World War and English culture.* London: Bodley Head.

Inglis, K. S. (1998). *Sacred places: War memorials in the Australian landscape*. Melbourne, VIC: Miegunyah Press.

Kelly, P. (2011). The next Anzac century. *The Australian*, April 23, 2011. Retrieved from https://www.theaustralian.com.au/national-affairs/the-next-anzac-century/news-story/eab21527c4f28fc9927b388631eecbc7

Kerby, M., Baguley, M., & MacDonald, A. (2019). And the Band Played Waltzing Matilda: Australian picture books (1999–2016) and the First World War. *Children's Literature in Education: An International Quarterly, 50*(2), 91–109.

Kerby, M., Baguley, M., MacDonald, A., & Lynch, Z. (2017). A war imagined: Gallipoli and the art of children's picture books. *Australian Art Education, 38*(1), 199–216.

Kerby, M., Baguley, M., & Tuppurainen-Mason, E. (2016). Interpreting the Anzac legacy: Reflexive accounts of artistic practice. *Australian Art Education, 37*(2), 116–132.

Kerby, M., & McDonald, J. (2018). Landscape and memory: An exhibition at the Toowoomba Regional Art Gallery. *Australian Art Education, 39*(2), 236–267.

Kerby, M., Tuppurainen-Mason, E., Baguley, M., & Lynch, Z. (2017). *Voices from the trenches*. Toowoomba, QLD: Ellipsis Media.

Lake, M. (2010). Introduction: What have you done for your country? In M. Lake & H. Reynolds (Eds.), *What's wrong with ANZAC?: The militarisation of Australian history* (pp. 1–23). Sydney: University of New South Wales Press.

Lamb, J. (2018, April 19). Tribute to land and memory. *Whitsunday Times*. Retrieved from https://www.whitsundaytimes.com.au/news/tribute-to-land-and-memory/3390724/

Larsson, M. (2009). A disenfranchised grief. Post-war death and memorialisation in Australia after the First World War. *Australian Historical Studies, 40*(1), 79–95.

Loftus, T., & Lamb, J. (2018, August 10). Legends of Proserpine. *Whitsunday Coast Guardian*, pp. 1, 4.

McKenna, M. (2007, June 6). Patriot act. *Australian Literary Review*. Retrieved from http://www.theaustralian.com.au/arts/patriot.

McKenna, M., & Ward, S. (2007). 'It Was Really Moving, Mate': The Gallipoli Pilgrimage and Sentimental Nationalism in Australia. *Australian Historical Studies, 38*(129), 141–151.

O'Reilly, M., Eldridge, S., Tuppurainen-Mason, E., & Kerby, M. (2015). *Boys in khaki*. Boondall, Brisbane: St Joseph's Nudgee College.

Reynolds, D., & Reason, M. (2012). *Kinesthetic empathy in creative and cultural practices*. Chicago: Intellect Books.

Scates, B. (2006). *Return to Gallipoli: Walking the battlefields of the Great War*. Cambridge: Cambridge University Press.

Seed, J. (2017). *I asked artists about empathy: Here is what they said....* Retrieved from https://www.huffingtonpost.com/entry/i-asked-artists-about-empathy-here-is-what-they-said:us_587bbac0e4b094e1aa9dc740

Siegesmund, R. (2013). Art Education and a Democratic Citizenry. *International Journal of Art & Design Education, 32*(3), 300–308.

Stephens, J. R. (2012). Recent directions in War Memorial Design. *The International Journal of the Humanities, 9*(6), 141–152.

St Joseph's Nudgee College. (2015). *The sound and the Fury: Nudgee College showcase evening, 24 October, 2015* [Catalogue].

Twomey, C. (2015). Anzac Day: Are we in danger of compassion fatigue? *The Conversation*. Retrieved from https://theconversation.com/anzac-day-are-we-in-danger-of-compassion-fatigue-24735

Twomey, C. (2013). Trauma and the Reinvigoration of Anzac: An Argument. *History Australia, 10*(3), 85–108.

Winter, J. (2017). Käthe Kolwitz and the Art of War. In J. Bourke (Ed.), *War and Art: A visual history of modern conflict* (pp. 252–267). London: Reaktion Books.

14

Pedagogies of Empathy-Building: Canadian and Azorean Perspectives on Film-Viewing in Higher Education

Amélie Lemieux, Casey Burkholder, and Josélia Mafalda Ribeiro Fonseca

Introduction

Film-based exercises generate transformative discussions when used as learning tools in classroom settings. As three assistant professors working in post-secondary research and teaching universities, we describe how we have incorporated film within our teaching at the undergraduate and graduate levels. In particular, we present three cases of film-viewing initiatives that took place as part of teacher education classes. When we were students—from elementary school to university—we experienced film

A. Lemieux (✉)
Faculty of Education, Mount Saint Vincent University, Halifax, NS, Canada
e-mail: Amelie.Lemieux@msvu.ca

C. Burkholder
Faculty of Education, University of New Brunswick, Saint John, NB, Canada
e-mail: casey.burkholder@unb.ca

J. M. R. Fonseca
Faculty of Education, University of the Azores, Ponta Delgada, Portugal
e-mail: joselia.mr.fonseca@uac.pt

© The Author(s) 2019
G. Barton, S. Garvis (eds.), *Compassion and Empathy in Educational Contexts*,
https://doi.org/10.1007/978-3-030-18925-9_14

271

within the classroom as ways to learn from different perspectives and explore narratives multimodally (Rowsell, 2013). From Sao Miguel to Montreal and Calgary, the three of us reminisce about being both relieved and overjoyed when a teacher would wheel out the shared television and rewind a VHS to play a film for the class. Our experiences were not so isolated. A study from Butler, Zaromb, Lyle, and Roediger (2009), for example, showed that 93% of pre-service teachers who participated in their study had taken a class in which the instructor used film as a pedagogical strategy. In addition, the authors noted that film was traditionally employed to generate discussions around content areas like historical fiction. Similarly, Howell (2014) highlighted the benefits of using historical movies to develop pre-service teachers' interest in history and social sciences. Beyond pre-service teacher courses, film propels immersion in narratives. That is, sonic dimensions, ever so present in movies, propel aesthetic experiences in ways that can foster empathy (Barton & Unsworth, 2014; Unsworth, 2014). Similar conclusions can be drawn from arts-informed research, where empathy is fostered through collaboration, art-making, and art-viewing (Cole, 2017; White & Costantino, 2013).

In parallel with these studies, there is a need to examine pre-service teachers' perceptions of films, specifically as to gather insights that look beyond simple portraitures of teaching. It is useful to consider film as a generative tool rather than a passive exercise to replace lecture time, or to assess content knowledge through fill-in-the-blank worksheets (Delamarter, 2015). In this chapter, we show how film can be used as a springboard to reflect on values that teacher candidates will adopt in their daily work lives. In this way, we contribute to the literature grounding film use in higher education as the needs for such practices emerge, providing "more opportunities for educators and students to use a particular hardware, software, space, or approach not necessarily as packaged, but as needed" (Abrams, Chen, & Downton, 2018, p. 131).

To this end, we use a thematic approach in this paper by presenting three autoethnographic cases based on our discussions with students that emerged from viewing *Mr. Lazhar* (2011), *Stories We Tell* (2012), and *Freedom Writers* (2008). We begin by contextualizing recent research that frames moving-image narrative stories (film, streaming series, weekly episodes) as relevant for classroom settings as they present moral issues, discussions about pedagogical practices, and the place of empathy in classrooms. Then, looking at the three cases, we consider relationships between empathy, choice, decision-making, agency, and critical analysis by using film in higher education. We de/center "the self as research subject" (White & Costantino, 2013), focusing on autoethnographic accounts (Ellis, 2004; Ellis, Adams, & Bochner, 2011) of our experiences teaching with film in order to generate empathetic discourses in the BEd and MEd courses we taught over the past three years.

Film, Netflix, and Empathy Development

Recent research has analyzed critical discourses in Netflix series. For example, Toliver (2017) dismantled the ways in which popular films have negatively framed blackness and massively perpetuated the harmful stereotype that black male youth are illiterate or literacy-deprived. Toliver subverted this stereotypical narrative by highlighting how Netflix's *Luke Cage* provided rich opportunities to understand black male literacies, drawing on social justice issues and equity, and delving into empowering literacy practices, defined as situated literacy events taking place in lived, cultural and social worlds (Street, 1984). Toliver's work invites teachers to consider critical rhetorical analysis when introducing popular culture materials in educational settings. Such practices have the potential to portray and promote empathy in ways that highlight representations of marginalized populations on screen. Netflix did not renew *Luke Cage* as of Fall 2018, and this decision highlights how shows like these are typically helpful in expanding understandings of literacy worlds and narratives.

Empirical studies have investigated the transformative potential of film implementation in classroom settings and higher education. In one case, Trier (2006) introduced secondary English teacher-educators to discursive sociocultural and multimodal literacy theories to deconstruct traditional views on teacher-training and literacy practices. This study provided additional evidence that pre-service teachers could frame literacy education in more open, inclusive, and accessible ways, thereby encouraging empathy through varied modes. At the elementary school level, Australian researchers Mantei and Kervin (2016) found that short films were effective in helping students reflect on themselves and how they perceived others, thereby fostering empathy. These students carried out digital media production with iPads and engaged in reader-viewer response as they crafted stories on meaningful messages based on the films they watched.

In applied classroom settings, Domke, Weippert, and Apol (2018) explored film adaptations as legitimate, autonomous artworks, steering away from the rhetoric of comparing original print-based narrative versions to their digital counterparts. Again, this evidence supports the value of employing film adaptations for educational purposes through critical film analysis, including consideration of music choice, editing and design platforms, and cinematography. In this chapter, we explore how three film narratives have changed our own understanding of teaching with film and, in some cases, how considerations involving aesthetics and camerawork play a role in empathy awareness and development.

Lessons on Empathy: Pedagogical Discourses in *Monsieur Lazhar*

What we have come to explore is how human experiences can crack the screen open and offer possibilities to question values involving empathy and moral issues. It is thus not a surprise that aesthetic experiences are closely related to empathy development, in that empathy, to some extent, can result from one's aesthetic relationships and relational engagements with an object or a concept (White & Costantino, 2013).

I (Amélie) begin with a reflection on a project that took place in a Winter 2016 class with 20 pre-service teachers studying to become ESL teachers in a mostly Francophone province, Québec. Students in this class were enrolled in the Bachelor of Education TESOL program at McGill University and came from diverse linguistic and cultural backgrounds. Sitting quietly in a room, facing the screen at the front of my class, teacher candidates not only connected with images in motion, but also with the dialogic layers (Bakhtin, 1983) embedded within themselves—processing the movements on screen, bodies and colors mingling, depicting the dialogue spoken in Québec French and making associations with moral values. They connected memories with images and sounds, processing what was relevant and what was trivial for them, extracting meaning and producing sense at the same time.

Film-viewing stimulates the imagination and shapes, albeit momentarily, views of the world through selected moving frames and sounds. Countless thoughts are at play in film-viewing, engaging in a multimodal dialogic dance. As an ESL teacher-educator at McGill University, my role was to mediate those inner and outer voices to bring together multiple perspectives on teaching. Film triggers those dialogic layers in viewers when they are engaged in the narrative. I sometimes see myself as a mediator of these values in my classes, one who both guides and is guided by felt reflections-in-motion. As Costantino (2013) maintains, "empathetic relationships foster teachers' understandings of students' lives so that they can develop relevant curriculum and instructional strategies and address individual learning needs" (p. 205). And so, empathy as a situated, yet relational, emotion was one of the topics we discussed over this course.

Elsewhere, I have argued my rationale for teaching with film in higher education as an exercise that propels discussions on empathy and moral values (Lemieux, 2017). Choosing movies that allow students to reflect on empathy, moral development, and ethics is perhaps the most difficult task. The challenge comes with carefully selecting meaningful content that encapsulates the moral issues and teaching values to be addressed in relation to the teaching profession. Falardeau's *Monsieur Lazhar* is one of those movies that has stuck with me because it speaks to human and societal values in teaching. For Griffith and Hébert (2015), *Monsieur Lazhar* challenges human and societal values and focuses on such matters as pedagogical approaches, social justice, societal integration, and assessment practices in relation to the characters in the film. These predispositions spark dialogues in higher education regarding "good" or "desirable" teaching practices.

When I introduced the film to the pre-service teachers in my ESL course at the end of the term, my objective was to leave students with food for thought regarding their future role in the teaching profession. What type of teachers would they be? Did their moral and ethical values linked to teaching change over the semester? Could the movie ignite more reflective thoughts on these questions? My hope was that *Monsieur Lazhar*, a film that depicts the story of a recently immigrated refugee who lands a last-minute replacement teaching gig in a Montreal elementary school, would help my students reflect on these questions. Viewers learned, at the end of the film, that Lazhar did not hold a teaching certification and was hired in a rush to replace a teacher who had committed suicide.

In the movie, Bachir Lazhar's teaching practices are at times dubious and often polemical. Among these practices, Lazhar uses an outdated model of oral dictation, sticks to rigid techniques for classroom and behavioral management, is unprepared for parent meetings, and adopts punitive grading. However, Lazhar at times shows warmth and laughter, engages students in philosophical discussions, trains students in writing and reading rigorously, and goes the extra mile by introducing additional canonical literature to advanced students. Lazhar showed care for his students in those cases, or what most would call "tough love". The rhetoric of "tough love" in teaching often frames perception around the flaunted pedagogical ethos of sweat-and-reward and is associated with "good teaching". Engaging in dismantling these portrayed representations of "good teaching" is necessary to debunk those myths.

After the film screening, the pre-service teachers exchanged thoughts about such topics as how moral issues were tackled in the film. For example, did Lazhar's dual pedagogical and personal nature make him a "good" teacher (Ayers, 2001)? And by understanding Lazhar as a good teacher, did it mean that he was empathetic, efficient, or both? The discussions pointed to Lazhar as an untrained teacher, even as he occasionally presented personality traits that would be caring. Pedagogies of caring (Agne, 1999) resurfaced in the discussions and implied that a caring teacher, nowadays, would not assign dictations to assess writing and listening. Other teacher candidates in the classroom found such activities productive, and that implementing them showed care that aligned with Lazhar's teaching philosophy. Additional conversations focused on the quality of the acting (young and more seasoned actors performing roles), as well as the lighting and technical work to encourage the development of further understandings of aesthetic transactions (Rosenblatt, 1978) between human (viewers) and object (film) (or nonhuman in recent terms), or what Barthes (1977) would call the discovery of, and engagement with, the obtuse meaning of images in motion. In other words, these transactions between viewers and film yield multiple meanings to be unfolded, discovered, and discussed. This is where class discussions become important as dialogue can produce an exchange of such topics as empathy and moral values.

Thinking About the *Stories We Tell* with Pre-service Social Studies Teachers

I (Casey) have shown the film *Stories We Tell* twice in three social studies methods courses for pre-service secondary (Grade 7–12) social studies teachers, and once for pre-service teachers at the primary level (Kindergarten to Grade 6) between 2014 and 2016. In Prince Edward Island, social studies encompass the study of Canadian studies, history, geography, politics, law, and economics (Government of PEI, 2018). However, there is a greater focus on history and geography, particularly in the elementary years. After three years of teaching pre-service social studies teachers, there are a few observations I can make based on our conversations about social studies in general. The first observation is that most of the pre-service teachers found their experiences as learners of K-12 social studies to be boring. The second observation is that most remembered social studies as a class where dates, geographies, people, and facts were memorized, tested, and then forgotten. The final observation is that social studies was a place that encouraged an uncritical view of Canada as a multicultural paradise. My responsibility as a teacher-educator is to disrupt these practices and work with learners to create social studies classrooms that encourage critical memory-making and to work together as teachers for social action. Social studies, in my estimation, is a place where learners can become adept at reading for context, acknowledge discourses at play (Gee, 2014), complicate histories, and learn to speak and write back to power (Hooks, 2014).

The film *Stories We Tell* (Lee & Polley, 2012) begins with a montage of mixed footage edited together to evoke the passage of time. During the montage, the documentary's narrator, Sarah Polley's father, Michael, recites a quote from Margaret Atwood's (1996) *Alias Grace*:

When you're in the middle of a story, it isn't a story at all but rather a confusion, a dark roaring, a blindness, a wreckage of shattered glass and splintered wood, like a house in a whirlwind or else a boat crushed by the icebergs or swept over the rapids, and all aboard are powerless to stop it. It's only afterwards that it becomes anything like a story at all, when you're telling it to yourself or someone else. [00:30–01:06]

Stories We Tell (Lee & Polley, 2012) has stuck with me from the moment I first viewed it. As a huge fan of Sarah Polley's acting and directing work, I looked forward to seeing the film before I was even aware of its theme or content. When I saw the film—an examination of Polley's family history that blends stories both as remembered by people in her family and as moments that are imagined and fictionalized—I felt compelled to immediately watch it again. This second, more critical viewing, led me to think about how the film might be used, in my practice as a teacher-educator of social studies methods at a university in Prince Edward Island, to encourage the development of empathy in teaching and in understanding others' points of view.

As Andrea Doucet (2015) argues in her review of the film for *Visual Studies*, "at least five stories unfold within and around the film" (p. 98). First, the film reflects on how the documentary itself came into existence. The second story delves into Sarah Polley's mother, Diane, who passed away when Sarah was a child. The third story centers on the process of making the film, which includes the ways in which Polley is present as an interviewer, writer, and director. The fourth story "focuses on processes of storytelling and listening and how these are linked with the making and remaking of family histories and relationships. And finally, there is a larger theoretical, epistemological, and ontological narrative that frames the film and touches upon questions about what stories are, who they belong to, how they change in the telling, how listeners and audiences matter, and what stories *do* within families" (Doucet, 2015, p. 98, author's emphasis). By accessing these five stories, the viewers learn to put themselves in each of the roles and empathize with the diverse layers of storytelling, stakeholders, and contexts presented in the film. Each storyteller has a different connection to the story, and there are different stakes in relation to how the story is told and remembered. The ways in which the narratives relate to one another within the film, how storytelling itself is political and situated in a time and space, and the ways in which specific speakers highlight one moment and downplay another are fruitful concepts to discuss in social studies teaching.

While I acknowledge that history and social studies teaching has, at least in the academic literature, moved beyond memorization (Engle, 2003; Ercikan & Seixas, 2015; Hawkins, 2017; Kumashiro, 2015; Seixas, 2017; Seixas & Peck, 2004; Smith, 2017; Tuck, McKenzie, & McCoy, 2014), it is important to disrupt many of the teaching practices that pre-service candidates absorbed as students with a view of teaching social studies for a more equitable and empathetic society. In order to promote social studies teaching that encourages empathy and social action, I encourage the pre-service teachers to reflect on their experiences as learners and think about those students who are not served by prioritizing certain stories in Canadian history over others. For example, the Confederation narrative that specifically ignores the civic and activist contributions of: Indigenous peoples, Black Canadians, Asian and South Asian Canadians, the dis/abled, queer folks, working-class people, and girls and young women, among others.

To address these ongoing historical exclusions when I teach social studies methods, there are a few questions that I ask learners to consider: what does social studies do? How does the social studies curriculum encourage the inclusion of certain memories and exclusion of others? What stories are told? Whose stories are downplayed? What does this selective memory do for the building of a provincial consciousness in the context of Prince Edward Island? To address these questions, learners undertake various types of inquiry throughout the semester. They engage in personal history writing by creating a timeline of important life events, and then curate specific moments to highlight from their life experiences. They are also tasked to think about themselves as historical actors and work to place themselves in relation to specific moments in Canadian and Island history. Then, to build on these in-class personal histories, I share the film *Stories We Tell* in the middle of the semester. The documentary is incredibly useful in the social studies classroom as it disrupts the notions that a definitive truth can be found in a story, which can complicate the master narratives that are often told in history teaching. The film makes visible that what is true for one speaker may be different for another. Even within the same family, Polley's mother was remembered and understood differently depending on the perspective. The film magnifies the ways in which stories are passed on in families and through friends to piece together memories of a person who is no longer around. The ways that Polley's mother is memorialized is also informed by the perspective of the speakers. For example, one of her friends is quite judgmental about Polley's mother's behavior, which she describes as wild and reckless, while another friend remembers her as boisterous, full of life—an enormous, warm figure. *Stories We Tell* also complicates the viewers' understanding of truth and evidence. For example, archival footage is mixed in with new, fictionalized archival recreations that emerge from the memories of family members and friends. It is not until later in the film that the viewer begins to doubt the authenticity of some of the video footage. The viewer, on the first watch, then, is made to retroactively doubt the veracity of the video evidence from earlier in the documentary. It is this mixing of fact, fiction, and interpretation that makes the film so potent for pre-service teacher education.

After viewing the documentary, I ask students to consider a series of questions: What might this film teach us? How do we remember? How does social studies prioritize certain memories over others, and how might we work with learners to think about the stories that are not told in social studies? What techniques does Sarah Polley employ to encourage the audience to empathize with the people in her family, particularly her mother? To follow the film, and these series of questions, I asked learners to look at their family histories in relation to the larger narratives in Prince Edward Island's social studies curricula. Students interviewed elders from their families, including parents, aunts, grandparents, and great-uncles, to understand the kinds of stories that were told in their own families, as well as to get a sense of the ways in which social studies teaching and content has both changed and stayed the same over time. Students created short cellphilms (cellphone coupled with video production, see Dockney & Tomaselli, 2010; MacEntee, Burkholder, & Schwab-Cartas, 2016; Mitchell & de Lange, 2013), audio diaries, and podcasts, while others chose to write about what they had learned from these interviews. Ultimately, *Stories We Tell* serves as an important prompt to question the practices of memory-making and storytelling within social studies education. If nothing else, the film can be contextualized to prompt critical thinking about evidence, about story and narrative, about empathy, and about the ways in which we try to make sense of the world over time.

Reflecting on the Use of Films in Education for Values and Citizenship: The Case of *Freedom Writers*

I (Josélia) showed *Freedom Writers* as part of the Transdisciplinary Education and Civic Education course of the Master's program for Childhood Educators and Teachers at our university. I emphasized values and citizenship education throughout the course. The students who take this course have not yet begun their internship in kindergarten education. According to my observations, most teachers at the beginning of their career are afraid to adopt a constructive approach to teaching and learning citizenship and values. It is easier and safer for them to use a prescriptive approach and teach values and citizenship through instruction that conforms to conventional rules and norms in Azorean culture. Since values education develops ontologically, it is important to foster valuable, empathy-based relationships between students and teachers. The objective of showing *Freedom Writers* was twofold. First, it supported the ongoing process of developing the autonomous moral consciousness of my students as future teachers, during which they learned about values and citizenship based on moral autonomy as a process and not as a product. Second, the film's content offered lessons on how to educate young citizens about empathy, based on values awareness and discussions around representations of "good" teaching (Lemieux, 2017).

The use of film in values and citizenship education is conceived as a pivotal pedagogical strategy. Films are multimodal narratives (Rowsell, 2013), wherein hermeneutics favor not only the unveiling of students' personal values, but also provide, through sociocognitive conflicts, a critical reconfiguration of values as they pertain to education. *Freedom Writers* is a relevant film to address values and citizenship in educational settings, because it shows how it is possible to build on students' experiences to de/construct values through empathy. While this movie can be interpreted in ways that frame the teacher as a "white savior" (Hughey, 2010), we propose the idea that the teacher's role in this movie was also that of a learner who worked on developing her identity and values as a novice teacher.

Freedom Writers, Empathy Development, and Citizenship Education

Inspired by the 1999 book *Freedom Writers Diaries*, *Freedom Writers* is a film based on the true story of Erin Gruwell, an American teacher who is assigned a teaching load in a low-income Los Angeles urban school, with a student population living in a small, inward-facing community. At Wilson High, students are regularly accepted as to fill multicultural quotas. Unlike Gruwell, her fellow teachers convey stigma and prejudices toward students, who are seen as difficult cases. In addition, the classroom itself is divided into distinct territories. In the beginning of the film, boundaries are created and enforced, thus engendering classroom clusters. The first step to provoking empathy arose in the film when Erin introduced a game where everyone shared their negative experiences with racism, gang fights, drugs, and death. Students realized they had more in common than they thought, having suffered from racial segregation, and they started to be more empathetic toward each other.

A turning point occurs at the beginning of the film, when students analyzed Anne Frank's life. The *Diary of Anne Frank* proved to be of great importance to clarify their value systems and to reflect on their performed identities. Writing a diary was an evocative process for students, helping them narrate their life stories, problems, fears, and anguish. Articulating those struggles helped them feel empathy toward each other.

Freedom Writers made me think about Nussbaum's (2002) argument on democratic education, which is based on three capacities: critical thinking, living with and understanding each other and our differences, and the narrative imagination. Gruwell encouraged her students to think critically as they read Anne Frank's diary and as they write their own. That is, they relate to her diary, and upon writing their personal narratives, they clarified their values, fears, and desires to better understand themselves. This paves the way to becoming good citizens, as Nussbaum explains (2006):

> Democracy needs citizens who can think for themselves … who can reason together about their choices rather than just trading claims and counterclaims … Critical thinking is particularly crucial for good citizenship …

We will only have a chance at an adequate dialogue across cultural boundaries if young citizens know how to engage in dialogue and deliberation in
the first place. (p. 388)

By asking her students to read Anne Frank's diary and engage in discussions about struggles, Gruwell creates conditions to foster empathy in
her students. They become aware that others can experience similar problems as their own, and these problems exist because people lack humanity
and acceptance of others. Her students are encouraged to develop what
Nussbaum defines as the second dimension of a free citizen: "citizens who
cultivate their capacity for effective democratic citizenship need ... to see
themselves ... as bound to all human beings by ties of recognition and
concern" (Nussbaum, 2006, p. 389). Finally, Gruwell's work also promotes the development of narrative imagination, the third capacity that
Nussbaum (2002) describes as "the ability to think what it might be like
in the shoes of a person different from oneself, to be an intelligent reader
of that person's story" (p. 390). The narrative imagination is bound with
empathy, and the film propels reflection on what empathy is and what
it could be.

For my Master's students in kindergarten and primary school education, this film turned out to be an important experience on several levels.
First, the film screening was a strategy to promote citizenship education
with my students and help them clarify their own values by critically
reflecting on them. This allowed them to reconfigure the concepts and
practices they might use in their classrooms. Teaching through film develops citizenship and ethics in ways that sometimes written text cannot:
films tend to portray situations that can be lived and imagined by viewers
as they dis/identify with fictional characters. I thus contend that, in
higher education and especially in pre-service or graduate education
courses, educators must have opportunities to reflect on their own educational philosophies so that they, in turn, can devise strategies to help
children clarify their own values. When viewing the film, my students
realized that, to successfully implement these strategies, there needs to be
positive student-teacher relationships, because students will only express
themselves freely in a situation where they feel they can trust authority
figures. *Freedom Writers* allowed me to work with my students to caress

the idea of empathetic pedagogical relationships. Students in our university's Master's program for Childhood Educators and Teachers understood that nurturing empathetic relationships with their own students is not synonymous with being permissive. Rather, through empathy they can create trusting environments that encourage well-being and a sense of belonging. The film-viewing conditions I created for my students, as future educators, introduced empathy in the classroom as an ontological process rather than a fixed concept.

The Place of Empathy and Film in Future Research and Praxis

Films about pedagogy often portray performed moments of empathy through teacher-savior narratives, instances of caring and intentional listening, or solution-oriented situations in teaching and learning. When dismantling, even frame by frame, those scenes with students, this is where empathy has the possibility to become a hard-wired reflex. That is, the more time spent on debunking representational myths around teaching, decolonizing stories, imagining alternative scenarios and solutions, adding and deleting character features, questioning situational intentions, and playing with narrative story worlds, the more engagement there will be in empathy toward humans in pedagogical settings. In this chapter, we offered examples of films that were used to encourage empathy in higher education. We assessed the potential of three specific films and the discussions they may generate in situated contexts. First, Amélie described her use of the film *Monsieur Lahzar* in a class with pre-service ESL teachers in Québec. In this example, *Monsieur Lahzar* encouraged pre-service teachers to think critically and interrogated their preconceived notions of what constitutes good teaching and empathy development. The learners in her classroom noted the differences and similarities between being a good pedagogue and being an empathetic person. The use of *Monsieur Lahzar* encouraged learners to examine and unsettle their ideas about empathy in the classroom. In Casey's case study of the use of *Stories We Tell* (2012) with pre-service social studies teachers, she argued that asking learners to contemplate issues of voice, audience, perspective, and motivation was necessary when teaching history. Using *Stories We Tell* as a learning artifact, learners were asked to empathize with multiple characters and perspectives while, at the same time, to expand the application of these concepts to the context of teaching social studies. If within one family, there is no clear true story, what does that mean for social studies, and what does that mean for the stories that are told in Canadian history about minority and otherwise marginalized groups? How might we become empathetic and thoughtful educators with the stories that we have told, the stories that we tell, and the stories that we might tell in the social studies classroom regarding the territory that is currently called Canada? Finally, Josélia used *Freedom Writers* in a Masters of Education classroom to interrogate the structural inequalities in schools and encourage learners to examine their own complicities in maintaining and reproducing similar instances of inequity, as well as to think about what makes empathetic citizens within stratified systems. Film provides important visual entry points to examine teachers' lives and pedagogies. These three examples of incorporating film in post-secondary teacher-training brought forth deep personal reflections, critical considerations of our own relationship to teaching and learning, and bolstered thoughtful discussions on the meaning of being empathetic teachers and citizens.

Films

Déry, L., McCraw, K. (Producers), & Falardeau, P. (Director). (2011). *Monsieur Lazhar* [Motion Picture]. Montreal, QC: Microscope/Seville Pictures.

DeVito, D., Shamberg, M., Sher, S. (Producers), & LaGravenese, R. (2007). *Freedom Writers* [Motion Picture]. Hollywood, CA: Paramount Pictures.

Lee, A. (Producer), & Polley, S. (Director). (2012). *Stories We Tell* [Motion Picture]. Toronto, ON: National Film Board of Canada.

References

Abrams, S. S., Chen, X. J., & Downton, M. P. (2018). *Managing educational technology: School partnerships and technology integration*. New York: Routledge.

Agne, K. (1999). Caring: The way of the master teacher. In R. P. Lipka & T. M. Brinthaupt (Eds.), *The role of the self* (pp. 165–188). New York: State University of New York Press.

Atwood, M. (1996). *Alias Grace.* Toronto: McClelland and Stewart.

Ayers, W. (2001). *To teach: The journey of a teacher.* New York: Teachers College Press.

Bakhtin, M. M. (1983). *The dialogic imagination: Four essays.* Texas: University of Texas Press.

Barthes, R. (1977). *Image, music, text* (S. Heath trans.). New York: Hill and Wang.

Barton, G., & Unsworth, L. (2014). Music, multiliteracies and multimodality: Exploring the book and movie versions of Shaun Tan's *The Lost Thing*. *Australian Journal of Language and Literacy, 37*(1), 3–20.

Butler, A. C., Zaromb, F. M., Lyle, K. B., & Roediger, H. L. (2009). Using popular films to enhance classroom learning: The good, the bad, and the interesting. *Psychological Science, 20*(9), 1161–1168.

Cole, A. L. (2017). Understanding caregiving and Alzheimer's disease through the arts. In G. Barton & M. Baguley (Eds.), *The Palgrave handbook of global arts education* (pp. 431–458). London: Palgrave Macmillan.

Costantino, T. (2013). Cultivating the social imagination of pre-service teachers through aesthetic reflection. In B. White & T. Costantino (Eds.), *Aesthetics, empathy and education* (pp. 205–220). New York: Peter Lang.

Delamarter, J. (2015). Avoiding practice shock: Using teacher movies to realign pre-service teachers' expectations of teaching. *Australian Journal of Teacher Education, 40*(2), 1–15.

Dockney, J., & Tomaselli, K. (2010). Third screens, third cinema, third worlds and triadomania: Examining cellphilm aesthetics in visual culture. *Communistas, 15*(1), 97–111.

Domke, L. M., Weippert, T. L., & Apol, L. (2018). Beyond school breaks: Reinterpreting the uses of film in classrooms. *The Reading Teacher, 72*(1), 51–59. https://doi.org/10.1002/trtr.1677

Doucet, A. (2015). Ontological narrativity and the performativity of the *Stories We Tell. Visual Studies, 30*(1), 98–100.

Ellis, C. (2004). *The ethnographic I: A methodological novel about autoethnography.* Walnut Creek, CA: AltaMira Press.

Ellis, C., Adams, T. E., & Bochner, A. P. (2011). Autoethnography: An overview. *Forum: Qualitative Social Research, 12*(1), Article 10.

Engle, S. H. (2003). Decision making: The heart of social studies instruction. *The Social Studies, 94*(1), 7–10.

Ercikan, K., & Seixas, P. (Eds.). (2015). *New directions in assessing historical thinking*. New York: Routledge.

Gee, J. P. (2014). *An introduction to discourse analysis: Theory and method*. New York: Routledge.

Government of Prince Edward Island. (2018). *Social studies curriculum*. Retrieved from https://www.princeedwardisland.ca/en/information/education-early-learning-and-culture/social-studies-curriculum

Griffith, J., & Hébert, C. (2015). Un/bearable witnessing: Sex scandal, historical trauma, and literature of historical witness in *Monsieur Lazhar*. In N. Ng-a-Fook, G. Reis, & A. Ibrahim (Eds.), *Provoking curriculum studies: Strong poetry and arts of the possible in education* (pp. 173–184). London: Routledge.

Hawkins, J. M. (2017). Breaking out and going beyond the celluloid closet: LGBTQ media for the social studies classroom. *Social Education, 81*(3), 159–161.

Hooks, B. (2014). *Teaching to transgress*. New York: Routledge.

Howell, J. (2014). Popularising history: The use of historical fiction with pre-service teachers. *Australian Journal of Teacher Education, 39*(12), 1–12.

Hughey, M. W. (2010). The white savior film and reviewers' reception. *Symbolic Interaction, 33*(3), 475–496.

Kumashiro, K. K. (2015). *Against common sense: Teaching and learning toward social justice*. New York: Routledge.

Lemieux, A. (2017). In-class film-viewing for empathy development in higher education. *Canadian Review of Art Education, 44*(1), 64–73.

MacEntee, K., Burkholder, C., & Schwab-Cartas, J. (Eds.). (2016). *What's a cellphilm? Integrating mobile phone technology into participatory arts-based research and activism*. Rotterdam: Sense Publishers.

Mantei, J., & Kervin, J. (2016). Using short films in the classroom as a stimulus for digital text creation. *The Reading Teacher, 70*(4), 485–489.

Mitchell, C., & de Lange, N. (2013). What can a teacher do with a cellphone? Using participatory visual research to speak back in addressing HIV & AIDS. *South African Journal of Education, 33*(4), 1–13.

Nussbaum, M. C. (2002). Education and democratic citizenship: Capabilities and quality education. *Journal of Human Development, 7*(3), 385–395.

Nussbaum, M. C. (2006). *Frontiers of justice: Disability, nationality, species membership*. Cambridge, MA: Harvard University Press.

Rosenblatt, L. M. (1978). *The reader, the text, the poem: The transactional theory of the literary work*. Illinois: Southern Illinois University Press.

Rowsell, J. (2013). *Working with multimodality: Rethinking literacy in a digital age*. New York: Routledge.

Seixas, P. (2017). Historical consciousness and historical thinking. In M. Carretero, S. Berger, & M. Grever (Eds.), *Palgrave handbook of research in historical culture and education* (pp. 59–72). London: Palgrave Macmillan.

Seixas, P., & Peck, C. (2004). Teaching historical thinking. In A. Sears & I. Wright (Eds.), *Challenges and prospects for Canadian social studies* (pp. 109–117). Vancouver: Pacific Educational Press.

Smith, B. (2017). Methodologically historicizing social studies education: Curricular filtering and historical thinking as social studies thinking. *Canadian Journal of Education/Revue canadienne de l'éducation, 40*(2), 1–26.

Street, B. V. (1984). *Literacy in theory and practice*. New York: Cambridge University Press.

Toliver, S. R. (2017, December). Unlocking the Cage: Empowering literacy representations in Netflix's *Luke Cage* series. *Journal of Adolescent & Adult Literacy* (online first). https://doi.org/10.1002/jaal.721

Trier, J. (2006). Reconceptualizing literacy through a discourses perspective by analyzing literacy events represented in films about schools. *Journal of Adolescent & Adult Literacy, 49*(6), 510–523.

Tuck, E., McKenzie, M., & McCoy, K. (2014). Land education: Indigenous, post-colonial, and decolonizing perspectives on place and environmental education research. *Environmental Education Research, 20*(1), 1–23.

Unsworth, L. (2014). Interfacing visual and verbal narrative art in paper and digital media: Recontextualising literature and literacies. In G. Barton (Ed.), *Literacy in the arts: Retheorising learning and teaching* (pp. 55–76). London: Springer.

White, B., & Costantino, T. (Eds.). (2013). *Aesthetics, empathy and education*. New York: Peter Lang.

Index

CPI Antony Rowe
Eastbourne, UK
January 10, 2020